The Unpromised Land

The Unpromised Land

Agrarian Reform and Conflict Worldwide

Demetrios Christodoulou

Zed Books Ltd
London and New Jersey

The Unpromised Land was first published by Zed Books Ltd,
57 Caledonian Road, London N1 9BU, UK, and 171 First Avenue,
Atlantic Highlands, New Jersey 07716, USA, in 1990. Edition
for India published by Manohar Book Service, 1 Ansari Road,
Daryaganj, New Delhi 110002, India, in 1990.

Cover designed by Andrew Corbett.
Cover photograph by Mark Edwards.
Typeset by Mudra Typesetters, Pondicherry.
Printed and bound in the United Kingdom
by Biddles Ltd, Guildford and King's Lynn.

British Library Cataloguing in Publication Data

Christodoulou, Demetrios
  The unpromised land : agrarian reform and conflict
worldwide.
  1. Agricultural land. Land tenure. Reform
  I. Title
  333.33'5

ISBN 0-86232-778-4
ISBN 0-86232-779-2 pbk

Library of Congress Cataloging-in-Publication Data

Christodoulou, Demetrios.
  The unpromised land : agrarian reform and conflict
worldwide / Demetrios Christodoulou.
    p.   cm.
  Bibliography: p.
  Includes index.
  ISBN 0-86232-778-4. ISBN 0-86232-779-2 (pbk.)
  1. Land reform. 2. Land tenure. 3. Farm tenancy. I. Title.
HD1332.C47   1989
333.3'1—dc19   88-31885
               CIP

Contents

Tables

*To my wife Sylvia who has
sustained this labour of love*

Acknowledgements

This being a book derived from a lifetime experience the author's debt spreads out widely in time and in the range of persons and institutions. In the final analysis the main debt is to the rural people, among whom I was born, brought up and spent much of my life. I tried to serve them as teacher, professional public servant and ultimately as government minister in my own country and as an international public servant worldwide. This book may atone for some of the past failures in that service.

FAO with the opportunities offered to travel and for meeting people and attending conferences and technical meetings served as a good school and its library as an unparalleled information and professional back up. The UN and other Specialised Agencies and the World Bank either in co-operation or in their service also helped broaden experience.

Cambridge University with its libraries and academic excellence proved a wonderful haven for quiet learning. I went there first in 1981 under a Vivien Stewart Bursary offered by the Department of Land Economy and owe grateful thanks to all concerned, especially the Head of the Department, Professor G.C. Cameron. Dr. C.F. Kolbert and Dr. Henry W. West of the same Department have been specially helpful.

My niece, Mrs Frosoula Christophidou, has been of immense help in producing the final version of the typescript under difficult circumstances, and in numerous other ways.

My wife, Sylvia, more than deserves the dedication of this work, something she has earned many times over.

Preface

The theme and thesis of this book are of intrinsic universal importance, above all for the life chances of more than half the people in the world, especially the underprivileged majority. The poor have always been with us and the analysis given here suggests that they will remain so, for much longer. Poverty, in essence still primarily rural, has intermittently been studied, deplored or even "tackled" at national and international levels. Some limited telling facts, many theories and an international conference or two, are the main intellectual crop yielded by these efforts.

In 1984 the prevailing indifference took a severe knock from the disturbing and incredible news, broadcast with horrifying pictures on television screens at home, of "the greatest calamity that has ever befallen the world". A biblical catastrophe had *visibly* afflicted Africa in the shape of famishing millions, many of them dying of starvation *en masse*. This shocking tragedy stirred the conscience of ordinary people in many countries, triggered off action by individuals, groups and organisations, and forced governments to act. Such massive help could attenuate the immediate problem and save many lives in the short term, but the long-term problem of providing an essential guarantee that this would not occur again remains. The world is not unprepared; it has simply not exerted itself to achieve this goal. Ironically 1984 was the target year by which the 1974 World Food Conference had decided that "no child would go to bed hungry, anywhere in the world". That target was set before the Conference by the head of the delegation of the richest nation on earth, Dr Henry Kissinger.[1]

Five years later the 1979 World Conference on Agrarian Reform and Rural Development produced a *Plan of Action*, still being implemented, targeted on eradicating rural poverty and underdevelopment. There is no need to recall the colossal national and international efforts of the last 40 years in social and economic development and the massive investments involved. Nor need one point out the vast growth of literature, theories and practices in this field.

Since 1974 the present writer has maintained[2] that development strategies and practices adopted to date, which have been geared to generating economic growth, contain a built-in flaw and fundamental weakness. They tend to benefit and to build on those groups, usually a minority, who are already in possession of assets. Invariably, the "Matthew effect", which ensures that "to those that have shall be given", has come into operation. Along with the backwash effect it widens the gap between the "haves" and the "have-nots". The latter, the overwhelming majority in many countries, become more and more marginal to the development process; with less, if possible, political clout, they are reduced to an almost inert social force, as their poverty and marginality become both depressive of their progress and quasi-permanent.[3]

The world's poor and underprivileged are mainly rural; if one includes recent migrants who have flocked, and continue to flock, into shanty towns and other "blighted" urban areas, then the plight of the rural areas clearly becomes the essential problem of underdevelopment. There is little hope of effectively tackling such underdevelopment, or even of avoiding new mass starvation, unless the problem of assets is squarely faced, competently assessed, and its implications successfully incorporated into development strategies.

The key asset of rural people, the indispensable resource for food production and the focus of power, has always been the land. In consequence, it has never been free from conflict. This agrarian conflict is a main key to our understanding of rural underdevelopment, to freedom from hunger and to peace.

Agrarian conflict is endemic to rural society; yet the intellectual community's interest in it, never very strong, has waxed and waned over its long history. While agrarian discontent simmered and pressures built up in many situations, virulent outbreaks were relatively few and could "safely" be ignored.

The modest professional interest of recent years focused on other, "new" ventures, with rural development currently enjoying an "appalling" popularity. *As cultivated and pursued*, this has become an all-embracing, comforting concept and form of action, capable of attracting broad consensus, such as that achieved at the major event of the 1970s in this field, the World Conference on Agrarian Reform and Rural Development at the FAO, Rome, in July 1979.

The tragic events of 1984 may now bring interest in agrarian conflict into fashion, for it refuses to go away. Not only does it blight the life of billions and control the fate of developing nations with acute agrarian iniquities; it also returns to plague industrialising and even industrialised societies, such as the European Economic Community and in 1985 even the US. Whether the agrarian problem is the dog or the tail of the socio-political system, the conflict it generates still wags the system.

One cannot, in fact, study agrarian conflict, and efforts to contain it, in isolation from the socio-political system. Agrarian shocks are most opportune moments for observing the workings and reactions of the socio-political system when touched on its raw nerve. A proper study of agrarian conflict and reform provides a rare vantage point from which to watch the whole system coping with provocation.

At the heart of agrarian conflict is the issue of land as property which generates the shock waves. Samuel P. Huntington observed[4] that the industrial worker was interested in asserting his claim to an appropriate share of the economic product, while the peasant had no alternative but to attack the existing system of ownership and control of the means of production, namely land.

The root of agrarian conflict lies in the misery, inequality and injustice under which billions of people feel themselves undeservedly condemned to live. Famines are only dramatic manifestations that attract outside attention; endemic grinding poverty and powerlessness are "normal" features of their lives. In the cause of agrarian reform millions of rural poor have died or suffered torture and imprisonment. Agrarian reform is generally opposed by privileged land-owning interests and their supporters; their hostility and opposition is instinctive and "natural". Those close to the land, whose livelihood and welfare depend on it and who are aggrieved by existing agrarian relations, naturally yearn for improvement and change.

It is often assumed that supporters of agrarian reform are to be found among the left of the ideological spectrum. This is not always true, as will be seen later. Samir Amin, for example, has often linked[5] agrarian reforms with "Kulakization", i.e. with the creation of capitalist farmers, while Paul A. Baran[6] sees many dangers in agrarian reform, especially if it takes place in the midst of general backwardness, in which case it will retard rather than advance a country's economic development. This, Baran argues, results from the creation of rural slums, the strengthening of the feudal grip and the frustration of the accumulation of capital, thereby eliminating the possibility that development will be accompanied by a rapid advance to industrial capitalism.

The role of agrarian reform depends on the nature of the conflict that generates that reform, "on the conditions under which it takes place and on the forces by which it is propelled", as Baran himself observes. The drama built round access to land is vital, the problems it raises many and complex. The whole issue has not received the attention it deserves. Land as a crucial asset and its critical connection to the socio-political system; the key force that agrarian conflict tends to be in shaping many a country's destiny; the deeper meaning of agrarian conflict management; the controversy and the wide implications for the social forces flowing from stands adopted towards agrarian reform – these and other weighty issues require analysis and evaluation, but make overwhelmingly difficult any treatment of the subject that is both comprehensive and effective.

Existing writings on the subject tend to be specific to a small number of cases: some are only historical treatments of concrete agrarian conflicts and reforms within an analysis of causes and events of wider scope; others, monographs of specific agrarian problems and reforms, some containing comparative studies of limited scope; but the few evaluations of reforms are usually of an unsatisfactory statistical nature and often based on normative or classificatory schemes. They are useful sources, but have left the field patchily cultivated.

The historical and geographical horizons of the present study are wide, the international dimensions are treated as an integral and fundamental part of the probem. Our concern here is to examine underlying situations and likely causes and sources of conflict; to identify forces and processes at work; to look at the dramatis personae and the supporting cast; to sketch in the stage for events and its control system; and to illustrate these with examples of conjunctures and action. The aim is to probe to the fullest extent that situations are known or understood by the writer. This study is concerned with pertinence, not with norm-setting. Lessons, even important lessons, may thereby be drawn, but indirectly and perhaps more firmly.

In retrospect it may seem inevitable that this book should come out. The author was actually born into the agrarian problem and brought up with it; this shaped the life of his family. His parents inherited chronically indebted land as their share of an already very small holding. As part-time farmers they sought a variety of jobs and in the process the author experienced the real rural poverty of some of the poorest villages of Cyprus. These were the hard years of the 1920s and 1930s when the colonial economy of the country was experiencing acute neglect and underdevelopment. Even the house in which he was born was lost in the process for very little through the fraudulent manipulations of a lawyer's clerk.

The author can recollect no bitterness, conflict or agrarian discontent. Everything seemed to be taken as part of the "natural" order of things. The predominant sentiment was nationalistic, anti-colonial, with outbreaks of agitation, some of it violent. He "contracted" awareness of social and related political matters from poor farmers and artisans when he was their young village teacher and the Second World War was forcing *de facto* relaxation of the prevailing draconian ban (down to petty detail) on any political activity and social organisation.

His acquired taste for political economy began when, as a student in England, especially of applied economics, he had to learn and absorb all those white papers and debates engendered by the actions of the first Labour Government in the latter half of the 1940s; appreciation of the attributes of land came from the study of geography at the same time. His study in land use for a PhD degree at the London School of Economics and the courses he attended in London deepened and broadened understanding of these issues.

He cut his teeth in land reform as the first land consolidation and development officer in Cyprus, when he faced the acute problems of making sense of the complexities and conflicts and of devising operational tools for acceptable and effective action. His vision and the scope of his work, as well as responsibility, was vastly expanded when he joined the FAO of the UN as land tenure and settlement specialist. In a 20-year career with the FAO he moved on to become senior agrarian reform officer and ended as agrarian reform policy adviser.

The vast world canvas with its bewildering contrasts and complications requires any practitioner to put some order into his conception and method of work if his actions are to become relevant and effective, and not merely a formal response. Exposure to the real problems *in situ* is the best education.

The author's experience became both rich and painful. The divorce between diplomatic niceties and ugly realities; the comfortable conferences which contrasted with the urgent needs of humanity outside; the deceptions practised by politicians concerning real problems; and the low, if not at times negative, returns for colossal efforts and considerable funds – these and similar goings-on compelled in the author a profound reappraisal of policies, methods and attitudes and a search for real causes. He began to prepare himself for the days when, unencumbered by an official's limitations with their cramping effect on thinking and comment, he could probe into matters. His term as Minister of Agriculture and Natural Resources in his own country's government delayed the work but gave insights into political practice.

This book is not of course the author's memoirs or a subjective view of the world but can be read as a reaction based on experience; it is also a positive attempt to put the core issues where they belong and an invitation to view matters from where the real dynamic is generated. The main thrust of the book's argument is to emphasize that the dynamic behind structural changes is conflict, and that the intensity, direction and effect of that dynamic varies with prevailing conditions, contending forces and institutional instruments in what in essence is a power struggle. That essential truth has been silently passed over through diversions into at best elegant technocratic research or emphasis pointed at secondary issues or through sophisticated, and even crude, misinformation.

Notes

1. A year later he broadened his call. At the Paris Conference on International Economic Co-operation he said: "Our deliberations here must address the plight of one-quarter of mankind whose lives are overwhelmed by poverty and hunger and numbed by insecurity and despair . . . ." Quoted by Fagen 1978b p. 290.
2. E.g. in his 1975/1977 paper.
3. The widening gap has been generally recognised. Widely known as the "Kuznets curve", it acknowledges that in the early stages of economic growth there is increasing inequality, which is later expected to diminish. This eventual diminution has not yet been significantly confirmed outside the socialist system.
4. Huntington 1968 pp. 298–9.
5. See e.g., Amin 1976 pp. 299 and 349.
6. Baran 1957 pp. 169–170.

1 Introduction

The Nature of Agrarian Conflict and Reform

If the importance of land in history and politics is acknowledged, agrarian conflict has been ignored and agrarian reform often given a minor role in social and economic development. For this the technicians and experts are responsible. Their "sophisticated" analysis or argument does not, however, deceive the real, especially the primary, actors, who know instinctively where the crunch lies. The experts need no longer sigh in despair that agrarian reform is plagued by politics. For the conventional – nay official – wisdom of more than a decade has proclaimed authoritatively from prestigious platforms that agrarian reform is about *power*.[1]

Land is at the heart of agrarian conflict and reform and is the pivot of power. More precisely, the problem is one of human or social relations in respect to control and use of land and access to the accruing benefits. The land system is a network of these relations in institutionalised form. Land becomes the pivot of power because people depend on it for their vital needs: the greater the dependence, the more strategic becomes control of land and the more power it confers. Monopoly control of land may lead to monopoly control of power over people.

Institutionalised control of land operates through the political system. The reciprocal relationship between the land system and the political system makes them interdependent; the land system becomes a pillar – in agrarian societies the main pillar – of the wider socio-economic and political system; the latter, the guardian and supporter of the land system. Landowners have always ensured that the political system comes under their control or influence.

It follows that, whenever those who have no privileged access to land, especially those who are wronged or oppressed by the system, find it unacceptable, there is no *easy* way to change that system. Landowning interests, especially if they are privileged and entrenched, will not give up their privileges or power unless they are forced to do so. Only an acute conflict and shift in the power structure will bring about significant change.

That, in simple outline, is the nature of agrarian conflict and the political economy of reform. Because land has a special role as a means of production,

1

2 The Unpromised Land

while its use satisfies vital needs, the concept has persisted over centuries, if not millenia, that land is a free gift of nature and, therefore, meant for all inhabitants.[2] Appropriation of land for private use is thus in some way "unnatural" and "wronging" to others. On this tenet of land as a free gift of nature are based some classical economic concepts and the related moral stand, that land has social functions and cannot be appropriated for exclusive and selfish use and profit by some at the expense of others. Since the 1960s the Roman Catholic Church, taking its cue from Latin American ecclesiastical and supporting thought, has given official utterance to this repeatedly. On 20 February 1981, Pope John Paul II reportedly called land the gift of God.[3]

It is also worth observing that land has been the locus of group, and even national, identity. A tribe or nation, even an extended family, has ensured its identity, as well as its security, by defence of its territory and even linked its group continuity with ancestral burial grounds, whose inviolability was held sacrosanct. Some thinkers even ascribe to man an instinct of territoriality.

The agrarian probem, and the conflict and reform that arise, vary tremendously from place to place and over time in the same place. Even at their most moribund, land systems are live media, as are the connected political systems. The two interact under the influence of stimuli generated by themselves or by outside agents. They are in constant evolution, if usually at different rates and in different directions. They re-adjust to each other, often fitfully. The land system tends to be sluggish and thus to create problems for the rest of the economic and social system and to have repercussions on the political system. Mutual re-adjustment and accommodation is not, however, reform as understood in this study. Agrarian reform is a drastic, planned public intervention aimed at bringing about a new structure of access to land more adequate to the requirements of the socio-economic and political system for which it serves as support or with which it is closely linked. Thus agrarian reform inescapably involves the whole network of power relations and brings into play a vast range of forces.

One can illustrate the process schematically by describing two distinct and contrasted societies: (a) in the first, the overall socio-economic and political system is modern, advanced, strong, fairly adequately and equitably functioning, and therefore, rests on a structure of access to land (and water) resources free from *serious* pathological defects. Agrarian reform can thus be confined to a skilful operation to remove the slack in the land system and bring it into line with the overall system. This operation remains a "repair and maintenance" action with no far-reaching repercussions on the overall socio-economic and political system. (b) in the second, the overall socio-economic and political system is arrested, underdeveloped and poorly functioning. It rests on a structure of access to land (and water) resources in which those resources are concentrated in the hands of a small class of large owners; the economy is predominantly agrarian and the influence of the landowning class on the overall system decisive. Here agrarian reform becomes a critical element, even the spearhead, in a complete transformation of the total system.

Agrarian reform does not happen "naturally", in the sense of an automatic process. It is even riddled with benign or acute vicious circles. With the strong overall system of our first example, there is more than enough capacity in the system to carry the periodic "repair and maintenance" operation without undue difficulty. With the second, the complexity and magnitude of the task of an urgent and drastic transformation is barely within the capacity of the system and also faces strong opposition from powerful and entrenched landed interests. Normally effective action is avoided, the situation continues to deteriorate until mounting pressures lead to an overthrow of the system. Thus radical transformations of this type tend to occur on specific historical occasions and as the result of events of considerable magnitude and impact.

Between these two cases lies a wide range of combinations of conditions and circumstances, and a complexity of processes and dynamic interactions, that provide a rich backcloth to the drama of agrarian reform.

The Seeds of Agrarian Conflict and Reform

Since agrarian conflict concerns control and use of land and the distribution of its benefits, including their extension to social and political power, the question arises as to how conflict originates and, more particularly, how it is perceived.

Within a society itself, the conflict is first perceived as an incompatibility between existing arrangements and one's own essential interests and aspirations. Reform in turn is perceived as a way out of existing arrangements. In practice, since the status quo appears to many as a law of nature and incapable of alteration, social conditioning makes origination of both stages of perception difficult.

Perception need not, however, originate with those directly affected. Once the incompatibility and the possibility of a way out, i.e. of an alternative order of things, are effectively articulated and propagated, those affected may easily be alerted and thus stimulated to thought and action. The seeds, therefore, of the conflict and its elimination lie less in the perceptions of internal participants or external observers than in the realities of the situation. The embers are there, the fire has only to be fanned and fuelled.

The basic incompatibility concerns ownership of the means of production, i.e. land and water, and the social relations of their use. The most extreme example would be of monopolistic ownership and extortionate relations of production with the monopolist taking the lion's share. Incompatibility is aggravated when pressures mount with the increasing disparity between the rising potential for production (and therefore for higher incomes and social advance) and the restraints placed on production by the institutionalised land system, e.g. the monopolist prefers a low income and social prestige from his large land ownership to the risk involved in investment in new methods of land use.

The real situation is, of course, much more complex and varied, but it should be stressed that the basic incompatibilities tend to worsen when a socio-economic system is not stagnating but on the move. The only truth in the conspiracy theory is that outsiders may, to some extent, make people adversely affected by the inherent incompatibilities, aware of them. The seeds, however, are engendered by the malfunctioning of the system.

Notes

1. McNamara 1973 p. 19.
2. Rousseau expressed powerfully this "collective claim from natural law . . . Land is the gift of God, and land property did not enjoy the same legitimacy as property acquired by labour". In his *Social Contract and Discourses* he wrote: "The first man who, having enclosed a piece of ground, bethought himself of saying *This is mine*, and found people simple enough to believe him, was the real founder of civil society". Offer 1981 pp. 3 and 1.
3. Jeremy Bentham, another eighteenth-century writer, in his *Principles of Civil Code* suggested that "land was not the gift of God, but the gift of the state . . . Property was a social construct which was only justified by expediency; what had been granted could be taken away". Ibid. p. 1.

Part I: The Setting

"First Citizen: We are accounted poor citizens. The patricians good. What authority surfeits on would relieve us. If they would yield us but the superfluity, while it were wholesome, we might guess they relieved us humanely; but they think we are too dear: the leanness that afflicts us, the object of our misery, is as an inventory to particularise their abundance; our sufferance is a gain to them . . . for the gods know I speak this in hunger for bread, not in thirst for revenge."
Shakespeare *Coriolanus*, Act I, Scene I.

"The poor man hath title to the rich man's goods; so that the rich man ought to let the poor man have part of his riches to help and comfort him withal."
Latimer, preaching in the 1530s.

"The poor that have no land are left still in the straits of beggary, are shut out of all livelihood, but what they shall pick out of sore bondage . . ."
Gerrard Winstanley, mid-17th century England.

2. Rural Classes

Rural Classes in Relation to the Land: General Considerations

It is well known that, in developing countries, the vast majority of the population, in some cases over 90%, live in rural societies, from which the urban and industrial sections of the population also originated. As rural societies are predominantly agrarian and thus dependent on land, control of land is the strongest force in shaping their economic, social and political structure. To understand the nature and dynamics of these societies it is therefore essential to examine them in relation to the land.

Many people think of land control as combining ownership with use and the prototype land user as the owner-cultivator. It is thus surprising to discover that individual ownership of land, now widely diffused in rural society, is a relatively recent phenomenon. Historically, ownership of land was the prerogative of the ruler as part of his sovereignty over the territory, while the cultivators used the land as his tributaries. Between sovereign and cultivators were intermediaries, usually favourites, local commanders or provincial representatives, who extorted the surplus from the cultivators over and above the ruler's tribute and other exactions. They were part of the sovereign's apparatus for controlling the territory, ensuring the collection of tribute and raising armies to fight.

Remarkably, this arrangement, with variations and different emphases, is found in practically all ages and parts of the world. It may be considered a universal form of the administration of power in agrarian economies where land and its productive capacity are the mainstay of the economy and society. Sovereignty over the land, therefore, could not belong to the private individual. This is true not only of medieval societies, to which the whole concept of land ownership is alien,[1] but also of African societies, where sovereignty may extend over a whole kingdom or be confined to an extended family. The system existed in Indian societies before the discovery and conquest of the Americas, and in tributary states such as the Minoan Kingdom in Crete and the Asian polities of the past.

This fact – that widely diffused individual ownership of land is a recent phenomenon – must be kept constantly in mind in order to retain a true perspective of the modern emphasis on private ownership, especially where the individual quest for land is ideologically raised to the status of an instinct.

Data on Rural Classes in Relation to the Land

All approaches to the identification, classification, quantification and portrayal of rural classes *vis-à-vis* access to land have proved unsatisfactory. Identification is practically impossible because of their great variety and the tremendous overlap between them. For similar reasons classification tends to give untidy results and to leave out important inter-relationships,[2] while quantification is even more unsatisfactory because data do not exist in sufficient detail and coverage; those available are invariably unreliable or omit essential aspects; many are even contradictory.

The most widely used source of data is the census. Those who have had the opportunity to design and hold an agricultural census know both the pitfalls and inadequacies of even the most "reliable" results. Those who have used these to formulate or implement policies know that reliance on census data brings many assumptions and seeming certainties to grief. Too many users, however, are victims of hidden traps in the data. A common trap is insufficient awareness that agricultural censuses are based on the holding and the holder. A holding is defined as the total of a unit *operated* by a person, actual or legal, and the holder is the *operator*. The operator may own the whole unit which he operates, or part of it, or none of it.

Access to land is thus obscured by the "holding" approach of the census. Efforts to get at real relationships to land and so build up a profile of land ownership face many difficulties, even on a local scale. Ownership is surrounded by secretiveness; records are usually non-existent or, if they exist, not open to scrutiny; if open to scrutiny, the work of compiling meaningful aggregates is far too laborious and the records often outdated, sometimes by generations.

These observations are intended to qualify much of the information given here and to alert the reader to the degree of completeness or reliability of the data.

It is useful to divide rural classes in relation to the land into *cultivating* and *non-cultivating* classes. This classification is difficult to make with any precision and, in the light of modern farming, perhaps out of date, given that many "cultivators" do most of their work in or from their offices. For practical purposes, "cultivating" is defined here as referring to those classes whose activities or occupations have a direct bearing on agricultural production on the land itself or within the holding or farm; application of the definition will also be pragmatic.

Similarly, for purposes of analysis the term "class" refers to a relatively coherent category of people who share significant socio-economic attributes and status in society, but does not imply that they are necessarily conscious of themselves as a distinctive group.

The Cultivating Classes

Owners: As already noted, widespread private ownership of land is a relatively recent phenomenon. It is probable that in the past *de facto* individual ownership spread as central control broke down. In the last century or two increased commercial links, the development of capitalist production in agriculture, and the emergence of a parallel ideological orientation towards property-owning by a larger section of the population under the impact of the rise of the middle classes, the bourgeoisie, have led to a widening of land ownership in an accelerating process. The right to property and to its inalienability was often further safeguarded by inscription in the constitutions of states created in the nineteenth and twentieth centuries with the advent of independence under the impetus of bourgeois ideology and nationalism. This inscription served the interests of property owners, actual and potential; and in some cases even the right to vote was confined to actual property owners.

Many attributes of owner-cultivators are relevant to questions of agrarian conflict and reform: the size of their property holding; the size of their production or value added; the patterns of management and labour use; the destination of production; and the distribution of surplus. Of these the most critical are labour on the land and the relations of production.

A fundamental weakness of censuses based on the holding and the holder is that they tend to understate both large properties, sometimes to a marked degree, and very small ones. In the census a large property wholly or partly leased out for cultivation to a number of dependent holders vanishes as such or appears only as a diminished holding. At the other end of the scale, when small owners lease in other land to add to their own, they appear in the census as larger holders than they would be if only their own land were included; and when landless people obtain land for cultivation under lease or another dependent relation, even for a season, they appear as holders, however precarious their status. The resulting overall impression is that land properties are not so large or so small as they are in reality.

Table 2.1 should, therefore, be read with great caution and with the above reservations in mind. It is of interest in that it shows that owner-cultivatorship is not universal. It should be noted also that owners of land tend to have other strategic production advantages such as access to water, inputs and marketing, and to the institutions that administer them. Table 2.1 does not show cases of customary tenure where group ownership prevails.

Non-Owners: Table 2.1 also serves to show the proportion of holdings and land in use by holders who are not owners; for tenants and sharecroppers actual percentages are given; for the rest it can be deduced to some extent. This category can usefully be divided into (a) those who are holders but not owners, and (b) those who are neither. The former hold land in lease, sharecropping or other dependent tenure form; the latter are workers who provide an owner or holder with their labour but have no managerial duties.

A more systematic treatment of the whole range of issues arising from the

Table 2.1
Holdings by Tenure and World Census Year
(Number of Holdings as % of all Census Holdings; and Land Area as % of all Land in Holdings)

	Owner-Operated Holdings				Holdings Operated by Tenants and Sharecroppers			
	No. of Holdings			Area	No. of Holdings		Area	
	1970	1960	1950	1970	1970	1960	1970	1950
Region								
North and Central America[1]	61.7	58.8	59.2	37.2	11.4	19.1	11.8	24.3
South America[2]	61.9	65.9	78.1	80.6	17.3	18.4	6.2	10.1
Asia[3]	85.8	68.1	52.6	83.9	5.9	9.1	5.9	37.3
Europe[4]	67.7	64.1	44.2	58.9	9.0	11.5	12.5	15.4
Country								
Canada	68.6	72.9	77.3	44.7	5.2	5.7	5.6	7.2
USA	62.5	57.1	57.4	35.3	12.9	20.5	12.9	26.9
Costa Rica	84.5	76.3	81.1	90.8	5.0	4.0	1.2	4.1
Dominican Republic	54.7	58.8	—	—	10.1	28.9	—	—
El Salvador	35.3	—	—	77.1	24.0	—	7.2	—
Honduras	66.2	—	—	84.7	22.6	—	5.3	—
Panama	12.3	24.6	14.1	26.0	4.4	6.0	3.5	9.3
Brazil	60.4	69.7	79.3	82.6	20.4	17.3	6.1	9.1
Colombia	68.7	62.4	—	74.6	14.2	23.3	5.3	—
Peru	62.2	68.1	—	82.1	8.7	15.7	4.5	—

Uruguay	58.6	49.9	50.3	52.7	22.9	33.3	34.7	19.0
Venezuela	60.9	39.8	—	82.4	5.6	13.1	—	2.1
Jordan	67.3	—	—	72.7	14.9	—	—	12.2
India	92.0	72.7	—	91.5	4.1	5.5	—	2.4
Indonesia	74.8	64.1	—	76.2	3.2	6.8	—	2.1
Pakistan	41.7	41.1	52.6	39.5	34.5	41.7	37.3	29.6
Philippines	58.0	44.7	—	65.6	28.9	39.9	—	21.4
South Korea	66.5	73.6	—	66.1	9.5	—	—	6.7
Austria	73.0	—	—	77.3	1.9	—	—	0.9
Belgium	28.0	26.8	18.9	7.1	23.9	24.8	29.2	27.8
France	41.5	45.0	—	—	14.7	20.7	—	—
Fed Rep. of Germany	39.9	42.6	42.0	29.8	6.8	5.0	5.7	9.0
Italy	81.8	73.9	—	76.2	6.7	8.7	—	7.6
Malta	9.5	7.7	—	4.3	73.9	72.2	—	68.1
Netherlands	38.1	37.1	—	27.9	22.5	30.4	—	26.9
UK	51.6	53.9	44.9	43.4	27.5	34.3	44.5	30.8

Note: The important category "Holdings under more than one mode of operation" has not been included above. Average figures for regions are derived as follows: [1] For holdings 7 countries; for area 11 countries; [2] For both 6 countries; [3] For holdings 5 countries; for area 10 countries; and [4] For holdings 10 countries; for area 12 countries.

Source: Tables 5.2 and 15.7, pp. 94 and 284 respectively in FAO *The 1970 World Census of Agriculture*, Rome. 1981.

conditions under which these classes operate or work is given in the discussion of production relations (Chapter 4). To complete the data, such as they are, concerning the cultivating classes it is appropriate to consider the non-rural cultivating classes.

Urban: This is a very mixed category. It comprises: those cultivating classes who live permanently in urban areas and practise, or are engaged in, agriculture in the neighbourhood of the town or even within its boundary; those who may commute periodically, maintaining their links with their land; and those traditional large owners or new entrepreneurial interests who operate from an urban environment.

Figures published by FAO[3] based on population censuses indicate an urban labour force in the agricultural sector ranging from 0.3% of the total labour force in Bangladesh to 10.2% in Algeria. Nicaragua with 6.5%, El Salvador with 7.7%, Peru with 9.2% illustrate the urban character of the large land-owning class. Countries for which figures show trends present a variable picture. In Poland, where there is a tendency to part-time farming, the proportion of the urban labour force in the agricultural sector has increased in the post-war period; in India with a rise in both part-time farming and entrepreneurial agriculture the proportion has risen fairly markedly.

The Landless: Literally speaking, landlessness sounds a simple concept. It is, however, a complex tool to fashion and handle for purposes of analysis and policy making. Any meaningful approach must concentrate on those classes which need to work for a living but have no access to land or whose access is such that it deprives them of making a living appropriate to the general level in their area.

For reasons already discussed landlessness is largely undocumented and, as a politically sensitive issue, unpublished. The data in Table 2.2 are derived from a systematic survey of existing information, published in a comprehensive study[4] which also provides safeguards in appraisal and use of the data for comparative purposes. With all their imperfections the figures give a general picture of landlessness and near-landlessness in the rural societies of 20 developing countries. The "landless" are defined as "members of the rural labor force who own no land but must sell their labor in order to earn income; the near-landless are those whose access to land or whose holdings are insufficient to provide a family livelihood and who must, therefore, spend a substantial proportion of their labor time working for others".[5]

The results indicate an almost universal rise in the absolute number and proportion of the landless among rural populations throughout the world.[6] Among the reasons for this are: the rapid increase in overall population compared with the fixed quantity of land and its loss to agriculture; eviction of precarious holders from land; rural indebtedness; the spread of entrepreneurial agriculture among landlords and urban interests; and slow or distorted overall economic development.

Table 2.2
Landlessness and Near-landlessness in Selected Countries

Country	(1) Landless as % of Rural Labour Force	(2) Near-Landless as % of Rural Labour Force	(1) & (2) Combined
Bangladesh	28	61	89
India	32	47	79
Java	60	29	89
Malaysia	12	39	51
Pakistan	43	45	88
Philippines	55	26	81
Sri Lanka	54	19	73
Thailand	10	40	50
Argentina	24	46	70
Bolivia	38	45	83
Brazil	40	19	59
Colombia	20	46	66
Ecuador	28	45	73
Mexico	30	20	50
Peru	23	37	60
Costa Rica	35	15	50
El Salvador	38	52	90
Guatemala	29	59	88
Dominican Republic	35	52	87
Jamaica	24	56	80

Source: Esman and Associates 1978 Tables 2 and 4, pp. 36 and 36d.

Non-cultivating Classes in Rural Areas

There have always been non-cultivating classes in rural areas but in recent years their numbers have rapidly increased both absolutely and as a proportion of the rural population. In the past they were closely or loosely related to agriculture, either as rentiers or as artisans and providers of services. In recent decades, especially in developed and in rapidly developing countries, the numbers of residents in rural areas with few connections with agriculture or even with rural activities have grown and are fast growing. In the UK in the 1940s and 1950s they were known as the "adventitious population".

FAO have published[7] data on the rural labour force in non-agricultural sectors which show that as a percentage of the total rural labour force they varied from 6.3 in Mali, 9.3 in Turkey, 11.8 in Nicaragua, 14.2 in El Salvador and 14.8 in India to 27.7 in Indonesia, 30.8 in Malaya, 31.0 in Pakistan, 32.7 in Algeria and 38.5 in Spain. In developed countries they were 59.1 in Hungary, 61.5 in Sweden, 68.3 in the Federal Republic of Germany and 88 in the United States. As Naiken[8] observes, the figures clearly indicate "the increasing trend of non-agricultural participation in rural areas as the share of the agricultural labour force in the total economy is reduced".

Notes

1. Simpson 1961 p. 84.
2. Concerning problems of classification and an attempt at such a classification, see Christodoulou 1970/1972 pp. 41–51.
3. Naiken 1977.
4. Esman and Associates 1978.
5. Ibid. p. 35.
6. A critical study of available figures in India and Bangladesh concludes that in India those owning no arable land at all dropped from 30.8% of rural households in the 1954–55 National Sample Survey to 25.6 in that of 1971–72, while together with those with less than 0.4 ha of arable land the percentage (around 45) barely changed. The figures are described as an informed guess. For Bangladesh the Sample Survey of 1978 leads to the conclusion that 28.8% of rural households own no arable land; combined with those with 0.4 ha of arable land or less these reach 62%. From Cain 1983 pp. 149–167.
7. Naiken 1977 Tables 1 and 2.
8. Ibid. p. 6.

3. Access to Land

Institutionalisation of Access to Land

Control over land has, over the millenia, contained an element of force or assertion of power. This is connected with the vital role of land in sustaining human society and with the scarcity of productive land in relation to needs. It is also probably due to the rough ways in which disputes could be settled among early (and not only early) human groups. The habitat, or territorial domain, of the group had to be defended and martial qualities and mores were deemed appropriate.

Institutionalisation is a way of setting norms or agreed positions to smooth the path of human relations. Control over land must have been affected early in human social development by such institutionalisation in the form of customary arrangements regulating human relations in connection with control and use of the land. Customary arrangements have survived in many societies to this day,[1] notably in Africa.

Assuming that the African experience of institutionalisation of access to land in customary land tenure systems is universally valid, the key norm would be that he who clears and brings land into cultivation could claim exclusive use of the area, by himself and his family and usually also by his descendants. In the course of time this tends to form a constellation of such group land units and the need arises for a coherent and common approach to the protection and defence of the land pertaining to a wider kinship group of early pioneers. This becomes a rudimentary land administration and may be merged with wider quasi-state powers used to regulate other affairs of the wider kinship group.

A basic right is that every person born into the smallest cell of the group, or later in the territory of the wider group, whose parents are members of the group, should receive sufficient land from the group land to ensure the subsistence of his nuclear family. Co-ordinate with this is the obligation to *use* the land; otherwise it reverts to the group and is liable for allocation to other group members in need. This takes place especially if the person to whom land has been allocated leaves the area; he has, however, the right on return to receive land, though not necessarily the same fields as he had before he left.

15

This process explains the growth of sovereignty over given areas of land. Cumulatively and in the course of time the picture becomes more complex and a hierarchical system of sovereignties develops. The process assumes, of course, a natural growth undisturbed by intrusions, conquests or plundering by marauding groups or by invading superior forces.

The ecological approach to the institutionalisation of access to land has the merit of emphasising the two main aspects of the problem: the "natural" need for regulation of access and the corollary of power to enforce, and change, the rules. Land tenure institutions, therefore, reflect the needs of society and the pattern of exercise of power.

Where no enforceable customary or statutory regulation of access to land exists, force and sharp practice decide acquisition and holding. Enforceable regulation which is equitable and protects the weak can exist only with a minimum equality among the interested population or when strong and fair state legislation and administration exist and operate well. Those conditions rarely existed in the past and are rarer today than surface indications lead observers to believe.

Modern land tenure institutions have evolved from past conditions under the impact of social, economic and political developments, including violent changes due to war and revolution. Some institutions are the offspring of institutions transplanted from the mother country to colonised areas, progenies of both the grafted and the old stock. The variety of land tenure institutions is enormous; an indication of some basic distinct types should perforce suffice.

Contemporary Land Tenure Institutions

Existing land tenure institutions reflect their current stage of evolution. They cannot remain as they are now for ever. The most praised land tenure form existing today is private ownership, which is often described as ideal and suited to human nature.

Private Ownership of Land
As seen from Table 2.1 agricultural land owned privately can reach and even exceed 90% of all land in holdings included in agricultural censuses. There are, however, lower percentages. In most socialist countries, and above all in the USSR, private ownership is much reduced, sometimes to 2–3% of all agricultural land.

Private ownership implies total or ultimate control over the given land with rights of unfettered disposal. However, ". . . dependence upon the sovereign dents the perfection of ownership. . . . Landed wealth is especially vulnerable, owing to its visibility, immobility and durability".[2] Furthermore, "Roman law and English common law set land apart as a superior prototype of property, in acknowledgement of its primacy among the assets of agrarian societies".[3] Ownership and control over it require the protection of the state, which is normally secured by registration and often guaranteed by a provision in the constitution.[4]

Private ownership has evolved from the decay and supersession of previous systems – the feudal system in Europe, hybrids in colonial possessions, or large tributary polities in Asia. The decay is due to the previous system's losing momentum owing to its exhausting its own potential for renewal, and to the impact of more dynamic new systems, the most dynamic historically being the capitalist system. Thus private ownership is an offspring of both disintegration and a new thrust. The offspring of mere disintegration tends to be a stagnant subsistence owner/cultivatorship almost by default; on the other hand the offspring of early capitalism in agriculture is thrustful and on the ascendant, taking over the stagnant "cousin". In what is now the USA, the Pilgrim Fathers escaped from the vestiges of feudalism, from primogeniture and entail in England, to an apparent *tabula rasa* in land institutions. Their concern was to own their own land, to be their own men and to ensure that their descendants could continue to be so. In addition land was plentiful. "Individual freeholding could not have gained ascendancy in the US if land had not been cheap, so that men of modest means could own it. Gradually the frontier vanished, and land became more costly. The potential effects on our system of agriculture were blocked as it became conscious policy of the U.S. government to defend traditional small-unit agriculture."[5] The concluding observation contains the important truth that private ownership combined with the capitalist thrust in agriculture carries its own blocking mechanism.

Private owners can be cultivators, partners with cultivators or merely rentiers. The boundary between such divisions is blurred; an owner of land can be all three. Table 3.1 summarises some of the characteristics of owners of land who are cultivators; while Table 3.2 adds to the attributes of land owners by pointing out some relations to cultivators of their land. Table 3.1 indicates that landownership can be large, medium or small; individual or in partnership; and can concern legal or physical persons. These attributes are important and raise many issues discussed in subsequent pages.

Finally ownership can be secure or insecure; absolute or qualified; real or on paper. Such attributes are closely related to formal land administration and law; but also to respect for rights by the state or by powerful interests and general acceptance by all concerned. Faulty law and poor land administration cause insecurity through inability to establish proof of title or clarity of position. This generates confusion and encourages abuses. A "soft" state and aggressive practices by élites create the conditions for social commotion provoked by abuses.

Tenancy of Land

In simple terms tenancy of land is permission by its owner to another party to use the land against payment. Many speak of it as a contract. Those who subscribe to the tenet that land is a gift of nature and that what it yields is the result of somebody's labour, consider tenancy as exploitative practice by

Table 3.1
Categories of Cultivators Who Own the Land of their Holdings

Owner	Type of Holding	Predominant Mode of Operation	Market Orientation
Kinship Group	Small or Medium	Family labour and traditional mutual aid	Subsistence and/or for sale
Poor Farmer	Small	Family labour	Mainly subsistence
Middle Farmer	Medium	Family and hired labour	Mainly for sale
Rich Farmer	Large	Mainly hired or dependent labour	For sale
Entrepreneur	Medium	Hired labour (and management) with some mechanisation	For sale or for processing in own plant
Entrepreneur	Large	Hired labour (and management) with mechanisation	As above
Company	Large	Hired labour (and management) with mechanisation	As above
Company	Plantation	Hired labour (and management) and mechanisation	Export (usually to home country if the company is foreign)
Co-operative	Medium or large	Member's labour	For sale
State	Large	State employees	For sale/supply to approved enterprises/customers
Religious or Cultural Institution	Any size	Members or inmates (and hired labour)	Subsistence or sale

somebody (the owner), who has no more right to the land than the exploited person (the tenant) and the rent as an extraction from the fruit of the labour of the user. Most conventional economists consider rent as the share of one factor of production, in this case land, in the output. The problem then shifts to assessing the right share. In practice this ideological dispute is solved by the bargaining position of the parties involved.

Rent is paid in the form of money, share in the crop, services to the owners of the land or a mixture of all three. The tendency is towards cash payment in line with capitalist concepts and practices.

Tenancy is the most elusive land tenure institution and has proved most resistant to effort to regulate it through legislation, registration and administration. The main reason is that the parties tend to be so unequal in bargaining position and in social and political clout. This is particularly important since tenancy is so widespread in the world (Table 2.1). Tenancy and its problems will feature prominently in subsequent pages.

Table 3.2
Categories of Cultivating· Holders Who Do Not Own the Land of their Holdings

Cultivator's Tenure	Owner of the Land	Type of Relationship
Partner	Various	Partnership Contract
Tenancy	Various	Contractual; payment of rent
Sharecropping	Various	Contractual; sharing of produce
Emphyteusis	Various	Contractual or traditional; payment of nominal rent
Customary	Kinship Group	Traditional; virtually permanent and free occupation
Squatter	Various	Informal and clandestine
Colono or bonded labour	Traditional Latifundio or other large owner	Traditional free labour and other services offered to the landlord in return for small holding to operate
Perpetual use	State	Approved cooperative or collective farm (paying tax and subject to quota deliveries to the state)
Contractual among Partners	Individual partners	Employees and/or partners

Emphyteusis mentioned in Table 3.2 requires explanation. Literally it means "implantation", which must denote that it originated with colonising new lands, such as the Greek colonies in Sicily or on the Black Sea Coast. Today it signifies a very long-term tenancy at rent which becomes nominal over that period which may be as much as 99 years. It is still found today in Malta and Italy.

Customary Land Tenure

Contemporary customary land tenure is largely confined to Africa south of the Sahara. Its presumed origins were described earlier and I have given a fuller account in a paper[6] to the World Land Reform Conference in 1966, and discussed recent trends and tendencies in an article.[7] Here it is worth recalling that these tenures were an institutional accommodation to conditions of subsistence lived in isolation, at times a kind of siege economy, in a tropical agricultural environment with relative abundance of virgin land, thus encouraging initiative to bring land under cultivation, group solidarity and territorial identity. Regulation was flexible, the polities hierarchical and gerontocratic, but subsistence conditions enforced a certain homogeneity in levels of living. Land administration was vested in the hierarchy, mainly the chiefs and their council of elders; it followed certain customary norms, hallowed by religious beliefs connected with ancestral spirits and ancestral burying grounds. Members of each kinship group had basic rights: land enough to support their nuclear families and claim to such land allocation on their return even after a long absence. The land allocated had to be used or

it would be returned to the group for allocation to others. Periodic realloca-
tion among the families was carried out, especially if shifting cultivation was
practised.

The flexibility and adaptability of customary arrangements were useful to
relatively isolated communities whose numbers were kept fairly constant by
a sort of Malthusian process. Under colonial occupation, white settler
settlement, the rise of local élites favoured by colonial rule, and the takeover
by these élites after political independence, these qualities of flexibility and
adaptability proved the Achilles' heel of the system. The local rightholders
were displaced, defrauded, exploited and deprived by superior force and
power, not infrequently under a legal guise, as will be seen later. The
vestiges of customary tenure in Africa are still under continuing pressure in
the interests of modernisation, which is often no more than thinly disguised
plunder. The security of tenure that prevailed in the past is now usually
ensured for some, usually the well-to-do, through registration; for the rest
the road to eviction for indebtedness is open. Thus landlessness, unknown
in the past, is now appearing and growing. Customary tenure is formally
vanishing; in the minds of most rightholders there is confusion.

State Land

State land exists in every country for various reasons. It may be property
previously belonging to the sovereign or the crown; it may be the result of
conquest or expropriation. Land expropriation for agrarian reform is a
special and important measure used by the state to acquire land for redistribution, so that the land is rarely kept as state land for long; if the state does
keep the land, it is often intended as a reserve power to influence land
utilisation. Tanzania nationalised the land a few years ago but its effect on
access to land has been very gradual. On 29 March 1978 the Nigerian
Federal Military Government issued a decree which in effect nationalised
the land. Under its terms the military governor of each state would award
certificates of occupancy to those who have customary rights (usually over
agricultural land) or statutory rights to a particular plot. Occupancy would
be limited to 0.5 ha of undeveloped urban land, to 500 ha for agricultural
purposes or to 5,000 ha of land for grazing purposes.[8] The *Financial Times*
observed that urban professionals, in spite of difficulties put in their way by
customary tenure in the past, had increasingly invested in commercial
agriculture in their home areas in recent years. It added that the decree may
facilitate the trend, especially if they are able to exert influence on the
bureaucracy.

Three years earlier, in 1975, the land reform Proclamation in Ethiopia
affirmed "all rural lands shall be the collective property of the Ethiopian
people". The Ethiopian government has since experimented with setting up
co-operative and state farms. All socialist countries have maintained much
land as state property, for use as state farms or allocation to co-operative
groups for use in perpetuity. Some, notably Poland with an overwhelming
proportion of land in private ownership, have legislation that the state

should have first option for land which will be sold or transferred because the owner has ceased to farm.[9] Thus gradually state property in land is increasing.

The most extensive state land is to be found in the USSR. According to Soviet law[10] the right to own land, mineral resources, forests and waters passed into the hands of the Soviet state. This nationalisation, which was without compensation, was decreed on the day after the victory of the October Revolution. It did not automatically confiscate the land from all land owners, but only from landlords, members of the Czar's family and "other exploiters".

Land is allotted for a definite purpose and "only for gainful use". The principal agricultural land users are collective and state farms. Collective farms are allocated land for use in perpetuity, and this is composed of land in common use and of household plots. The household land is for personal, ancillary farming by the collective-farm family without the employment of hired labour, and is not transferable to other persons.

Notes

1. Norman Stone in *The Times Literary Supplement*, 27 May 1983, p. 532 mentions Teodor Shanin's view (and Chayanov's) that the peasant repartitional commune in pre-revolutionary Russia served the purpose of giving strips of land to men with large families; when the children grew up, the land was repartitioned, and parcelled out to other large families.
2. Offer 1981 p. 2.
3. Ibid. p. 5.
4. Securing private property rights by the state "has the advantage in terms of legal, fiscal and coercive power to define and enforce property rights at a lower cost than voluntary groups." Holton 1985 p. 54. Of course, groups do the enforcing in many situations, as in large traditional estates in Latin America or when there is strife between landlords and tenants and the latter try to invade landlords' lands, when the cost is in blood and death.
5. Breimyer 1964 p. 934.
6. Christodoulou 1966.
7. Christodoulou 1977, esp. pp. 4–6.
8. *Financial Times* 30 August 1978. In the northern states almost all land had been under state control since 1962. Allowances and other aid under the regime brought about by the decree enabled influential people to become substantial farmers. Senior army officers, including the head of state, Obasanjo, retired to become "large production farmers" See Ohiorhenuan 1984 p. 21.
9. "Between 1971 and 1979, the State Land Fund [in Poland] received 1.8 million hectares of land from private farmers while selling them less than 600,000 hectares in return." Cook 1984 p. 410.
10. See Syrodoyev 1975.

4. Social Relations in Production

Social Relations in Production from the Land

Land is, of course, not only a factor of production but also wealth, which, throughout history, has provided perhaps the strongest base for social and political power. Landed wealth may have diminished in importance with the growth of other sources, but is still coveted by those seeking a hedge against inflation,[1] even though their interest may not be in agriculture.[2]

Its productive capacity has largely made agricultural land the bone of contention and root cause of agrarian conflict. More wealth, certainly far more fabulous fortunes, have been made from land for urban uses. Opponents of agrarian reform often maintain that for reasons of equity (or "horizontal justice") *urban* land reform should be instituted at the same time as rural land reform. As far as is known only the Philippines and Nigeria have attempted to legislate urban land reform. The fact remains that rural land generates acute agrarian conflicts, affects a very large number of people and spreads over a far wider area. The urban problem is acute, but more than land is involved – namely accommodation, which can, and does, rise high above ground.

Production relations in the use of land are of vast variety and tremendous complexity. Not all of them are known and many of their problems have escaped the attention they deserve. Here some important types are indentified and discussed as a crucial ingredient of agrarian conflict.

Family Farm and Peasant Farm: Ambiguous Concepts

The family farm has been idolised, even venerated, in the literature on agrarian problems. The concept, however, is ambiguous. Literally it refers to a unit pertaining in some way to a family. It is not always clear whether the family owns the farm land, rents it, or even squats on it. Usually it means that the land is owned. But then the conditions of production remain unclear. Does the family work it without hiring labour? Or is it merely managed from an office or even from farther afield? The scale of operation also makes a tremendous difference. A very small unit run by a poor family in severely undercapitalised, if not technically very backward, conditions which does not fully utilise available family labour, and produces barely

22

enough to meet debts, let alone feed the family, is a far cry from a US farm[3] covering a thousand hectares and having a turnover of some million dollars, which is operated with ultra modern technology by a PhD degree holder, largely from the office and benefits from highly developed services and markets (and even subsidies).

Perhaps the general consensus is to include under this concept an owner-operated farm employing family labour and achieving viable status. This is still vague because it does not specify how much of the family labour is fully employed and for how long; furthermore, it does not resolve the difficulty of defining viability which may refer to full employment and/or to sufficient income being obtained to sustain the family at a stipulated level, also to be defined.

The family farm is often invested with sterling qualities in that, if widespread, it provides a socially stable class with qualities of moderation, thrift, a sense of responsibility and attachment to the fatherland. Many agrarian reforms have been advocated with this aim in mind: the Stolypin reform in the 1900s, the Japanese reform in the 1940s and that in Italy in the 1950s.

The family farm is frequently equated with the peasant farm, thus making the concept even more ambiguous. Using the limited data available for such a heterogeneous region as Latin America, Ortega[4] considered peasant agriculture as comprising those units where cultivation was carried out by the family. Such agriculture accounted for half the rural population in the mid-1970s, i.e. 60 to 65 million people, with 13.5 million productive units on somewhat less than one-fifth of the agricultural land. Nearly 40% of those units were less than two hectares each and Ortega considers this figure indicates the level of semi-proletarianisation, i.e. combining work on the family holding with wage employment outside it. Where work is not available, the family are simply poor peasants, as are many in El Salvador and Jamaica. Even though census figures are disputed, Ortega thinks they suggest that small holdings are increasing.

There is considerable merit in discussing small producers together since they share many attributes and face similar handicaps. For instance, they have to produce whatever the market demands in order to live; their labour potential is fixed; their bargaining position in employment, sales or purchases very weak, etc. Some of these problems and the characteristics of the peasantry are discussed later (Chapter 7). But the ambiguous concepts of family farm and peasant farm will be avoided in analysis.

Owner-operated and Family-employing Small-scale Agricultural Units

This is a less ambiguous concept which, however, does not lend itself to precise quantifiable definition. In the systematic land tenure studies carried out in Latin America in the 1960s under the auspices of the Inter-American Committee for Agricultural Development (ICAD), units of this kind were classified as family-sized and sub-family sized. The former were defined as having sufficient land to satisfy the basic needs of a family at locally-defined levels and to provide remunerative employment for 2 to 3.9 man/years at prevailing technical levels, on the assumption that most of the work was done by family members. The sub-family unit was one unable to satisfy such needs or provide employment for up to two man/years. Percentage of families in these two categories[5] are shown in Table 4.1

Table 4.1
Percentage of Agricultural Families Owning and Operating Farm Units

Families	*Argentina* (1960)	*Brazil* (1950)	*Chile* (1955)	*Colombia* (1960)	*Ecuador* (1960)	*Guatemala* (1950)
1. Owning Family-Sized Units	16.4	12.0	14.8	17.9	8.0	6.6
2. Owning Sub-Family Units	13.1	5.0	5.3	33.2	43.1	38.0

Source: ICAD Studies

The definition and Table 4.1, despite the coverage of one region only, bring out features common to problems of study of these issues in many countries: on the one hand, the requirement that the operating unit should ensure income and employment levels sufficient to satisfy family needs in both, on the other, the difficulty of quantifying such levels in relation to expectations, size of family and type of technology, all of which are compounded by insuperable obstacles in obtaining data. Except for limited localities such work has not been attempted and observations generally rely on impressions.

Table 4.1 shows the limited proportion of agricultural families operating family-sized units in contrast to those in the sub-family category. The situation is, of course, dynamic and changes in technology and organisation of production could change the proportions considerably.

By definition this category is characterised by intra-farm production relations confined very largely or exclusively to the family, whose members are self-employed. The head of the family is often said to exploit its members with arduous and long hours of work and low remuneration (Chayanov's Law of self-exploitation). More accurately, exploitation of the family is the work of outsiders and occurs in a number of ways. Low remuneration may result from low prices for the produce, low·production and low productivity. Low prices are in turn due to numerous factors: the state wants cheap food for urban consumers; market relations are adverse because the produce is offered when supplies are relatively abundant and prices low, but the producer is forced to sell urgently on account of family needs or because he is indebted or cannot store the produce; the buyer may be an intermediary in a monopsony position, a creditor, a processing firm in a strong position to depress the price, or even an incompetent or corrupt institution such as a co-operative or marketing board.

Low production is due to the small scale of operation arising from the size and/or quality of the land in the farm, including its layout, e.g. its fragmentation; from out-of-date techniques and lack of capital (physical and financial), and at times from the poor quality of labour, the result of undernourishment or disease. Necessity often forces families to spend large amounts of labour, which they may possess in some abundance, to achieve higher production (and yields) than would occur in other types of farm organisation using different factors of production.

High inputs of labour together with other limited factors of production result in low returns to labour, which are not compensated for even by higher yields.

Finally, remuneration from production has to be compared to expenditure on production inputs and, of course, on living. Small-scale producers also operate in adverse market conditions when buying.[6] Griffin makes the case that the rural capital market operates against the small-scale operator, especially if his land tenure status is weak; he is also handicapped in access to fertiliser, water and technical knowledge.

Thus this category suffers from severe structural defects which vary with the extent of deficiencies in the structure. The category is, however, far from homogeneous and one cannot easily generalise about it. Families cope with their situation in a number of ways, a common one being outside employment by all members part of the time, or by some all the time.[7] Significantly this enables them to sell their labour on the farm through the produce or/and outside the farm even more cheaply than they would otherwise. Many commercial farms and plantations and mining, industrial and service concerns use this labour and often *encourage* families to work their own land in addition to their employment with them. Conversely, some small-scale farms employ additional labour from outside the family, at least seasonally at peak periods.[8]

Owner-operated Large-scale Agricultural Units

This is a varied category, difficult to treat comprehensively. It embraces:

1. Modern agricultural units managed by the owner, increasingly with the help of mechanisation, including computerisation, and with decreasing, almost minimal, employment of labour. Many "family" farms in developed countries are now of this type. Intra-farm production relations are with family members and with permanent, and occasionally seasonal, wage labour. As operators, large owners enjoy advantages of scale both inside and outside the farm. They have better access to inputs, including credit (at more advantageous terms) than small-scale operators and are better equipped to deal with marketing. They are better organised and can use government and other public institutions effectively. They enjoy a strong bargaining position in relation to their employees, except where the latter are organised and there is especial demand for their labour. Generally the wages of agricultural workers are lower than (often half of) those in other comparable categories.

One force is superior to this category, even in developed countries – agribusiness (or other corporate agricultural enterprises) which, through contract farming and other forms of controlled co-operation, is able to ensure it a dependent position.

Under entrepreneurial or capitalist agriculture larger producers dominate and displace smaller ones, while processing or marketing interests exert strong influence on development and the distribution of benefits.[9]

Modern agricultural units are fast spreading in the developing world with the expansion of high yielding crop varieties, and the accompanying capitalised farming of the "Green Revolution". This causes considerable changes in the structure of rural society and generates new forms of agrarian conflict.

2. Traditional large units managed by the owners have dominated many developing countries, especially in Latin America, Asia, the Mediterranean and the Near East, and to a smaller extent in Africa. They are relics of past socio-political and economic systems fast superseded under the spreading impact of capitalism. Since they lack modern means of cultivation, they tend to employ large numbers of workers under varied conditions. Slavery is no longer openly practised but dependent, or bonded, labour, is common, with the labourer paid in kind and offered minimum welfare support in the form of housing and, where he also offers domestic services, food. There is not much information on this form of labour which under modern conditions may be declared illegal. Under the "Hali" system of tied labour in Gujarat farmers provide subsistence and sometimes education for labourers and their children in return for total command of the labour supply of the labourer's family.[10]

Writing of India as a whole Das Gupta[11] describes bonded labour as follows:

> Hired attached labourers are normally employed for a year at a time and perform agricultural, non-agricultural, as well as domestic, work for the employer . . . [They are] normally heavily dependent on one particular family for work, so much so that in some cases the relationship closely resembles a 'serf system' in terms of those restrictions placed by village landholders on their attached employees' right to leave the work . . . Although the 'bonded labour' system has been legally banned in 1975, . . . it would take long to implement it at the village level as long as the employers of bonded labour continue to dominate the social and political life of the village community.

The most widespread forms by which owners of traditional large estates operate them are in conjunction with tenancy, sharecropping and other dependent cultivation. This is especially true of the latifundio of Latin America.

3. Latin American latifundio. There is a voluminous literature on this subject and only outstanding features are highlighted here. The latifundio

referred to is the Latin American hacienda, or traditional large estate, comprising the landowner's home farm and his tenants' holdings, the latter forming more than half the cultivated area; the landowner retains the grazing lands for himself.[12] Tenants pay rent by working on the landowner's home farm. The commonest way of tying the cultivator to the hacienda is to give him a small parcel of land for a house and garden. The cultivator is obliged to work for a very low wage, or no wage at all, for a fixed number of days in the year, or to deliver to the landowner his agricultural produce at a low price.[13]

The land given to tied workers is so little that it keeps them dependent on their surplus labour and thus in bondage to the landowner.[14] They have in fact no alternative but to seek the work and shelter offered by the land-owner. Work and rent agreements ensure that any increased productivity or unexpected gain always accrues to the landowner. Permanent improve-ments such as buildings or fruit tree planting belong to the landowner, even though the cost was defrayed by the cultivator.[15]

Production relations in this category are, therefore, the most unequal and oppressive in existence today. The extreme lack of assets and weak bar-gaining position of those who have only labour to offer under adverse conditions are set against the monopoly of assets, employment and services enjoyed by all-powerful landowners. This inequality in production relations is matched by inequality in social and political power.

Data on large-scale production units, usually derived from Agricultural Census figures, suffer from the limitations discussed earlier. For the seven countries of Latin America,[16] large landowners concentrate in their hands much more land than appears from data on farm-size. They own or control various production units[17] through their families or commercial relations. The figures given in Table 4.2 thus understate the case.

Table 4.2
Large Multi-Family Operational Units in Seven Latin American Countries

Country	% of All Agricultural Families	% of the Country's Agricultural Land
Argentina (1960)	0.4	36
Brazil (1950)	1.8	60
Chile (1955)	3.0	79
Colombia (1960)	1.1	45
Ecuador (1960)	0.3	42
Guatemala (1950)	0.1	40

Source: Barraclough and Domike, 1966, Tables 3 and 8A.

The figures do not distinguish between modern and traditional units (haciendas). The contemporary trend is to move from the latter to the former.

Corporate Large Units

This category results from the entry into agriculture of finance capital which takes advantage of the industrialisation of methods and organisation in food and raw material production and of the integration of linkages downstream and upstream in production, processing and distribution.

Finance capital is provided by mercantile, industrial, banking, insurance and other financial interests who tend to enter profitable, usually modern and pioneering, lines of agriculture. Because of the scale, complexity and nature of this category, relations with external interests are present from the start or are sought after. These units thus tend to come under the influence of foreign interests, often multinational enterprises. Although the situation is complex and neat divisions not possible, colonial, post-colonial and multinational relations and influences will be discussed in considering the international dimensions of agrarian conflict and reform.

Corporate large agricultural units are run by hired managers under the control (real or fictional) of the board of directors. Management is advised and helped by a cadre of technically qualified personnel who enjoy privileged conditions. Work is done through the employment of regular, and in most cases also of casual, labour. Conditions of work and the level of wages tend to depend on the labour market. When there is a reserve army of un-employed or underemployed, labour conditions are poor, especially for casual labour. In such conditions organisation of labour is difficult and its bargaining position consequently weak.[18] Corporate bodies benefit also from employing smallholders or members of their family who supplement income from their own farming with wage labour for the corporate units and are thus capable of subsisting on lower wages than they would otherwise.

Corporate large agricultural units need not always be private, or exclusively so. Where parastatal bodies, such as Development Corporations, either alone or in partnership with private interests, engage in agricultural production, relations are rarely different for the workers, but the cadres and managers tend to belong to the parastatal, or state, bureaucracy with secure and well-paid employment.

It is perhaps legitimate to include here the *combinats* and agribusiness developed and spreading in countries with socialist forms of agriculture. An agro-industrial enterprise organically integrates agricultural and industrial production. It has a single integrated management system and common finances and functions as an independent legally recognised entity. In the USSR[19] the commonest form of this organisation combines a manufacturing establishment with a state farm. By the beginning of 1975 there were 56 agro-industrial firms and 512 agriculture-related enterprises (excluding state and collective farms with subsidiary smallholdings for processing agricultural products) which employed more than 760,000 workers. Agro-industrial enterprises were expected to increase rapidly.

This development in socialist agriculture illustrates more the integration of agricultural production with processing, but does not affect significantly the relations of production for the workforce which are governed by the regulations and practices concerning state farm employment; it may, however, enlarge employment and investment opportunities and make possible higher earnings, especially where there is greater autonomy for enterprise.

Co-operative Agricultural Production
This is a very varied category. Members of a co-operative unit may together own the land, may have pooled their private land for the purpose, or may lease the land from others; in socialist countries the land may be state land given to the co-operative in perpetuity. Co-operative units may vary in size and assets, including the quality of the land.

In theory internal production relations are governed by the general will of the members and managed by their elected representatives. In practice these "elected representatives" may be the real employers. In theory rewards are based on each member's contribution in land, inputs and above all labour. In practice they may be manipulated. The general principle is for the co-operative unit to avoid employing wage labour, but in practice many often do, and can even be harsh employers. Production relations within these forms should be ideal but rarely are.

Production relations with others outside the unit depend on the context in which the unit(s) operate. In market or capitalist systems they have to compete with other producers and may face hostility (mainly ideological) in the inputs and credit supply systems; even state organs may be unsympathetic. A federation of co-operative units may achieve economies of scale of operation and a good bargaining position.

In socialist systems co-operative units are dominant forms of agricultural production or at least widespread. Their performance has varied enormously and they have had to face all the problems and changes of state policy, and of integration into a planned economic management system. The issues involved will be taken up later.

Tenancy, Sharecropping and Related Production Relations
These have been considered the most notorious production relations in agriculture and are often the most exploitative and oppressive, frequently on a vast scale. It must not, however, be taken for granted that a tenant is automatically the weak party[20] or that he is simply the victim of evil times or conditions. Advancing capitalist agriculture, fuelled especially by high-yielding varieties of crops and modern production techniques, has enabled strongly-placed entrepreneurs to bid for land to lease, sometimes on a large scale, at the expense of small tenants and even from small landowners. In developed countries especially, where tenancy is a commercial relation,

tenants can hold their own and young farmers prefer to lease their land rather than buy it, thus saving their capital for operational purposes.

In general production relations are grossly unequal; owners of the land, the landlords, possess practically all the means of production, while tenants and sharecroppers usually own only their labour, if that. The landlords are unwilling, unable or prefer not, to engage in cultivation, while the tenants and sharecroppers need to earn an income, often as subsistence for their families. The main difference between tenants and sharecroppers lies in the form of payment to the landlord for use of his land: the former pay a fixed rent, usually in money, no matter what the level of production; share-croppers, as the name implies, pay a share of the crops obtained, in proportions agreed in advance. A tenant does not have to pay more if he has been successful or fortunate enough to produce more than anticipated but pays the same amount even if the crop has been disastrous. A sharecropper pays less if there is a crop failure, but much more if the crop is a bumper one.

There is a vast amount of literature on the merits and defects of tenancy and sharecropping[21] – either treated together as a production relation or as contrasted forms. The general conclusion is that sharecropping discourages the cultivator from exerting himself or spending on inputs to raise productivity because this increases the return to the landlord, while tenants are discouraged from raising productivity through fear that the landlord may increase the rent in future contracts. Despite this, one school of thought maintains that conversion of sharecropping to tenancy is a progressive step and much legislation has focused on this, as in the Philippines in the 1950s and 1960s.[22]

The sense of injustice and even extortion perpetrated against those labouring on the land for the benefit of idle landowners can be strong and universal.[23] The worst conditions of exploitation tend to develop in areas where land is concentrated in a few hands and there are vast reserves of labour who have no land or insufficient land to support themselves.

Legislation to regulate tenancy and sharecropping has almost invariably failed because landlords tend to be in a position to evade its provisions, tenants and sharecroppers too weak to take advantage of it, and the enforcing authority at the local level too unsympathetic with the law and too much under the influence of the landlord class to implement it.

Thus this system of production relations is perpetuated with all its adverse effects. In South Asia[24] the landlord usually escapes taxation on income derived from ownership of land, and typically performs no agricultural work himself, not even supervisory work. Rarely does a large landlord operate a home-farm with hired labourers; usually he lives in the town, turns over the working of the land to sharecroppers and other tenants, and delegates rent collection to local agents; he has no forceful inducement to invest, as he can obtain a comfortable return without doing so.[25]

The tenant, especially the sharecropper, "enjoys" all the disadvantages. He is fearful all the time that his precarious position may become catastrophic by losing his only source of survival, through eviction, since there are other hands to take his place. Many are indebted to their landlords, having lost the status of owner-cultivatorship through debt. There are cases[26] in Indonesia, Malaya and Bangladesh in which an indebted peasant leases out land to his creditor at a low rent and the land is then leased back at a much higher rent.

A sharecropper is tied more closely to the landlord and it is not unusual for the share-rent to be twice as high as a cash rent or even higher still.[27] This applies also in Ecuador.[28] But there are worse cases to record. Under the *namumuisan* system in the Philippines, an intermediary pays a fixed rent to the landowner, thereby eliminating all risk to the latter, and enters into a sharecropping agreement with the tenant. The risk is thus shared between tenant and intermediary.[29] The sharecropper now has to provide surplus both for landowner and intermediary. There is often a hierarchy of tenancy and sharecropping.

> In several regions of Colombia it is common for landowners (*patrones*) to delegate authority to a farm manager (*encargado* or *administrador*), who in turn assigns land use rights to a number of share-renters (*vivientes* or *contraristas*), who then arrange for sub-share-renters (*socios* or *compañeros*) to furnish labor and small amounts of capital, who often in turn work out labor trading arrangements with other individuals (*peones, obreros*, or *jornaleros*) to supply additional labor at harvesting and planting time.[30]

A profile[31] for the Philippines of 112 rice landlords shows the socio-economic position:

Upper Class: 21% of the sample. Had more than 100 ha of farm; were owners of a major business or major stockholders of corporations; had two or more cars, two or more houses, a vacation and trips abroad; members of international and national organisations.
Upper Middle Class: 34% of the sample. Had 51–100 ha; were executives or officials of a large business or in government, owners of a large retail business; had one/two cars/jeeps; their residence was worth 25–50,000 pesos; had vacation in the Philippines; were members of national and local organisations.
Lower Middle Class: 34% of the sample. Had 11–50 ha, white-collar jobs; grade school teachers, first level supervisors, owners of retail business with employees; house worth 10–20,000 pesos; members of local organisations; had several household appliances.
Lower Class: 5–10 ha, engaged in small business without employees; no signs of high level living.

(Table 4.3) shows social stratification in Indian agriculture:[32]
A recent analysis of laborious and thorough Land Occupancy Surveys in Bangladesh in the late 1970s arrived at four "meaningful" strata in the countryside: (a) large landowners (over two ha) accounting for 6%

Table 4.3
Land Area Belonging to Each Group as Percentage of Total Area

	West India	East India	South India	Total India
Absentee Landlords	16	13	4	13
Peasant Landlords	23	22	32	24
Other Peasants	59	55–60	56	58
Agricultural Workers	2	5–10	8	5

Source: Myrdal 1968, Table 22-2, p. 1059, based on Government of India figures referring
to the 1950s.
Data for Latin America appear in Table 4.4 and additional information in Table 4.5

of rural households and 45% of cultivated land, much of which they give out
for sharecropping; (b) middle farmers (1–2 ha) 17% of households, owning
33%; (c) small farmers (0.2–0.8 ha) 30% of households owning 20% of land
and taking in as share as much land from stratum (a); and (d) the landless
(less than 0.2 ha of land) who form half the households and own 2–3% of
the land.[33]

Sharecroppers and workers who own no land are held in low esteem,[34] but
at least the sharecropper works for himself and is not directly supervised by
the landlord, even though his average earnings may be lower than those of
hired workers in districts where labour is scarce. The sharecropper may,
however, be frustrated[35] in that he cannot make his operations run evenly
because of the constraints of his position: small-scale operation, uncertainty
of status (he is often only a one-season at a time cultivator), and indebtedness into which he may sink lower *with* every season, as his produce may be
mortgaged before it is even produced and sold at the lowest prices, although
he may pay the highest prices for production inputs.

Tenants may match this position. The *Kishans* of West Bengal,[36] i.e.
tenants with virtually no land of their own, little or no capital for production
and generally no security of tenancy for more than one production cycle, yet
who constitute 40–50% of the cultivators of the land, are almost always
indebted to their landowners. A substantial portion of their legal share of
the harvest is taken away immediately after harvest as repayment of past
debt, at the lowest prices ruling at that period. The remainder of their share
is usually insufficient to enable them to survive until the next harvest and
they are forced to borrow to buy their food. Indebtedness accumulates and
keeps them perpetually in thrall. No wonder they rebelled.

Non-availability of land is often institutionally induced. Larger landowners
in India, aware that expansion in the acreage under cultivation may lead to
upward pressure on wage and a reduction in rents, practise monopolistic
restriction of cultivation which, partly at least, explains why privately owned
land in the vicinity of villages is unutilised;[37] while much arable land in Latin
American large estates is still natural vegetation.[38] Furthermore, many tied
tenants are not allowed to plant trees (e.g. coffee) on land allocated to
them to use, for fear that they may strengthen their bargaining position as

Table 4.4

Agricultural Families Classified by Socio-economic Status in Six Latin American Countries (percentage of total)

Status	Argentina (1960)	Brazil (1950)	Chile (1950)	Colombia (1960)	Ecuador (1960)	Guatemala (1960)
Upper Class						
a. Operators of large-size farms	0.4	1.8	3.0	1.1	0.3	0.1
b. Operators of medium-size farms	4.8	12.8	6.5	3.9	2.1	1.5
Middle Class						
a. Managers of large- and medium-size farms	1.3	2.1	2.1	1.5	—	2.2
b. Owners of family farms	16.4	12.0	14.8	17.9	8.0	6.6
c. Operators of family farms who are not their owners	16.2	2.9	2.9	5.4	1.5	1.2
Lower Class						
a. Owners in indigenous communities	—	—	16.6	—	1.3	—
b. Operators of sub-family size farms	25.9	8.6	6.5	47.0	52.3	63.6
c. Workers without land	35.0	59.8	47.6	23.2	34.5	24.8

Note: The above data overestimate the numerical importance of both the upper and middle classes, while they underestimate that of the lower class.

Source: Barraclough y Domike, 1966, Table 2.

tied labour.[39] Thus Alexis de Toqueville was right when he reflected that "human prosperity depends much more on the institutions and the will of man than on the external circumstances that surround him."[40]

Agricultural Workers

References have already been made to agricultural workers and some data given in Tables 2.2, 4.3 and 4.4. Although a very important class and increasingly and rapidly becoming a very large force, they are extremely difficult to define. Landless and assetless people, for example, take up any occupation available and may, in the course of the year practise more than one, quantification and classification thus become difficult.

Moreover, as already discussed, those with land may be partly operators using their own labour and that of their family, at least part of the time. There are the further difficulties of defining and separating those who provide labour under the constraint of quasi-feudal obligations or of debt and in lieu of rent or even in lieu of a share in the produce.

Esman and Associates[41] divide agricultural workers into permanent and casual. They define the former as having steady, year-round, stable employment for a single employer; the latter as those with no stable employment. Permanent workers are divided into "free" and "bonded", while casual are described as local and migrant; migrant are then distinguished as seasonal, permanent and intermittent.

Table 4.5 is taken from Esman's figures; even though these are drawn from various sources and years and based on varied definitions, since their deficiencies and therefore reliability are accounted for and evaluated by the authors, they constitute an able attempt to give the best available up-to-date picture.

Table 4.5
Landless and Near-landless by Occupation or Tenure in Latin American Countries (percentage of total category)

Country	Permanent Workers	Temporary Workers	Cultivators	Tenants	Land Reform Beneficiaries	Artisan, Other
Argentina	21	20	30	28	—	2
Bolivia	12	24	54	—	—	10
Brazil	19	31	12	20	—	18
Colombia	13	13	54	16	—	4
Ecuador	15	17	40	22	—	6
Mexico	5	43	24	—	17	11
Peru	5	18	28	12	22	15
Costa Rica	10	44	16	—	—	30
El Salvador	16	20	17	37	—	10
Guatemala	10	23	57	10	—	—
Dominican Republic	15	20	30	25	5	10

Source: Esman and Associates, 1978, Table 4, p. 333.

In production relations the freedom of the worker to offer or not to offer his labour is very important. Tradition-oriented landowners enjoyed the privilege and prestige of a large retinue of attached workers, who were treated as their own servants, and who brought them plentiful, docile and thus very cheap labour. The system implied some obligations on the land-owners' part towards their workers. For the workers this meant at least a home and a plot of land and thus secure employment, admittedly at a very low income, and with very low social status. It is not surprising that, in spite of the acquired right to leave the hacienda, which was recognised in the nineteenth century, owing to the scarce alternative employment opportunities available and to their lack of education, many attached workers saw this more as a threat than a promise of improved position.[42] In Ecuador, "free" dependent labour or casual labour aspire to become *huasipungueros*, or attached cultivators, because of the enhanced security.[43]

The spread of opportunities for commercial agriculture, especially for export, reinforced by modern inputs and mechanisation, has encouraged an entrepreneurial outlook on even traditional estates (somewhat like Lenin's "capitalist Junker economy"[44]). Entrepreneurial classes find traditional obligations irksome, the fixed (and excessive) labour supply uneconomic; and when labour becomes restive or demanding, they find it dangerous and troublesome. The possibility of agrarian reform enhances fear of trouble and danger.

Some landowners wish to have it both ways. They welcome the distribution of government land provided that sufficient land is offered to the workers to tie them to it but not enough for them to be able to dispense with additional employment. This ensures for the landowners a supply of "free" labour, "contented" with low wages supplemented from their own cultivation.[45] In Peru in the 1950s even sugar plantations wanted labour tied to them by advancing loans to harvest workers.

Entrepreneurial agriculture has, however, its own logic. Wishing to expand activity and the rate and size of his profit, the entrepreneur looks for more land and land-augmenting methods and inputs; he is anxious to reduce his labour and other operating costs, and aims at increasing returns through large output and better prices. Land reforms can help in this. Joshi argues[46] that in India the impact of land reforms combined with new technology to accentuate the ascendancy of larger producers and the insecurity of small peasants, especially tenants. Moreover, commercial tenancy, based on leasing-in of land from small by big peasants, gained importance. Thus a more production-oriented but aggressively acquisitive landed class, unrestrained by any sense of obligation to the larger community or to the weaker sections of society, came to dominate the rural scene. The mild agrarian reform introduced by Ecuador in 1964 was intended to accelerate agricultural production to support industrialisation, by concentrating on the abolition of tied labour such as the *huasipungo* and raising minimum rural wages.[47]

Other publicly assisted investments in agriculture also fuel the process because they encourage larger landowners and others from outside agriculture to acquire land as a productive investment. Similarly, Rudra remarks[48] that in India this leads to increased concentration of assets and income among the bigger producers, that small tenant farmers will either be evicted or work under the owner's supervision in the same conditions as those of farm servants, and that workers will not be freer, since "freedom" results in poverty and leads them into debt. He predicts "an ever expanding sea of poverty and unemployment".

The much-boosted "green revolution" has also played its part. "Typically, much of the increased income from the new high-yield varieties is a residual return to the landowners; only a small proportion derives from greater use of labor."[49]

The process, therefore, which concentrates assets and income, has as its obverse, the "backwash effect" namely deterioration of the status of working cultivators and their tendency to proletarianisation and ever-increasing underemployment and open unemployment. Esman and Associates stress the rapid[50] commercialisation and mechanisation of agriculture in Latin America,[51] the result of switching from labour intensive crops to mechanised production crops (e.g. in Brazil) with consequent general displacement of labour[52]; they quote Abercrombie's highly conservative estimate that 2.5 million jobs had been lost through mechanisation in the region.

There has been lively controversy over the last few years regarding mechanisation and the "green revolution" and the effect of both on employment. It is valid to conclude that overall there has been loss of employment, sometimes of dramatic proportions, and that, while some fortunate workers have managed to obtain permanent and well-paid employment, the vast majority are worse off.

Worst off are the casual labourers, some of whom migrate seasonally, often crossing frontiers for this purpose. Workers from India migrate to the Nepalese *terai* at harvest time.[53] In the Ivory Coast the bulk of the labour force, some 700,000, are immigrants from neighbouring countries, mainly Burkina Faso, and wages are Government controlled.[54] In Guatemala, an estimated 25% of the rural labour force is involved in annual seasonal migrations,[55] some of which are organised by labour contractors with whom the migrants must share their meagre wages.[56] In Java there is a similarly extortionate system[57] not involving migrant labour. This is the *Tebasan*, or middleman, system under which the farmer sells his entire rice crop to a middleman while the rice is still unripe; these middlemen are often local moneylenders who already have under recruitment landless labourers who will work for them at below-market wages as a means of paying off loans obtained in the past.

Thus the growth of landlessness,[58] unemployment and impoverishment of an increasing number of rural people is characteristic of both stagnant economies with increasing population, and growing, especially fast modernising, economies. Ghose and Griffin[59] explain the process as follows: if the rate of growth of per capita supply of food is less than that of per capita demand, the relative price of food will rise and inequality in the distribution of income increase, thus adversely affecting those who have to buy food from the market, i.e. deficit farmers and landless labourers. Money wages are not fully adjusted, hence real wage rates tend to decline. Furthermore, rising food prices may lead to the resumption of tenanted land by landlords. The rural surplus producers, i.e. the relatively large landowners, benefit doubly because, first, the product price rises and, secondly, the cost of food production relative to price tends to decline. This is particularly true in conditions of significant inequality in the distribution of productive assets, and where deficit farmers and wage labour are important in the population.

Meanwhile the numbers of agricultural workers are swelling. "Between 1961 and 1971 cultivators in India increased by four per cent while landless agricultural labourers increased by 80 per cent."[60] They are exploited in every way; if tenants or sharecroppers, they are evicted from part of their land so that they remain a reserve army of cheap labour; they are paid low wages; they face long periods of unemployment and short periods of feverish occupation; and they are divided into a privileged minority with steady employment and good pay, and a deprived large majority who are poverty-stricken, irregularly employed and badly paid. This takes place mostly amid conditions of fast growth and prosperity which are confined to the landed classes of medium and large producers.[61] Even the "second Marie Antoinette principle" does not save them.[62] No wonder that they often flock into urban areas where, living in fast-growing slums and shanty towns in acute poverty and squalor, they become at least a visible problem.

Non-agricultural Groups and Production Relations

Naiken identifies[63] the non-agricultural component of the rural labour force as comprising "those servicing the farm population (e.g. persons involved in the sale and maintenance of agricultural machinery or the sale of fertilizers, shopkeepers, artisans, doctors, etc.) and those who are completely independent of agricultural activities – the 'adventitious rural population' . . . which is becoming important in many developed countries". Figures given by Naiken[64] indicate that the share of the non-agricultural sector of the rural labour force reflects roughly not only the general development of the country (e.g. the USA has a percentage of 88, Germany 68, Sweden and Japan 61, while Mali has 6.3, Nicaragua 11.8, Bangladesh 12.3, and in the middle range Spain and Greece 38) but also the patterns of urbanisation and the location of non-agricultural activities (hence Turkey with only 9.3 per cent, but the Philippines 27.6). Naiken observes that

> not all those who shift from agricultural activities migrate to urban areas; a significant number remain in the rural area to take up employment in the non-agricultural sector of the rural economy. Mechanisation and the use of more industrial inputs in agriculture not only reduce the man-power needs in the agricultural sector, but they are also likely to increase the demand for services to the farm population, thus leading to an increase in the servicing population in rural areas.[65]

Qualitative changes, however, take place in the economy which affect employment and production relations.

> As agriculture becomes more commercialised one can expect greater specialisation and division of labour. Occupations will become more specific, social relations will become more distinct and the customary terms on which services are exchanged will tend to give way to formal contracts . . . The numerous people who formerly were exercising entrepreneurial functions on a small scale . . . will cease to be "penny capitalists" and will become a proletariat.[66]

These are the broad sweeps of change. Specific societies reflect the structures that compose them at a particular stage. Traditional landlords have large retinues of servants for prestige reasons. Commercial landlords shed their labour and the social obligations binding them together: labour and landlord will become "free". Concentration of land in response to capitalist development in agriculture makes even small owner-cultivators operators of even smaller and more fragmented holdings, and converts them into part-time farmers, or even "absentee" owners of small pieces of land, or small landlords to big entrepreneurial tenants. Artisans lose their *raison d'être* but the informal sector subsists on "taking in each other's washing", or on sweated family labour, or on even less fortunate labour, producing on a small scale new products or meeting small needs of the population.

Thus "black labour" and "submerged economies" develop and thrive.

Much of this reflects the affected people's asset position and capacity to operate within the system. Thus in Nepal

> Retailers, particularly those in rural areas, tend to be drawn predominantly from the local peasant population, coming into commerce either to supplement their farm incomes or, having raised the capital to open the business from savings or a loan, to run it as "a subsistence" enterprise. Larger merchants, however, tend to be members of the land-owning class . . . The hereditary aristocracy . . . invest in hotels, import-export businesses, tourist agencies, and other lucrative enterprises in Nepal and India.[67]

Middlemen also abound: they are notorious in the trade of agricultural produce. Tractor contractors enter production by helping part-time or absentee owners, then branch out in different directions – repair workshops, suppliers of spare parts, etc. Labour contractors exploit situations of peak demand for labour and the defencelessness of poor labourers seeking employment; they thrive on indebtedness and the preference of the landowner for a secure, trouble-free and profitable labour supply.

Usury is the great art in poor rural areas. Never in the world's economic history has any activity been so decried and combated, only to emerge unbowed and victorious. Government efforts to make it unnecessary through institutional credit have fallen foul of numerous combinations of circumstances: the rural poor have no tactical power because they are so deep in poverty and indebtedness and never earn enough to repay loans; they have no assets to serve as collateral; the middle and rich producers corner available credit, run its institutions and often default and bankrupt them; the usurer therefore emerges as the saviour of the poor in their plight and ensures that they continue to be poor and bound to his will.

According to a 1969 Reserve Bank of India Report[68] private money-lenders accounted for 46.6% of all farming loans. The money-lenders are large farmers, an influential upper class, who control the village trade and labour market, as well as village administration and co-operatives. An official study of bonded labour linked this illegal practice with usury; assetless people are bonded mostly in lieu of debts taken for domestic consumption. The motive behind private moneylending is primarily to create social obligations rather than profit from interest.

Notes

1. Reviewing the book *Men of Property* by Rubinstein, *The Times* of 22 June 1981 wrote ". . . landed wealth is the most permanent kind . . .", while *The Times Literary Supplement* of the same date wrote: ". . . landed and other forms of wealth remained intertwined, especially when land was associated with urban property as with the Westminster and Bedford estates . . ." The quest of land for leisure is fast increasing and such land tends to come into the hands of upper middle income and wealth groups, able to pay the leisure premium on it. See Hirsch 1976 p. 35.

2. "Buying agricultural land was all the rage among the City's financial institutions in the 1970s." *Financial Times* 8 February 1986.

3. The "mainstream of family-sized commercial agriculture" in the USA ranges in sales of output from $50,000 to $500,000 annually per farm. *Financial Times* 12 March 1985.

4. Ortega 1982 pp. 75–111.

5. Barraclough and Domike 1966 p. 239 y Cuadro 8A.

6. Griffin 1972 pp. 19–24.

7. The difficult problem of part-time farming and the issues involved have been tentatively investigated in Christodoulou 1982 pp. 373–380.

8. Dé Janvry 1981 p. 84 sees the agricultural sector of Latin America as characterised by a *functional dualism* between the capitalist sector which produces commodities on the basis of hired semiproletarian labour and the peasant sector which produces use values and petty commodities on the basis of family labour and delivers cheap wage labour to the capitalist sector.

9. "U.S. agriculture is today a multibillion-dollar industry, increasingly dominated by large corporations and conglomerates through direct investments, vertical integration, or contract farming". DeWind, Seidl and Shenk 1979 p. 380.

In a Report to Congress, the US Congressional Office of Technology Assessment stresses that new technology, which is costly and complex, is accelerating the US away from the traditional family farm and towards large industrialised production units. *Financial Times* 21 March 1985.

According to figures given in a paper prepared for the US Presidential Commission on World Hunger, entitled "Domestic Hunger and Malnutrition" dated 8 March 1979, p. 17, "Five percent of American farmers control more than 50 per cent of our farmland . . . In California, 52 percent of the crop land is owned by corporate farms".

10. Esman and Associates 1978 p. 218.

11. Das Gupta 1977 pp. 13–14. Positive discrimination by the government to help these underprivileged people in education and employment led to violent reaction by the privileged in the mid-1980s.

12. Klein 1977 pp. 42–44.

13. Barraclough y Domike 1966 p. 243.

14. Baraona and Associates 1965 p. 142.

15. Barraclough y Domike 1966 p. 245.

16. Ibid. p. 241.

17. The record must have been held by Iranian landowners before the reform. "The most powerful group consisted of 400–450 families, some of whom are reputed to have owned as many as 300 villages. According to one estimate, 37 families alone owned 19,000 villages, i.e. around 38 percent of the total." Halliday 1979 pp. 106–107.

In Nicaragua the dictator Somoza's properties amounted to 23% of the arable land. See Austin, Fox and Kruger 1985 p. 18.

18. For an analysis of the conditions of work and powerlessness of contract labour in the USA see DeWind, Seidl and Shenk 1979 pp. 381–383.

19. See Martyrov 1977 pp. 233–242.

20. In fact sometimes the plight of small landlords is used to counteract agrarian reform. On a visit to the Philippines in the 1970s I witnessed the fury of retired civil servants, widows and other old people concerned that the reform threatened their low income, some of which came from land rent. They were doing the work of larger ones who were busy evading the reform.

21. For an extensive treatment of sharecropping see Byres 1983 pp. 1–183.

22. Cline summarised (a) the traditional or "Marshallian" argument that sharecropping causes inefficient factor allocation, (b) Cheung's challenge to the effect that the landlord ensures maximisation of output and equalisation of what he pays labour with what it can earn elsewhere and (c) other contributions to the debate. See Cline 1977 pp. 281–335.

23. In mid-seventeenth century England, Winstanley, the Digger, put it thus: "the inferior Tenants and Labourers bear all the burthens in labouring the Earth, in paying Taxes and Freequarter above their strength; and yet the Gentry who oppress them live idle upon their labors carry away all the comfortable livelihood of the Earth". St. John Chrysostom, in his Homily on S. Matthew, exclaimed, "who could be more oppressive than landlords and their agents?"

24. Myrdal 1968 pp.1039 and 1065.

25. Sometimes he has no compunction. Sir Razik Fareed, Member of Parliament in Ceylon, opposing the 1958 Paddy Lands Bill, in contrast to the Minister's view on tenants being forced to *pay* excessive rents, cited his own practice: "I give . . . half the harvest". Mentioned in Herring 1981 p. 151.

26. Myrdal 1968 p. 1045.

27. Ibid. p. 1067.

28. Baraona 1965 p. 139.

29. See Griffin 1972 p. 19.

30. Adams 1966 p. 50.

31. Castillo 1975 pp. 274–276 reproducing a table from a study of E.A. Bernal.

32. Myrdal 1968 Table 22–2, p. 1057.

33. Blair 1985 pp. 1239–1240.

34. Myrdal 1968 pp. 1057–9.

35. Baraona 1965 p. 427.

36. Bhaduri 1973 pp. 121–123.

37. Myrdal 1968 p. 1063, f.1.

38. Barraclough 1970 p. 938.

39. See Hirschman 1963 p. 102.

40. Quoted by Myrdal 1968 p. 1058, f.1.

41. Esman and Associates 1978 pp. 20–22.

42. Barraclough y Domike 1966 p. 245.

43. Baraona 1965 p. 424.

44. Lenin 1964 p. 32.

45. In Latin America especially, this semi-proletarianisation, i.e. retaining a foothold in agriculture, is spreading and serves as "a shelter for labour force, which enters and leaves the labour market according to the conditions of the market". (Ortega 1982 p. 99).

On the other hand proletarianisation is also spreading since the number of workers living with their families on the farms has declined, mechanisation has reduced labour demand, and the combined decline in leasing, tenant farming and sharecropping has resulted in seasonal, wage-paid and even itinerant work predominating. Gomes and Pérez 1979 p. 68.

46. Joshi 1974 pp. 340–341 and 328.

47. Vos 1985 p. 1106.

48. Rudra 1978 pp. 399 and 404–5. See also Gaiha 1985 pp. 237 and 242 in which it is confirmed that the small landowners lose their lands to the large ones who benefit from

the new technology and public investments; furthermore rents and share costs have risen sharply for the poor.

49. Mellor 1976 p. 79.

50. Esman and Associates 1978 pp. 337–338.

51. Not only agriculture. In Peru besides the *yanaconas* (sharecroppers) the *huacchilleros* (sheep tenants) were also being proletarianised long before the reform. See Kay 1982 pp. 142–144.

52. See also extensive analysis in Ortega 1982 pp. 96–107.

53. Blaikie, Cameron and Seddon 1980 p. 53.

54. Den Tuinder 1978 pp. 6, 8 and 43.

55. Esman and Associates 1978 p. 79.

56. Ibid. p. 80. Concerning the USA, DeWind, Seidl and Shenk 1979 pp. 381–383, observe that the contract is between the Government of the workers' country, mainly Caribbean, and the growers of Florida and the Eastern States concerned, the workers having no say at all regarding terms. The ability of these governments to protect the workers is very limited.

57. Esman and Associates 1978 p. 243.

58. Dore, quoting Raj, mentions that landless agricultural labourers numbered 31 million in India in 1961 and 55 million in 1981 and their level of wages was unchanged. Dore, 1984 p. 70.

59. Ghose and Griffin 1979 pp. 3–4.

60. Asian Development Bank 1978 p. 55.

61. Miró and Rodriguez 1982 p. 55 see two stages in Latin America since the 1950s: an increase in wage-earning workers first; and a semiproletariasation later combined with a replacement of permanent workers by seasonal ones.

62. "the rich . . . must . . . eat more cake in order that the poor get more crumbs". Adler-Karlsson 1978 p. 167.

63. Naiken 1977 p. 6.

64. Ibid. Table I.

65. Ibid. p. 7.

66. Griffin 1972 p. 69.

67. Blaikie, Cameron and Seddon, op. cit., p. 82.

68. Roth 1983.

5. Historical Roots and Wider Relations

Colonisation, Colonial Agriculture, Settler-farms, Plantations and Multinational Agribusiness

The problems and situations discussed have deep historical roots. The vast majority of developing countries have been colonial dependencies. The New World was colonised by European settlers and the institutions transplanted there still strongly determine economic conditions. Developed countries achieved their present position of economic and political power with the advantage of centuries of dominance of vast territories.

The following examples illustrate the relevance of these historical roots: the USA fought a Civil War to assert the supremacy of industrial and commercial interests over plantation interests and their outlook, which was conditioned by exploitation of Negro slavery. "The abolition of slavery was a by-product . . . [The Civil War] was fought to check the ambitions of the Southern slave-owning oligarchy which wanted to escape from what was essentially a colonial relation to Northern capital."[1] Apart from its internal repercussions, this historic trauma still has important international significance. Professor Stipetic of the University of Zagreb argued that one reason why the United States was against land reform was that, in Latin America, United States ambassadors could talk to the gentry because they had much in common with them and little in common with the peasants. Professor Dovring agreed but ascribed this to the Southern syndrome, i.e. the backwash of the Civil War which saw "the entrenchment of Southern plantation interests behind the ideology of private property as inviolable. The Southern landed interests . . . gained disproportionate influence over national policy".[2]

In Latin America large landowning interests have held in their hands the organisation of agricultural production and control of the political, social and economic institutions for the greater part of the last four centuries.[3] These interests are represented by the landed aristocracy set up by the colonial powers of Spain and Portugal to ensure control and exploitation of the conquered lands and peoples. A "semi-indigenous" approach was adopted in the Philippines. "The Spaniards took to the Philippines the *encomienda* system which they used in their American possessions. A large part of the land, and the best at that, was thus handed over with its natives to the ownership of the Catholic Church or to Spanish or half-caste families, who were termed *Caciques*."[4] They served the Spanish conquerors as government officials; their powers enabled them to amass large landed properties. Some noble landholding families in Malaya and in former French Indo-China obtained exclusive rights to land as a reward for their assistance to the British or French.[5] For South Asia the authority of European admini-strators over titles to land was a powerful weapon that could be turned either to punishing those who were hostile to the colonial regime or to rewarding those who co-operated.[6] Control over land was a key to the exercise of colonial domination.

In most colonial territories land not given to favourites was sooner or later brought within the orbit of statutory law. This not only reflected the concept of land tenure of the administering powers, but also the interests of the dominant élites of the metropolitan countries. In Africa and South Asia especially statutory law was introduced into complex situations governed by customary tenures, which were flexible and practicable from the point of view of the users.

One principle generally applied with far-reaching effect was that "vacant" or "unclaimed" lands became "Crown" or public lands, even though in customary law they belonged to lineage groups or to communities as a whole. This opened the way for land to be taken both for company and public purposes and also to settle European farmers or establish plantations on the cheap.

White settler farming and influence played a marked role in economic development and political fortunes of many colonial countries. Kenya is a well-known example; Algeria, Mozambique, Angola and Zimbabwe have fought prolonged wars of liberation against the European governments with settler communities. Portugal's 1974 revolution was a direct result of the struggle of colonial peoples who could not be subdued.[7]

Plantations first based on slavery and then on indentured labour have left a mark on the composition of the population as well as on the agrarian structure in many Latin American, Caribbean, Pacific and Asian countries; while plantations by large multinational companies have been the main base for often overwhelming dominance in the economies of many countries, known pejoratively as "banana republics".

The rising tide of capitalism in developed countries also affected economic activities in colonial and semi-colonial countries so that these were gradually brought within the orbit of policies and decisions developed by the domi-nant interests of metropolitan countries. Many would, in fact, argue that this centre-periphery axis has existed for four centuries or more. One view of the development of the colonial state postulates that the state's increasingly complex and wide-ranging interventions in economic life constitute basically the use of state power to create and sustain capitalist relations of production with an adequate, stable and docile supply of labour. Its dealings, of course, had to reconcile relations between the metropolis and the colony and within the colony between introduced forms of capitalist production and various indigenous modes.[8]

Myint[9] makes the additional point that "the migrant labour system provided the mines and plantations with a very convenient stream of casual labour for which they did not need to take much care and responsibility. . . . Further, during the slumps in the export market, the redundant labour could be laid off and returned to the subsistence sector without continuing responsibility for them". The subsistence sector was also crowded in many places, such as the Kikuyu Highlands of Kenya and in Southern Rhodesia, owing to displacement by settlers of the inhabitants who then had to seek work on settler farms and plantations. The development on the one hand, of settler agriculture and plantations and, on the other, the restriction of available land for the indigenous people, coupled with taxation by the colonial state which had to be paid in cash, helped to usher in the capitalist form of agriculture in colonial territories and to forge links with the wider capitalist system.

The process also fostered native capitalism from which sprang practically all the élites of independent ex-colonial territories. Many succeeded to the lands of departed colonists or settlers, some under projects which became part of the independence agreement, as in Kenya. Élites were deliberately fostered by educational schemes, e.g. the Ecole de Fils de Chefs in French West Africa, or the relatives of Chiefs in British Africa. Missionaries also helped create such élites. This devolution was in essence a broadening of the base for political control by the colonial administrations. "The well-to-do élite, which historically benefited from the limited African participation in cash-crop production and educational facilities available under colonialism, has tended to provide the main pool from which have come new office-holders for national and local government posts."[10]

This early start by a small minority of élites from colonial territories is one of the key features in the development of the ex-colonial world. They acquired a momentum in economic advantage and political control after independence, including access to land. In Kenya "European farms were being purchased privately as intact units by members of the newly prosperous African (especially Kikuyu) political, administrative and business elite".[11] Further down the social scale other strata also benefited. Lists of large farm holders include members of parliament, senior government officials, ambassadors, senior police officers, executives of parastatals and church officials.[12]

> At the top there are a group of farmers, mainly in the high potential areas, who have rapidly increased their incomes over the past decade. These are for the most part farmers who benefited from settlement and irrigation schemes or from land registration. . . . These farmers appear to number some 225,000 or about a fifth of all smallholders. Theirs tend to be the holdings whose workers are hired on a full-time basis, and also on a seasonal basis to assist them with farm work.[13]

The first and only ruler of the Ivory Coast since independence is himself a wealthy planter and leader of the party which grew out of an association of African planters.[14] I have given further examples in another study[15] and earlier mentioned similar developments in India. The landowning élites of Pakistan, as a landed aristocracy, were reinforced by colonial rule so that, when Pakistan was created, they were already deeply entrenched in its political system.[16] Between 1947 and 1958, 68% of the legislative members were landlords, and between 1962 and 1969, 58% members of the land-owning élite. From 1947 onwards all Chief Ministers of Punjab, Sind and the North-West Frontier Province were themselves big landlords, while the officers of Pakistan's armed forces usually came from old, wealthy land-owning families.[17] Some prominent leaders of the military *coup d'état* of 1958 also had large landholdings. The fabled twenty-two families of West Pakistan who control industry, the civil service and the military establish-ment are from the rich landlord class. They became the continuing con-trolling force for the modernisation process which "provided many op-portunities for great profit and very rapid social mobility by relatively few families".[18]

In the Philippines the Spanish-speaking, and in part mixed descent, families, the *ilustrado*, consolidated their position of economic and social power and also acquired political power under American rule. Land was their main source of power and continues to be so. Not only the deposed Marcos' "cronies" had considerable landed wealth, but also, Mrs Aquino and others who deposed them come from such landed background.

Throughout the developing world the modernisation process could be instituted only on the basis of considerable and expanding reliance on the participation of superior interests from the developed countries who con-trolled the new technology and had the economic, technical and organisa-tional ability to apply it. Thus the ex-colonial dependencies could achieve development, based on modernisation, only by entering a new dependency. Such dependency has at least two major aspects, a normative and a struc-tural. The normative concerns adoption by the élites of developing countries of outlook, tastes, habits and aspirations borrowed from the developed world and acquired through association, education and acceptance of cultural norms. These élites of developing countries aspire to acceptance by the élites of the developed countries whom they consider superior and measure their achievement by such acceptance. The structural aspect concerns the integration of the two kinds of economic and production systems, the developing countries becoming increasingly dependent on the conditions and pull or push of the economies and policies of the developed.

Increasingly, the new technology, and the capacity to instal it, is con-centrated in the hands of multinational companies, whose economic power and room for manoeuvre exceed that of many modern states. This develop-ment powerfully influences international economic relations and strongly affects the production systems of developing countries; in agriculture it even induces the evolution of the *older* kind of plantation company. The élites of developing countries, who have developed a strong dependence on foreign interests for their economic prosperity and the survival of their control, increasingly gear their links to multinational companies, whose interests they share. In imperial Ethiopia the Awash Valley development through large modern plantations was a combined and complementary effort by the Mitchell Cotts multinational British firm, the powerful local Sultan, Ali Miral, and the Crown Prince of Ethiopia.[19] Interdependence between foreign and local interests in Liberia had a special twist. Firestone, which by the end of the 1960s accounted for 62% of the rubber plantation concessions and 50% of the employment in that activity

> could easily have paid double or triple the going wage rates and still have earned substantial profits. . . . Firestone is not in fact a free agent because it must take account of political repercussions. Many of Liberia's most important politicians and government officials (and their relatives) are independent rubber farmers who are reluctant to have their own wage bills increased. . . . The technique that keeps wage rates down without producing a severe labor shortage is involuntary labor recruitment under government auspices.[20]

In the Ivory Coast, Houphouet Boigny[21] chose a capitalist (though still nationalist) road which involved the maximum use of foreign capital and expertise even if that meant continued foreign economic domination. "I was negotiating a technical contract with the Government," said a US industrialist recently. "It wasn't until I got to the Minister that I actually met an Ivorian. Even the Minister's secretary was French." There are 20 French technical advisers in the private office of the Minister of Economy, Finance and the Plan; 120 in the Ministry as a whole. Of the steering group drawing up the next development plan there are reportedly nine French *cooperants* and one Ivorian. In fact there was overwhelming control of the country's economy by French interests. In 1978, 53% of capital in commercial enterprises was French and 30% of the industrial sector was in the hands of French nationals; 81% of profits in the modern sector went to French interests.[22]

Fagen asks of the profoundly penetrated and multinationalised Mexican economy, "Could a typical Mexican regime consistently decide in favor of impoverished *ejidatarios* when the interests of Mexican and international agri-business are at stake?" "The answers are rather obvious," he replies:

> to weave multinational corporations into the development scenario . . . is to significantly strengthen certain sectors of the domestic class structure while disempowering others. New class alliances with key sectors of the state bureaucracy are formed at home, reflecting the exigencies of attracting and facilitating investment capital. New socio-political forces are linked to those sectors of production and distribution which are most fully internationalized and on which aggregate growth depends. The highly tuned and high technology segments of the domestic economy become ever more susceptible to pressures generated externally but articulated internally by privileged classes and class fractions.[23]

Broad Social and Political Relations of Production

Analysis of production relations reveals both the essential elements of rural societies throughout the world and the ecological conditions for agrarian conflict. In their wider linkages production relations define social status and underpin political influence which in turn enhance and perpetuate economic ascendancy. Ideally there should be data to quantify and give accurate profiles of these crucial issues. Regrettably they do not exist. Even the 1979 World Conference on Agrarian Reform and Rural Development produced no data and no quantified insights into this problem. Myrdal's suggestion[24] that "the fact that rigorous inquiries . . . have not been sponsored officially must be partly ascribed to the vested interests in concealment" is thus perhaps vindicated.

Social and Political Power

We have noted already the pervasive and abiding power of large estate owners, who, as some of the wealthiest and most influential members of society, play a key role.[25] In addition to landed wealth, they control other production inputs, and, since the most influential also engage in finance and commerce, agriculture is often of only secondary interest. Furthermore, they maintain political positions in the state capital, and have professional and cultural interests remote from rural areas. Generally they reside in the city or even abroad.

In Ecuador,[26] which is typical of many Latin American countries, the landowner carries out functions which in practice pertain to the powers of a state: he inflicts fines, adjudicates over family or neighbours' disputes, administers justice, supervises private morality, enforces religious practice and unilaterally determines wages, rates and compensations. In fact the hacienda is "a society, under private auspices. [It] governs the life of those attached to it from the cradle to the grave".[27]

Nepal has similar features:

> The hereditary aristocracy still maintains ultimate control of affairs of state and hence of formal politics of Nepal today. Involved heavily in both the army and the administration, it remains a substantial land-owning group—although some members have taken advantage of their privileged position to invest in hotels, import-export businesses, tourist agencies and other lucrative enterprises in Nepal and India. This aristocracy is one section of a much larger ruling class of landlords and employers of labour. . . . Most members of the ruling class maintain close relations with the government service and many have houses in the capital.[28]

This pattern is replicated in many other countries. In Indonesia the power and ability to make decisions in all key issues rests with President Suharto and his wife together with a dozen trusted advisers, practically all of them military, and many from the birth place of the Suhartos.[29] The military are heavily involved in a wide range of enterprises including plantations.

To safeguard their position in an evolving agriculture many landowners switch over to capitalist forms, shedding as much as they can of the dependent labour force tied to them by traditional obligations, and opting for "free" labour.

The social stratification of plantation agriculture has been described[30] as "typically rigid, with a small, enclaved, upper class into which mobility is virtually impossible . . . most of the populace is part of a vast army of unskilled laborers, locked into economic, social and political deprivation". Multinational plantation companies, which

> are vertically integrated, have a fairly wide geographic compass, and have a cushion of political influence. . . . They are in a position to play different countries off against each other, particularly since they tend to operate in small countries that are largely dependent upon a single plantation crop. These conditions tend to buffer them somewhat against the winds of economic nationalism and the major risk that they run, expropriation.[31]

Other winds of change, however, have overtaken them. The spread of capitalist agriculture has brought new demands from developing countries: ". . . the old plantation firms tend to have their primary contacts and influence with long-standing ministries and élites (both at home and abroad), the new equipment, supply, and processing firms have more contacts and influence with the new national planning and development ministries and with the various national and international aid agencies".[32]

An example of the social stratification of landlords in the Philippines appears earlier (p. 31). Myrdal[33] gives a profile of the social pyramid of South Asian villages. At the apex are the landowners, while the lowest positions are occupied by those who own no land. Least enviable is the situation of persons entirely dependent on others for work as agricultural labourers. Landowners are of three broad types: (a) the big landlords, remnants of the feudal-type structure inherited or created by colonial policy; (b) non-cultivating owners to whom rents from land are often a supplement to other earnings. (These two groups are generally absentees but exercise a formidable influence on village life. Absentee land ownership is both a hedge against inflation and a sort of tax haven) and (c) resident landowners who are further subdivided into (i) those who have enough land to be able to lease out part of it; and (ii) those with enough land to employ themselves and their own families, with the possibility that some may employ a farm servant and some casual labour at peak periods.

In all these profiles the emphasis is on assets[34] as the basis for economic advance, social status and influence. In Nigeria the small class of wealthy farmers functioned as rural capitalists (moneylenders, merchants and farmers) and as representatives of the State at the rural level; they used their wealth as a launching pad into national politics, before the latest military coup.[35] In the last four decades development efforts by official bodies, including foreign aid, have benefited[36] those with assets, including medium landowners, some of whose rise to power has been impressive. As already observed, the modernisation process, and in agriculture the "green revolution", has fuelled this marked change of fortunes. Assets of course include not only land, which is of basic importance, but information (or knowhow) and links (or organisation).

It was mentioned earlier (p. 44) how, amidst general illiteracy and marginality, those who benefited from mission schools or from the education available to the offspring of indigenous élites in colonial dependencies gained a head start. That knowledge is power is now well recognised. Those who benefited from higher education, especially those who obtained it in metropolitan universities, gained not only technical knowledge but also social contacts and poise, all of which are of paramount importance in the modernisation process.

Perhaps it will drive home the lesson if, in the light of this analysis, we examine the plight of those deprived of assets. Knowledge of this is scanty. There are, of course, government services often directed specifically towards those with no assets. But do these services reach them? Or do they get diverted? "Even outsiders get grafted on as clients; for instance the village level worker, who is at the lowest rung of the extension hierarchy, and who is supposed to channel government help and services to the poorer rural strata, often becomes a client of the rich farmer and naturally favours his patron."[37] Public servants, the police and the army in areas of the traditional latifundio in Latin America are at the beck and call of the landowner. Churches and schools require his support in order to function.[38]

In general the small producer in Latin America must buy seed, fertilizers, tools, salt, flour and coffee from the local merchant or *hacienda* commissary, often at grossly marked-up prices. Frequently he has to sell his products at low prices to the landlord or to the merchant who has given him part-time employment or credit.[39] Discrimination in markets is widespread. In export crops, such as coffee, "when the situation on the international market becomes difficult, . . . the first thing that processors or exporters do is reduce their purchases from the small producers . . . so that [this] stratum becomes a sort of cushion which allows the medium-sized and large producers to regulate, in their favour the volumes marketed".[40] Isolated from the general system, the small producer is powerless to find channels to the market or to the public services owing to his precarious economic position and low status. Isolation is enhanced by lack of information as to where to turn and how to approach public servants or offices because of the great social gulf. This severe constraint leads to the practice of seeking a patron to whom he becomes client. The patron-client tie,[41] develops between two parties of unequal status, wealth and influence, depends on reciprocity in the exchange of goods and services, and rests heavily on face-to-face contact. Powell holds two underlying processes responsible for the establishment of these linkages: state centralisation and market expansion. "At the boundary of the little community stands the 'gatekeeper' – the landed patron. As the twin processes of state and market penetration of the peasant village occur, the patron becomes transformed into a broker, mediating the impact of the larger society on the peasant society." He adds that other local people with outside connections also begin to assume brokerage functions – bourgeois landowners, schoolteachers, physicians and pharmacists, priests, tax collectors and other local officials.

Esman and his collaborators make[42] a similar point concerning "inside" employment. "Temporary jobs and other forms of patronage financed by government may be distributed by local political bosses or local influentials with good ties to government to 'deserving' members of the local poor."

Countervailing power could of course be provided through organisation on the part of the mass of exploited people, who have on their side numerical strength of incalculable potential. Some political systems even seek their votes from time to time to form a political base. Why then is there so little effective action?

The issue of participation and equity in development, though fundamental, is a most difficult question and riddled with controversy. Many theorists have ascribed to the large groups of precarious and landless cultivators a low sense of "classness", meaning that they do not feel themselves compact and distinct enough to form a united and sustained fighting force against a clearly identified enemy. This may be particularly true of small owner-cultivators and commodity producers who are in the ambivalent position of believing that their interests lie more with larger producers than with those who offer their labour, and are more interested in prices than in higher wages. A large number of rice producers in Asia are on balance net purchasers of rice; in fact, the majority in the Philippines sell their crop immediately after threshing in order to meet immediate cash needs.[43]

Martinez-Allier ascribes[44] some of the failure of the peasantry to organise effectively against obstruction and intimidation by landowners and authorities to their treating peasant movements about to adopt a political character as having become dangerous bandits. In El Salvador[45] "there is little prospect of a mobilization of peasants to press more militantly for land reform. A small cooperative movement . . . treads more carefully to avoid being labelled Communist."

The repression of peasant and worker movements often takes the form of assassination of their leaders, as in Guatemala by the right-wing vigilante group "Mano Blanco".[46] A "mafia" kind of operation is reported from Punjab in Pakistan, where rich and powerful landlords with links with the police use local bandits to terrorise peasants[47]; and in Colombia "landlords organized private bands of 'fieles' ('faithful') consisting of laborers to replace the existing tenants or squatters".[48] In Brazil in 1986 hired assassins and gangs killed, kidnapped and generally terrorised both poor rural people aspiring to land under the announced reform and the Catholic Priests who supported them.[49]

A non-violent, far more effective and pervasive, way is the pre-emption of rural people's organisations by the élite or their agents; in fact, the initiative for setting up such organisations comes from the government, political parties and other institutions which thereby serve their own interests. Invariably the leadership and its accruing benefits are taken over by the land-owning class, political brokers or agents and other interests to the exclusion of those for whom the organisation, whether a co-operative, worker's union or farmers' association, is set up. Local "self-government" suffers the same fate: *panchayati raj* in India and the "cultivation committees" of Sri Lanka are well studied examples.

No wonder, therefore, that farmers are found to "have weak to non-existent feelings of efficacy toward political institutions which make no difference to their lives" as reported in a study[50] of two regions in Malaya and Sumatra. This attitude admirably serves the purposes of the ruling élites. In El Salvador: " 'The peasants here are very passive', a landowner, Ulises Gonzalez, said as a passing peasant lifted his straw hat in respect. 'They were even opposed to the land reform project because they knew it wouldn't work. But now they're back to working hard.' "[51] In Asia also "the tenant regards the landlord with awe and reverence . . . "[52] The net result is that power remains in the hands of large or otherwise powerful landowners who become power holders locally and power brokers nationally. In Latin America and the Philippines they call the system *caciquismo*; in Brazil, *coronelismo*.[53]

Vertical Distinctions and Cleavages

The structures previously examined concern the horizontal stratification of societies, which, as the social pyramid, provides the main key to the functioning and dynamics of human groups. There are, however, other distinctions and cleavages within societies which, although overall of minor, and even of local, importance, may on occasion assume major proportions and overshadow, however temporarily, all other differences. Basically, grievances and strife arising out of these divisions have socio-economic roots. Such vertical distinctions often affect minorities or disadvantaged majorities, which, although themselves socially stratified, unite in opposition to groups who dominate them. Serious socio-economic handicaps exacerbate vertical divisions, which may take on a virulent form, thus opening the way for exploitation by a fundamentalist leadership or by class enemies.

Sex Roles and Status. A division that cuts societies into two almost equal parts and is due to the "accident" of birth, is sex. The range of problems associated with socially determined roles and status allocated to people on the basis of sex began only recently to receive the attention it deserves, and there is as yet no full grasp of the precise nature, or of the quantitative importance, of these problems, let alone of their qualitative significance. The totality of implications in terms of deprivation, humiliation and pain inflicted, not to speak of loss to society of talent and of input of great value, has yet to be fully appreciated. The lack of knowledge[54] and insight into problems of such colossal significance is connected with vested interests who would not welcome probing into issues which may undermine their position. The present order has existed for so long that people take it to be the natural order. In reality, it is no more than the sex stratification system which ranks males as higher than females, and which "determines that men only will occupy major decision-making positions and will control the valued resources in the society."[55] It is this system which "permeates norms, values, and social structures . . ."[56]

The severe handicaps placed in the way of women in the fields of owner-ship of land, management of agricultural units (even though, as widows or emigrants' wives, they are often *de facto* running them), provision of credit, supply of inputs, marketing, agricultural education and extension, employ-ment and wages, allocation of agricultural and other work, participation in rural people's organisations such as co-operatives, farmers' associations and workers' trades unions, political activity and their role, social status and unprejudiced acceptance are only now being recognised and documented.[57] It is assumed here that it is a mistake to pretend that women are everywhere and at all times discriminated against in a *similar* fashion or to the *same* degree even within one country or region. The truth is that, within a given group, social category or class, occupation, or legal position, women tend to be more under-privileged (or less privileged as the case may be) or more discriminated against than are men within the same class, occupation or legal situation. This is borne out by studies like that of Dixon on South Asia, already referred to. In short, women share all the privileges and advantages or all the disabilities and handicaps of the class to which they belong, except that they tend to be worse off, sometimes much worse off, than the men of that group. It is thus tacitly implied that, when people or groups are referred to in this study, they include women as well as men and that in general the former are worse off than the latter.[58]

Ethnic Distinctions. Nationalism is a potent force which has assumed world-wide importance with the rise to prominence and power of the commercial, industrial and financial classes and the parallel spread of their ideology of removing handicaps on economic, social and political activity. As a liber-tarian call, it has been a liberating force. Constitutions proclaiming liberal ideals and safeguarding private property have been extracted from rulers, slavery banned, and the rhetoric of liberty been strong, especially in times of war, as an appeal to people to back the war effort. The struggle for freedom was not easy, as colonial peoples, one after another, discovered.

Despite the contradiction between the rhetoric at home and the practice in the colonies, these ideals have affected the emancipation of colonial peoples. Slavery and indentured labour left behind a vast residue of ethnic mixtures in Asia, the Caribbean, North and South America, and Africa. Under colonial domination white settlers, Asian and European merchant groups, plantation communities and other ethnic mixtures established themselves in countries far from their own as minorities, frequently privileged ones. The decay of empires, such as the Ottoman, left minorities in other countries, while the near extermination of indigenous peoples or their displacement on a vast scale took place in North America, Australia, New Zealand and Latin America and is continuing to this day in the Amazon Valley. Finally, in the carving up of Africa by European colonial powers many an ethnic group was severed by state frontiers that reflect the greed and capacity of imperial powers rather than any "rational" objective.

Thus ethnic divisions are numerous, vary greatly, and cause acute problems of conflict. Such conflict tends to exacerbate or be exacerbated by agrarian situations and contests, underlying or open. In Latin America social stratification often reflects ethnic lines: the "pure" European at the top, the Indios at the base and the *mestizos* (mixed blood) in the middle.

Colour and Race. This distinction is often one of the most pernicious and the cause of pathological tendencies. The White-dominated regime of South Africa is currently the most notorious and the key role of land tenure in bolstering it and perpetuating the race superiority complex is now better understood or at least recognised.[59] It is also at the root of the territorial separation, the so-called "Black Homelands", now promoted as a "solution". Slavery, indentured labour and the extermination of indigenous people were reinforced by, if not actually based on, colour and racial prejudice. The handicaps of coloured people and other racial groups in developed countries ("immigrants" and "gastarbeiters") are now recognised because they have become uncomfortable problems for the privileged "superior" racial majorities. Racial labels also have social significance. As Barraclough puts it for Latin America, ". . . class differences take an almost castelike appearance: peasants remain socially 'Indian' in Ecuador, Peru and Guatemala. Elsewhere distinctive dress, manners and skin-shading usually set the *campesinos* apart from the estate owners and administrators".[60]

Caste. Caste in the strict sense is well documented, especially for India. Although now illegal according to the Indian Constitution, in practice it is still a strong force, especially in rural areas. "Various studies of Indian village life show a very high correlation between caste ranking and superior and inferior rights to land",[61] and "studies on agricultural labourers show that a great majority of them belong to low and untouchable castes, while the landlords come from superior castes".[62] Moreover, "In India and Pakistan particularly, all but the lower strata can make common cause in obstructing the achievement of status and dignity by the dispossessed, for such efforts are typically regarded as scandalous violations of caste rules".[63]

At times horrifying crimes against low caste people hit the world headlines even today. State-sponsored "positive discrimination" to help low-caste people in education and other social fields as provided for by the constitution have sparked off riots owing to resentment by higher-caste groups.[64] The ability of high caste people to dominate economic, social and political institutions is well documented from Asian countries.

Religion and Ideology. Strongly held beliefs are a powerful force for motivation and mobilisation. Religious groups and other people held together by a body of ideas have often achieved feats of endurance in long and hazardous treks, in creating exclusive communities and reclaiming land for cultivation and settlement. Many such live in North America, while early Jewish settlements in Palestine were to some extent similarly motivated. Religious minorities, even deviant or sectarian factions of one church, are often the cause of strife, either through resentment on the part of majorities or through their own exclusiveness and "deviant" ways. Such strife is exacerbated by social cleavage, especially if the minorities are either distinctly more prosperous or decidedly under-privileged. Modern political systems adopt ambivalent attitudes to such problems, veering from tolerance or indulgence to repression and persecution.

Organised religion is an institution often of millenial history. Such institutions have shared the fortunes of the communities in which they operate, as part of either the ruling class or the oppressed, especially as a new religion or militant form of the church. The Roman Catholic Church in Latin America illustrates this ambivalence. In Ecuador "the landowning institutions of the Church are essentially of a *latifundista* character".[65] Indeed in Latin America the Church has generally been a major pillar of colonisation and administration over the centuries and has bolstered up all regimes by its undoubted wealth and prestige and by lulling, through its preaching, the sense of injustice felt by the oppressed.

Conversely, some churches or sections of them have sided with the oppressed and suffered from repressive regimes, including the assassination of clergy which extended even to the Archbishop in El Salvador. Sharpe analyses[66] the advocacy of agrarian reform by the Latin American Bishops' Conference of 1968, and the support by the bishops of the Dominican Republic for action in agrarian reform; he also stresses the limits of such support. The ambivalence of the Roman Catholic Church in Latin America to social issues is dramatised by the fortunes of "liberation theology"; especially resented by the Vatican and the local hierarchy is the application of its tenets by activist theologians and priests in basic communities through the concepts of conscientisation and praxis. Liberation theology sees the abolition of injustice and the building of a new society as coming about through effective participation in the struggle by the exploited classes against their oppressors.[67] In the summer of 1986 the bizarre move was reported in the press of the President of Brazil visiting the Pope in Rome to request that the Catholic clergy attenuate their support of oppressed rural people agitating for agrarian reform and being killed by thugs hired by landowners in the process.

Language. Language, and in general the capacity to communicate, is a medium that can bind together but also divide and handicap. Linguistic minorities cause headaches to the state and arouse friction with intolerant majorities. Efforts to create a lingua franca to overcome linguistic divisions within a population often create resentment and stir demands for autonomy by linguistic groups, especially if they are territorially compact. "Command of the lingua franca may itself give advantages to persons fluent in it, so its use has political-economic implications."[68] In Sri Lanka the rebellion of 1971 had some basis in the career disadvantages under which youths with inadequate knowledge of English suffered. Language may be associated with social ideology as happened in Greece where for decades the spoken form of Greek was associated with dangerous social doctrines and even with atheism, and outbreaks of riots and persecution recurred from time to time. "Particularly difficult problems arise when the national language is seen as one of colonisation, as the Oromo view Amharic in Southern Ethiopia, or when a langauge is identified with exploitation, as the Malay see Chinese in Malaysia".[69]

Notes

1. Baran and Sweezy 1975 p. 247.
2. Dovring 1974 pp. 509–533.
3. Barraclough y Domike 1966 p. 236.
4. Quoted from Robequain by Myrdal 1968 p. 1036, f.2.
5. Ibid. p. 1036.
6. Ibid. p. 1035.
7. See Christodoulou 1976 pp. 1–2. Note also the strife in New Caledonia, where the indigenous people are fewer than the settlers and immigrants were brought in to serve a settler economy.
8. Berman and Lonsdale 1980 pp. 58 & 60.
9. Myint 1969 p. 59.
10. Seidman 1974 p. 112.
11. Young 1982 p. 210.
12. Hunt 1984 pp. 287–288.
13. ILO 1972 p. 35.
14. Young 1982 p. 194.
15. Christodoulou 1977 pp. 4–6. See also Adedeji 1981 for examples from many countries.
16. Hussain 1976 p. 227.
17. Sanderatne and Zaman 1973 pp. 12, 14 and 19.
18. Papanek 1972 pp. 6–8.
19. Bezzabeh 1980 pp. 18–19.
20. Clower, Dalton, Harwitz and Walters 1966 p. 150.
21. *Financial Times* 9 December 1980. It took a financial crisis to alter things. The cost of expatriates officially recruited exceeded $100 million a year, of which the Ivory Coast

paid 80%. In 1985 it was decided to cut back the number sharply. *Financial Times* 23 January 1985. Already the country was heavily indebted, with $4.5 billion external debt and 36.9% of the GNP going to service it in 1982. See Fieldhouse 1986 pp. 187–188. In 1987 the Ivory Coast announced that it was suspending debt repayments because it could not pay the service. That service in 1987 was $1.2 billion. *Financial Times* 28 May 1987.

22. Campbell 1985 p. 286 quoting *Africa Confidential* 1 August 1979.
23. Fagen 1978b p. 294.
24. Myrdal 1968 p. 1056.
25. This paragraph is based on Barraclough y Domike 1966 p. 244; see also Barraclough 1970 p. 918.
26. Baraona 1965 p. 81.
27. Tannenbaum 1965 p. 28.
28. Blaikie, Cameron and Seddon 1980 p. 85.
29. Kieran Cooke in *Financial Times Survey: Indonesia* 10 March 1986.
30. Young 1970 p. 356.
31. Dahlberg 1979 pp. 109–110.
32. Ibid. p. 110.
33. Myrdal 1968 pp. 1053–1055.
34. It is interesting to observe that powerful as caste in Indian villages tends to be, "it is their position as landowners, rather than caste membership per se, that gives them status and power". See Lewis and Barnouw 1967 p. 131.
35. Ohiorhenuan 1984 p. 24.
36. See for example Chenery 1979.
37. Scarlett Epstein, T. quoted in Asian Development Bank 1978 p. 228.
38. Barraclough y Domike 1966 p. 244.
39. Barraclough 1970 p. 933.
40. Ortega 1982 pp. 83–84.
41. Powell 1970 pp. 412–414. Alavi takes objection to the reciprocity concept in this type of relationship. See 1973 p. 54.
42. Esman and Associates 1978 p. 83. See also Silverman 1967 esp. pp. 289–290, regarding the *mezzadria* landlords.
43. Castillo 1977 p. 44.
44. Martinez-Allier 1977 p. 53.
45. Alan Riding in *New York Times* 8 April, 1977.
46. Esman and Associates 1978 p. 336.
47. Alavi 1973 p. 56.
48. Hirschman 1963 p. 104.
49. As the *Financial Times* 26 June 1986 put it: "Indignant landowners, vigilantes and hired guns vie with thousands of ragged families backed by militant priests".
50. Gibbons, de Koninck and Hasan 1980 p. 196.
51. Op. cit.
52. Myrdal 1968 p. 1331.
53. The "network of controls exercised by large landowners over rural populations has become known as *coronelismo*. The *coronel* is a traditional politician, normally a landowner, [who] delivers the votes of those dependent on him and receives public powers in exchange". Cehelsky 1972 pp. 230–231.
54. Even global figures are eloquent. Two-thirds of the world's work and 60–80% of Africa's and Asia's food production are contributed by women; but they earn only one-tenth of the world's income and own less than one percent of the world's property. World Bank figures reported from the Nairobi Conference on women by Michael Prouse in the *Financial Times* 13 February 1987.
55. Safilios-Rothchild 1985 p. 312.
56. Ibid. p. 299.
57. Literature is growing. Besides the Safilios-Rothchild analysis, already cited, three other studies are worth mentioning: Deere Wilson 1985 pp. 1017–1035; 1982 pp. 795–811; and Dixon 1982 pp. 373–390.

58. One can anticipate and illustrate this by pointing out that the impact of agrarian reform on rural households is *not* gender neutral. Only male household heads are incorporated into the new agrarian reform structures, and it is mainly men who are the beneficiaries. Women are considered as unremunerated family labour possessing neither education nor farming experience. See Deere 1985 pp. 1037–1053.

59. United Nations 1976.

60. Barraclough 1970 p. 918.

61. Myrdal 1968 p. 1059.

62. Das Gupta 1977 p. 14.

63. Myrdal 1968 p. 1063.

64. "Gujarat's upper caste – the Brahmins and Patels, a once powerful landed community – has been overtaken by the rising Kshatriya caste, mostly small farmers and businessmen." Seeing their inherited privileges eroded they resented the positive discrimination in favour of lower castes and backward minorities, mainly the increase in the number of government jobs and college places automatically available to them; that was a root cause for serious and protracted rioting in the place where Mahatma Gandhi launched his campaigns which included love for the untouchables. *Financial Times* 15 May 1985.

65. Baraona 1965 p. 119.

66. Sharpe 1977 pp. 346–362.

67. See Gutierrez 1983 p. 307.

68. Uphoff, Cohen and Goldsmith 1979 p. 145.

69. Ibid. p. 146.

Part II: The Genesis and Nurture of Agrarian Conflict

". . . like two men quarelling across a fence in the common field with yardsticks in their hands, each of them fighting for his fair share in a narrow strip."
Homer: *Iliad*, Book II
(translation by E.V. Rieu)

". . . the rights and interests of the labouring man will be protected and cared for . . . by the Christian men to whom God in his infinite wisdom has given the control of the property interests of the country . . ."
George F. Baer of the Reading Railroad,
US, 1902.

6. Main Forces and Dynamics

Origins of Agrarian Conflict

The account of the structures of rural society; the examination of production relations in respect of access to land; the identification of land with power; and the resulting conditions of existence of the various rural classes and their socio-political roles foreshadow an inherent agrarian conflict of variable potential in a varied ecology. The view that agrarian conflict is an alien import cannot be sustained except in the sense that a dormant conflict can be awakened, fomented, and even managed (or manipulated) by outside forces. Nor can the facile assumption that given conditions yield specified developments, in a mechanistic cause-and-effect sequence, be entertained. It is unwise to isolate certain crucial variables in conditions where a number of factors have combined in the past, and can combine in other circumstances in many different ways. Agrarian conflict is viewed here as inherent in prevailing conditions, which are themselves the outcome of many factors in conjunction. Its development is conditioned by dynamics arising out of conjunctions of new factors and conjunctures of new events. A systematic probe into a great range of problems and their dynamic can illuminate situations and processes; combined studies of this type can suggest some principles and yield perceptive experience, enabling us to deduce some rules of the dynamics involved. This saves us from fallacies leading to policies which can prove costly and painful failures in situations already overwhelmed by misery and pain.

The master key to agrarian conflict is, by definition, the vital resource of land. Sufficient indications have already been given of the nature of the problem: the supreme importance of land as an asset and the basis it provides for social and political power; the unequal access to land strongly determines the character of both local and wider societies and provides the dynamics of relations between classes.

Some wider considerations must now be examined.

The importance of land has been enhanced by two opposing trends. Population has increased – of late at unprecedented rates; land (and space on earth) has diminished, both relative to population and, for agricultural land, absolutely. In spite of optimistic predictions the race between bringing

61

"new" land under cultivation and loss of agricultural land to other uses is not being won by agriculture. Land is a finite quantity, population on earth does not seem so at present. The productive capacity of land has been constantly increased by inputs, their effectiveness accelerated by science and technology. Level, location and composition of production are institutionally determined and this affects the satisfaction of basic needs of the poor.

These macro-effects provide the context within which agrarian conflict arises but are rarely its immediate cause. The genesis and progression of agrarian conflict are to be sought basically in the relations of production from the land: namely who controls the land, who works it and how the fruits yielded are apportioned. This network of production relations is enmeshed within institutional forms of great complexity: beyond production relations in connection with the land, but in complicated interrelationships, are other production relations: and all this is part of a wider social, economic and political, and even cultural, context of complex, and interacting, human relationships, usually institutionalised and of long standing.

It is essential, therefore, to keep constantly in mind that a given agrarian conflict has local seeds and genetic traits; its life, however has a wider habitat with a complex ecology of equal importance. All conflict arises when incompatibility persists within a given situation. Agrarian conflict is no exception.

Basic Incompatibilities in Production or Other Agrarian Relations

The basic incompatibility in production relations is that between potential and performance. In such cases production and income distribution are below what would occur if the potential could be more effectively realised. Thus returns, which could otherwise accrue to them are denied to all concerned. This gives rise to a pathology in production conditions and relations which sooner or later has deleterious effects. The first to feel the symptoms are the weaker parties in the system; later the malaise spreads to all who expect returns.

There is a limit to the level of social cost that can be demanded in any production situation; once this limit is exceeded sooner or later extra-production methods, especially repression, will be required to contain discontent. If, however, the production system yields the maximum obtainable, however much and in whatever direction production relations are reordered, discontent loses much of its objective force. Moreover, when the system performs at high levels, it can increase rewards all round and even bribe the better organised elements in the system, thus blunting discontent.

It is not easy to decide *a priori* the threshold of tolerance of any social group; too many considerations are involved. An interesting example is the "tunnel effect" mentioned by Hirschman.[1]

It is also advisable, as Hobsbawm suggests,[2] to maintain the distinction between socio-economic reality and class consciousness. Appropriate here is Mintz'[3] argument about the need to understand "how populations come to the recognition that their felt oppression is not merely a matter of *poor* times, but *evil* times – when, in short, they question the *legitimacy* of an existing allocation of power, rather than the terms of that allocation".

The case of the hacienda, discussed earlier, reveals many acute incompatibilities: resources, especially labour and land, are seriously underutilised, at least in production. The dominant landlord has no interest in higher production because he already has a high income from either land or other sources, but attaches high value to the power he commands and its trappings. The network of interlocking powers within the socio-political system gives to his position, and collectively to that of his fellow landlords, an oppressive solidity and quasi-permanence.

The oppressive and widespread poverty and powerlessness of the attached tenants, sharecroppers and servants produces a pathological state which, in their unchallenged position, the landlord and his class can manage for a very long time.

The undermining of the system comes from the less dramatic but truly revolutionary changes, often taking place in a wider context: they amount to a fundamental progress in production potential, due usually to changes in technology and organisation, often in response to a parallel change in demand for output. A significant rise in the trade of agricultural commodities encourages adoption of new technology, which in turn induces changes in the organisation of production and thus in production relations.

Both the hacienda, and the majority of medium to large landlord production units operating with the same order of priorities, face the challenge and the beguiling promises of commercial demand. They are forced, therefore, to adopt, or adapt to, new technology and organisation of production; in response, technology and organisation develop further. In modern times the capitalist form of production has been able to achieve remarkable success in both. The result is a radical departure from the priorities and institutional approaches of the old landlord-dominated systems.

New, commercially-oriented and production-minded, landowners have emerged and some old-type landlords switched over to the new system, adopting new technology and gearing the production system to market demands. Higher production, greater turnover, lower costs of production and higher returns become the rule. Labour now has an overt cost and a price. Flexibility in the combination of factors of production is prized. As mentioned earlier, the old notion of dependent manpower, a prestige and power symbol, bound to the land by traditional ties and obligations, is replaced by the need for freedom of action on both sides, as labour becomes a commodity for sale and purchase. Old ties and asymmetrical, but to some extent reciprocal, obligations are thrown overboard. Labour is now "free".

When it came, freedom was welcome to some, especially those who had land of their own; some may have even campaigned for it, but to many it meant the worst of both worlds; they remained indebted but had no means of employment and income, not even a house or place to stay. Writing about Ecuador, Baraona[4] distinguishes between the *colonos*, of somewhat freer status and with a certain amount of self-confidence, and the *huasipungueros* with neither.

Capitalism in agriculture has spread and is spreading worldwide. It has proved very successful in expanding production and has changed the nature of the agrarian conflict.

Another major system now being replaced by capitalist agriculture is customary land tenure based on group ownership of land and family-operated production units. As explained earlier, in customary systems those who wrested land from nature were deemed its owners and passed it to their heirs as property. The system was maintained by the development of simple polities with elders in command (gerontocracy) and some equality in conditions of life close to subsistence. These polities enjoyed stability and continuity in relative isolation. The major blow came from invaders with superior technology and organisation. Some countries were brought under colonial rule, thus bolstering the native landlord/tenant or sharecropper relationship and encouraging money economies and commercial orientation, often through settler farming, each with its own new agrarian conflict. The commercial sector gained ground supported by world trends and external forces.

Thus colonial rule and post-independence external economic ties have given impetus to capitalist expansion in agriculture.

Capitalist Agriculture and Agrarian Conflict

A universal system of much dynamism, capitalist production creates conflict in production relations both by its own nature and by the wreckage it leaves behind in its advance.

Its nature is characterised by the divorce between ownership of the means of production and those who work them as hired labour. Conflict arises in that the profit motive requires the owner of the means of production to pay a low price for labour to cut down cost, while the workers feel exploited since they believe that they are deprived of a fair reward for their contribution.

Conflict based on these motives and beliefs is aggravated by visible differences. In plantation agriculture, for instance, the well-paid foreign staff and the remote owners are visibly better off and often ethnically and racially different. They have taken over the best land and the indigenous people, severely deprived, live in acute poverty and suffer from land hunger.

In time new land owners, and converted old-style landlords, become visibly richer as the result of what is seen as a low price paid for labour. Upstarts in a rising capitalist production system become very visible indeed. Many of the smaller ones are strikingly more ruthless and in a hurry, and therefore make the workers more aware of the "evils" of the system.

The "freeing" of labour and the need to negotiate its price force workers to contest with the owners of the means of production in order to protect their employment, remuneration and conditions of work. This encourages, even compels, workers to organise to face the undoubtedly stronger economic, social and political position of their employers, thus opening a new field of conflict which has become such a marked feature of the system.

The advance of capitalism leaves much wreckage behind. In the search for profit based on low costs of production and high returns from output the system adopts certain defensive and offensive traits.

It tends to enlarge its scale of operation by horizontal and vertical expansion. Thus a capitalist agricultural producer acquires more land by buying out existing producers (smaller or indebted owners, advantage being taken of their temporary or lasting weakness) or by leasing-in more land by displacing smaller producers, whether owners or precarious tenants and sharecroppers. Under capitalism concentration of production in fewer and fewer units is a universal phenomenon and the wreckage widespread and varied. One outcome is the full or semi-proletarianisation of the mass of small producers. Hence the very visible phenomena of urbanisation and emigration in acutely difficult conditions, or part-time cultivation of their own land combined with employment, if available, on other farms and plantations or in non-agricultural work.

The process of concentrating effective production in fewer and more powerful units knows no limits, as the growth of modern agri-business demonstrates.[5] It also illustrates the other kind of expansion: vertical integration. Medium (and even smaller) producers are contracted by processing firms to deliver certain lines of their output which is produced under stipulated conditions and even under supervision. Processing firms may be producers in their own right or become so. Some may operate, and more and more do so, as multinational companies with economic power exceeding that of small states.

Very large firms, especially multinationals, deal with their own labour in two main ways: they pay, at least some of them, much higher wages than those prevailing in the country or area and thereby help blunt their militancy as divisions among workers increase; or they shift activity within their production complex in a way that shields them from militancy by any one section of their workers.

Another major tendency in capitalist agriculture is the economy in labour cost achieved through technology which enables a lowering of labour rates per unit of output. The result is to reduce employment. If labour is scarce and fully employed, this is a social gain, as well as a private advantage; if labour is abundant and unemployed, the social cost is enormous. Combined with the rapid process of proletarianisation, this tendency to lower employment cumulatively assumes catastrophic proportions.

An important aspect of the system is the choice of location, with preference given to places that ensure the greatest profitability for the firm or unit, e.g. those with the best quality land, the most appropriate location in relation to trade, and proximity to others to ensure low overhead costs.

Regional disparities are thus accentuated and richly endowed areas mono-polise all activity. Areas or whole countries become either tributary pro-ducers of the rawest material or complete backwaters. Areas which exported food become importers.

Combined with location is the shift of labour *en masse* from areas of no or low employment to areas of high employment. This involves mass migra-tions within countries and from one country to another and leads to en-hanced vulnerability of the workers in the new environment, rootlessness and malaise from the underprivileged cultural and social conditions in which they are compelled to live.

These phenomena are .reproduced in greater or lesser degree by all countries and often at all levels. The rise of the medium farmer class in areas of the "green revolution" and as a result of land reforms in India[6] has already been mentioned; this burgeoning of a powerful, middle-range capitalist producer class is so widespread throughout the world within the orbit of the market economy as to become the hallmark of our time. Combining numbers with the capacity to extract maximum benefits from the social and political system, they have become a powerful political force in most existing political systems. The question arises whether they will last very long in a process of concentration of economic activity and power and in a "multi-nationalised" world. In other words, will they become the future "peasants" of the new pyramid?[7]

Capitalist agriculture based on private property (inherited and/or amassed) is often linked with liberal democracy. But

> when the liberal property right is written into law as an individual right to [its] exclusive use and disposal . . . and when combined with the liberal system of market incentives and rights of free contract, it leads to and supports a concentration of ownership and a system of power relations between individuals and classes which negates the ethical goal of free and independent individual development.

In other words, once again the Matthew effect comes into operation, eventually denying the majority of individuals the right "to use and develop their capacities which is the essential ethical principle of liberal democracy".[8] In reality capitalist agriculture prevails under all the numerous authoritarian rightwing governments and dictatorships.

Centrally Planned Economies and Agrarian Conflict

In contrast to a capitalist economy, a socialist economy aims at abolishing private property as the major means of production and distribution, and substituting for it public ownership and/or control; the emphasis is on collective or state operation of the economy and the focus on reward for labour (and skill) expended in production, rather than on rent or dividends; reliance has hitherto been placed mainly on central planning and control rather than on the market.

In socialist countries, except for Poland and Yugoslavia, land is either nationalised or virtually publicly controlled, and is operated through the medium of state farms and collective or co-operative farms. In theory the means of production are owned (or controlled) by the people, there is no exploitation of man by man, and production and distribution are decided by public authorities on behalf of the people; with collective or co-operative farms policy is approved by all their members in appropriate assemblies.

Do such systems present any incompatibilities? The most pervasive is the variance between theory and practice. For instance, do the assemblies of collective farms decide production and distribution? Or, at a higher level, do the public authorities in deciding production represent the will of the people? Has exploitation of man by man ended completely?

Another incompatibility is the degree to which, in agriculture at least, interlocking centralised control allows sufficient scope for timely decisions and action to meet situations as they arise. As Wilczynski writes:[9]

> In the absence of private enterprise, there must be a dual system of decision-making – by planning authorities and producing units. . . . The challenge confronting a centrally planned economy is to evolve a mechanism ensuring an application of natural resources by farms and other enterprises that is in accordance with the maximisation of social benefit. The targets set in the national plan must be reconciled with the interests of the individual producing unit and its personnel, so that the latter do not act contrary to social interest. At the same time the executors of the plan must be able to influence planners according to changing conditions of production and consumption.
>
> The reforms being implemented in the European CMEA countries are designed to meet this challenge by a decentralisation of decision-making, the acceptance of profit as the main indicator of enterprise performance and a new system of material incentives to personnel.

CMEA is, of course, the socialist countries' economic co-operation bloc (known also as COMECON) embracing the USSR, Eastern European countries and developing countries such as Cuba and Vietnam.

These reforms refer mainly to the newly adopted Hungarian "New Economic Mechanism" and also to those associated with the name of Lieberman. As Clegg wrote soon afterwards:[10]

> Lieberman and his followers in Russia have followed Oscar Lange in pointing out the difficulty of exerting strict control over a sophisticated industrial economy. It is also felt that the profit motive instills greater desire to increase productivity than calls to serve the cause of socialism. Generally this decentralisation has . . . resulted . . . only in greater freedom for enterprise management and increased incentive payments to the workers.

Yet appeals to workers' idealism and to extra-economic motives have not been absent. Until the late 1970s the People's Republic of China was hailed for its success in mobilising the population on the basis of frugality and non-economic motivation. Cuba has laid stress on *conciencia* and the role of the *hombre nuevo* (new man) in the belief that "Genuine fulfilment of individual personality was not . . . contrary to the primacy of the collective interest, but instead was made possible by this primacy".[11]

It is generally agreed that there is still a gap between production potential and actual performance in the agriculture of centrally planned economies, which is highlighted by heavy imports of grain (especially feeding stuffs) by the USSR and by food crises in Poland. The USSR farm output by 1979 was 2.5 times 1950 levels, the average annual rate of increase being 3.5 per cent, nearly double that of the USA.[12] The reasons why the USSR has not been able to produce the quantities and quality of farm products necessary to meet domestic demand have been the subject of lively controversy for many years. The authors already mentioned diagnosed[13] low labour productivity and high costs of production, while Johnson identified[14] as the "major indicators of the disappointing performance of Soviet agriculture . . . the very high fraction of national investment devoted to agriculture [26–27%], the high cost of farm products, and the instability of output".

Hitherto criticism of the USSR by outside critics has been of *low* investment in agriculture and, of course, ideological opposition to collectivisation in general. Collectives have been seen as the villains of the piece. Some critics have gone so far as to assert that socialism and agriculture are incompatible. It is interesting that such an important economist and long-standing student of the Soviet economy as Johnson should reaffirm[15] that "I am now quite fully convinced that the socialized nature of agriculture is not the primary or even an important source of the inefficiency and high cost so prevalent in the Soviet Union". Griffin concluded that communal (or collective) tenure is more capable of promoting rural development than individual tenure through bringing together many desirable features under a single institutional framework.[16]

The technical argument has always concentrated on the need for smaller *working* units in agriculture. "Farming offers the opportunity to separate production activities into discrete functions or spaces," and this "would be consistent with the concept of a collective farm and . . . would bring a much closer correspondence between reward and effort than now exists."[17]

The process of decentralisation of decision-making and autonomy of operation at lower levels has been in operation for the last two decades or so. Hungary has been credited with pioneering ideas and practices. The adoption in 1968 of the "New Economic Mechanism" introduced "enterprise autonomy – which meant abandoning compulsory planning – and the transition to reliance on market signals (prices, interest rates, and taxation policies) to guide enterprise decisions".[18]

Many years ago the USSR was experimenting with links, i.e. a variety of sub-brigade production unit of 10 to 15 persons which was expected to become a typical unit for most labour intensive field and livestock operations[19] that autonomous work-teams were introduced experimentally in the late 1960s.[20] An area of land is handed over for the cultivation of given crop(s), together with the necessary equipment, to a small group (say five or six people) who are allowed to organise their own work, without having work-schedules imposed on them and are paid by results. In 1982 under the adopted "Food Programme" new "Incentives for peasants . . . include small brigades responsible for a range of tasks."[21]

This trend has been observed in socialist countries outside Europe. Cuba began to organise labour into brigades in the late 1970s, extending them rapidly in the 1980s. They are given the resources to accomplish given tasks; they organise their own labour and most of their wages are based on results.[22] In Vietnam in "1981 the key policy of subcontracting agricultural tasks to families was introduced". It "has shifted responsibility for production down from the level of the co-operative to the production team and from the team to the family". Furthermore incentives are provided for output to be increased "by setting a quota of production at averaged levels which is to be sold to the state at state prices. The producers can keep the surplus and dispose of it as they desire".[23]

The People's Republic of China has attracted considerable attention because it has embarked on a new course with far-reaching implications. Ma Hong, President of the Chinese Academy of Social Sciences and Adviser to the State Planning Commission, analysing[24] the new strategy, refers to the 1958 movement for the creation of people's communes when "the peasants were discouraged as a result of the stirring up of a 'communist wind', excessively high quotas for state purchases of agricultural products, and the issuing of arbitrary directions. Later on . . . private plots and country fairs [were abolished] and . . . a higher form of public ownership [was advocated] despite a poor development of productive forces". To correct such errors the new agricultural policy was adopted in 1978. "The decision-making powers of the production teams have been expanded, remuneration is now linked more directly to output, and different forms of the system of production responsibility have been set up." Other principles mentioned include: appropriate mechanisation consistent with full utilisation of the high rural labour force, and the use and development of draught animals; stable long-term policy on private plots and family sideline occupations; and narrowing of the gap between prices for industrial and agricultural products.

The communes were an amalgamation of former collective farms; they became a small economic region with a township and a number of villages administered together. The production brigade at the base is in essence an average village unit or group of hamlets, while the production team down the scale is a normal-size co-operative unit. Each of these three units had rights and duties set down officially, but in times of revolutionary zeal or fever the higher-level units tended to usurp much of the decision-making which by law belonged to the lower.

The ownership rights of these units are now protected by state laws. "As long as they operate within the guidance of the state plan all basic accounting units can cultivate whatever they like, decide their own methods of management and distribute their own products and income."[25] The most important basic accounting unit has always been the production team, now strengthened. Under the new policy the production team can enter into a contract with a small unit, usually a family,

> for the use of specific tracts of land for a predetermined production goal. Output up to the quota is sold to the state for a relatively low price and part of the proceeds go to the production brigade or commune. Output beyond the quota can be directly consumed by the contractor, sold to the state at a premium price, or sold in the free markets.[26]

It is estimated that over 90% of China's farmland is now cultivated on this family scale.[27]

The contract period is now for a minimum of 15 years. The production team responsible for the fulfilment of indicative plans conveyed to it by the local government is able to ensure their fulfilment through contracts with smaller units, i.e. families.[28] The team "remains the most important collective institution in rural China. [It] is the level of account, the source of work points, the owner of the land and draught animal power".[29]

In China, domestic sideline-occupations are officially encouraged among members in their leisure time. The most discussed issue, not only in Chinese agriculture but in all socialist agriculture in general, is the role of household plots. Critics, usually on ideological grounds, draw adverse comparisons in productivity between the collective sector and the household plots, implying inefficiency in the operation of the former.[30] Johnson disputes this, at least in the case of the USSR.[31] The fact is that socialist countries now encourage production on household plots. In China production teams are allowed to raise the size of these plots to 15% of the cultivated land.

Data for 1970 indicate that income from private plots and other receipts in the USSR was higher than what members received from collective farms.[32] The *Financial Times* (19 March 1985) gives the following Table regarding private farming in socialist countries of Europe:

Table 6.1
Private Farming in Socialist European Countries

	% of total arable farmland	% of total output
Bulgaria	12.9	25
Czechoslovakia	2.8	10
East Germany	5.1	5–14
Hungary	12	35
Poland	76.8	79.5
Romania	15	n/a

Hungary, the best farmed socialist country, has successfully integrated production from co-operative farms and private family farming activities.[33]

The inequalities that exist between and within collective farms and state farms is another problem and subject of lively debate. Differences are due primarily to location, which determines both natural conditions and labour on the collective farm. On its formation the collective farm took over conditions as they existed and had an obligation to employ this fixed labour force – a serious problem for many poorly endowed collective farms. As Johnson observes with regard to the USSR, the long-run solution would be either to encourage migration away from the farms or to bring a wide range of non-farm jobs within easy reach of the farm people. If hired labour were an acceptable practice, high-income collective farms could hire workers from low income collective farms. Another approach would be to charge or collect rent on land. The development in recent years of agrarian-industrial complexes has so far contributed a very small amount of employment especially off-season.[34] Concerning inequalities between the two forms of organisation, there is a trend towards conversion of collective farms into state farms, while measures have also been taken to narrow the differences between the two.

Of the two countries with a very high proportion of private farms, Yugoslavia opted for self-management, while Poland has had a chequered history of policy formulation and implementation. Poland tried collectivisation at first, relaxed it in the mid-1950s, and has had to tread carefully in relation to the private sector since that time. Essentially it has aimed at strengthening the socialised sector without weakening the private. Poland has been accused of going to the extreme of encouraging the growth of middle class farmers,[35] while, especially during the Solidarity (1980–1981) period, the pressure on the State was for guarantees of a permanent status for private agriculture and for improvements in the operating environment for private farmers through greater access to inputs and credit and autonomy for farmers' organisations.[36]

Finally, it is often argued that socialist agriculture has been introduced not only on ideological grounds, but also for urgent reasons of rapid development to safeguard the security and survival of the socialist state.

Emphasis on industrialisation was intended to change the nature of the economy from agrarian and backward to modern and independent. Dependency on other countries, especially for heavy capital goods would mean, it was thought, acceptance of military inferiority and increase the risk of socialism being destroyed by external intervention. Referring mainly to Soviet agriculture Galeski[37] gives the reason behind rapid collectivisation as the ambitious programme of industrialisation and thus the need to expand exports to purchase equipment; hence the further need to control prices. Galeski adds significantly: "since agricultural producers were not inclined to increase their marketable produce . . . it was necessary to use other measures to control the producers, their investments, their resources and their consumption".

Supporters of socialism believe it to be a higher form of democracy. To fulfil this role Horvat spelled out[38] three main requirements: equality in (a) production; (b) consumption, and (c) citizenship. Equality in production implies, in his view, social ownership of the means of production, the right to work, and the right to management of production. Equality in consumption means distribution of the product according to the results of work. Equality in citizenship implies a political democracy.

That socialist agriculture faces its own brand of incompatibilities is to be expected. In their evolution living societies present new problems; even old ones were not expected to be easily solved, as the founder of the first socialist state warned; "the mere conversion of the means of production into the common property of the whole society . . . *does not remove* the defects of distribution and the inequality of 'bourgeois law', which *continues to prevail* so long as products are divided 'according to the amount of labour performed' ".[39]

Notes

1. "Suppose that the individual has very little information about his future income, but at some point a few of his relatives, neighbours, or acquaintances improve their economic or social position. Now he has something to go on: expecting that his turn will come in due course, he will draw gratification from the advances of others – for a while. It will be helpful to refer to this initial gratification as the 'tunnel effect'." Hirschman 1973 p. 29.
2. Quoted in Mintz 1974 p. 322, fn. 7.
3. Ibid. p. 315.
4. Baraona 1965 p. 163.
5. In the USA in 1982 one per cent of the farmers absorbed nearly 60% of net farm income, while 87% of the farmers earned only 10%. The *Financial Times*, 21 March 1984.
    In Britain in 1973 holders of net wealth in the £100,000 plus class held 58% of all land (compared with 18% of total net wealth). Hirsch 1976 p. 33.
6. Bardhan summed up the position as follows: "In most parts of the country agrarian capitalism is sprouting . . . many families of capitalist landlords and rich farmers have also branched out into money-lending, trading, transport and other business services . . . strengthening their urban political and economic connections". Bardhan 1984 p. 48.
7. It is interesting that according to the *Financial Times*, 1 March 1985, a vociferous new farming lobby emerged the day before in Britain, the Small-farmers' Association, to combat the steady disappearance of Britain's small family farms, estimated as representing about 60% of holdings; they believed that the National Farmers' Union had not done enough for them and claimed that 10,000 farmers, all of them millionaires, obtained half the official price support available in Britain.
8. Macpherson 1978 pp. 199–200.
9. Wilczynski 1969 p. 557.
10. Clegg 1971 p. 13.
11. Archibald Ritter 1974 p. 270. In point of fact Ché Guevara was the promoter of socialist emulation to produce new attitudes, during the early years of the Cuban Revolution. By the 1970s attitudes began to change. On the twentieth anniversary of the attack on Moncada Barracks in 1973 Castro emphasised that economic incentives should not become the exclusive motivation nor should moral incentives become the pretext for some to live off others. See Jimenez 1987 p. 127.
12. Diamond, Bettis and Ramson 1984 p. 144.
13. Ibid. p. 143.
14. Johnson 1984 p. 114.
15. Ibid. p. 137.
16. Griffin 1986 pp. 165–191. He derived his conclusions from analysis of data from a number of countries, including 12 socialist countries, both developed and developing.
17. Johnson 1984 pp. 125–126.

18. Hartfort 1985 pp. 129–130.
19. Osofsky 1974 p. 234.
20. Nove 1983 p. 179.
21. Ibid. p. 185.
22. Jimenez 1986 p. 135.
23. Werner 1984 p. 49.
24. Hong, Ma 1983 pp. 36, 44, 50–51.
25. Saich 1981 pp. 216–217.
26. Trescot 1985 p. 208.
27. Gray 1984 p. 33.
28. Ibid. pp. 33–34.
29. Griffin and Griffin 1983 p. 226.
30. See *Financial Times*, 19 March 1985 (Leslie Colitt and David Buchan).
31. Johnson 1984 p. 124.
32. Johnson 1984 p. 174.
33. *Financial Times*, 31 October 1985.
34. Johnson 1984 pp. 120–121 and 132. See also Osofsky 1974 pp. 190–192.
35. See Piekakiewicz 1979 pp. 86–107.
36. See Cook 1984 p. 407.
37. Galeski 1977 p. 21. It is interesting that Yugoslavia in the crisis of its break with other Socialist countries in 1948 embarked on rapid collectivisation and tight control of agricultural production.
38. Horvat 1974 pp. 3–6.
39. Lenin 1969 p. 86.

7.   Rural Classes and Agrarian Conflict

Rural Classes and the Activation of Conflict

The systemic incompatibilities, discussed in preceding pages, provide the framework for agrarian conflict. Occasions, particular causes, and immediate reasons for conflicts, however, vary enormously. It is far from easy to account for and can best be understood by relating them to the rural classes already identified.

Casually Employed Agricultural Workers

This is the most detached and physically mobile social group, which is also often migrant and subject to scarce and most precarious employment opportunities and sources of income. Its members are rarely considered in programmes of land distribution, benefit little from development investment, and are often resented as migrants.

Accustomed from experience to being powerless and ignored, their stand in agrarian conflict is that of marginalised groups, reacting in different ways: (a) low expectations, e.g. struggling to survive through menial work, by offering the cheapest services to the better-off and by being submissive to them and to the system; (b) in rare and exceptional circumstances, revenge on the system through petty or bigger crime and indiscriminate violence; (c) offering strong-arm support to feuding families, repressive landlords, and local bosses; (d) with the benefit of good leadership, organisation for economic and social influence leading to political pressure directed at employers and political élites; and (e) migration. Their great numbers are a potential strength but have little chance of being put to effective use. Good leadership, class consciousness and effective class alliances can rescue the situation so that they become the vanguard for forceful challenge to the status quo. In Kenya they were the backbone and fighting force of the revolt in colonial days.

Sadly their marginality and deprivation, i.e. their precarious position, have often prevented them from achieving class cohesion and collective will and thus the capacity for organisation. Some have even allowed themselves to be used to frustrate other classes' efforts at agrarian reform.

The proletarianisation process combined with high rates of population increase have swollen this class to numbers which are causing concern to the élites, especially since they become visible by flocking into cities. They have not yet been paid attention by political élites, while theorists of revolution have possibly underestimated their potential.

Regularly Employed Agricultural Workers

This class is attached to a job and possibly to an employer, and thus has a regular income, however low. The employer may be a small-scale or a large commercial farmer, an agribusiness, a foreign plantation, or a state farm. Within this class are skilled and unskilled workers, often in practice with marked distinctions in pay and employment terms and preferment opportunities. Skilled specialists may have supervisory or even managerial responsibilities and may rise into that grade. Class homogeneity and cohesion are not, therefore, to be taken for granted. Where, however, large numbers work together, the potential for organisation exists. Class consciousness may develop among the workers especially if they have to negotiate wages and working conditions. They can thus become a key class in rural societies, ready to organise and with the capacity for action and sophisticated negotiation.

The very potential of this group may affect its class alliances. Organisation of better-paid, skilled workers or those favoured by their employers may go so far as to develop among them a narrow sectarian outlook and corporative pursuits, which tend to focus on benefits for themselves rather than the general interests of underprivileged groups. Some critics accuse them of lack of militancy, style them a "labour aristocracy", and even talk of the "embourgeoisement" of the working class. The record of this class, however, has been that it has often spearheaded and led working class action and militancy aimed at broad-based development and even radical transformation of the socio-economic system. Their weight in the economy, especially their strategic position in important lines such as valuable exports, makes them a powerful force which they can put to great effect through their capacity for strong organisation and sophisticated action.

Members of this class, especially if employed on large modern production units, are not so prone to clamour for land. As Martinez-Allier observes,[1] "That Andalusian and Cuban labourers demanded land is important, because this makes them in some way similar to 'peasants' . . . But, at the same time, there has been a 'proletarian' consciousness among Andalusian and Cuban workers shown in the demands for land *or work*, and in the demands for the socialisation or collectivisation of the large estates". He was, of course, referring to Cuba before the revolution. Mintz makes[2] fun of such distinguished socialist writers as Huberman, Sweezy and Sartre who, on visiting Cuba after the revolution, were surprised that Cuban workers did not want land, individually, i.e. a parcel of land each, and were content to work on state or co-operative farms.

The attitude of this class to land depends on the socio-economic context and political environment in which they work. Those wracked by uncertainty and inadequate employment may look upon land as a kind of social security, which gives them a chance to improve their employment (or that of the family) and the family income. Those organised and in conditions of reasonable employment may opt to demand no more than regular employment, fair remuneration, acceptable conditions of work and some dignity – demands which they may be in a position to negotiate fairly effectively. The few in privileged employment may wish no more than that their luck may hold. Those employed on large estates and plantations are often the main beneficiaries from the nationalisation of such units, as in the self-management sector in Algeria after the take-over of the *ex-colons* lands and in Peru with the expropriation of foreign enterprises.

Extra-economic issues also enter the equation. Some castes are condemned to being landless labourers and any efforts to enable them to get land are resisted as scandalous violations of caste rules.[3] More generally, "Even peasants whose holdings are so small that they need have no fears of expropriation from land redistribution join forces with those opposing reform proposals that would confer land on agricultural workers".[4]

Social status lends another twist to the situation. In West Bengal those

> strata in the rural hierarchy with a share, if only a modest one, in scarce land resources – that is to say the farm families – have been accustomed to leisurely working habits and to restricting their work participation. A considerable part of the work load has thus been shifted to landless people who have no means of livelihood other than wage labor . . . an extremely low level of wages . . . makes leisure very cheap.[5]

Racial and ethnic reasons condemn large numbers of workers to low status and acute poverty even on prosperous plantations, as with the Tamil tea estate workers in Sri Lanka whose conditions of work, pay and living have often scandalised world opinion.

Finally, organisation by agricultural workers is very difficult and in many cases most dangerous in the face of opposition by other, well-entrenched and powerful classes backed by the might of the state and, as already mentioned, at times helped by death squads.

Tied Agricultural Labour

Tied labour presents some variety; its common feature is that, for traditional institutional reasons, it is attached to a landowner or estate. The hacienda in Latin America is the leading example, with comparable conditions in countries of Asia. Even the tied cottage system in England resembles such an institution. Agricultural labour can also be tied by debt and other obligations.

The distinguishing characteristic of this category is that in return for their labour, the landowner allows workers to use land on his property.

A member of this class combines in himself the attributes of a cultivator and producer on his own account and of an agricultural labourer who is rarely paid any wages. Economic, commercial, political and juridical control is in the hands of the landowners concerned.

In practice permission is required to leave the estate. Because of indebtedness and the absence of alternative employment and income opportunities, when given their "freedom" they often cannot take it and leave. Loss of status may also be involved, especially in South Asia. "Some persons prefer semi-starvation on tiny plots of rented land to a higher real income obtainable from wage employment".[6]

In agrarian conflict this class tends in two main directions. As cultivators and producers they wish to obtain more land to improve their position and status. They also show interest in the prices of the produce and supplies. Those of free status or more secure position have challenged landowners and proved an important force for agrarian reform.

As tied labourers with inferior status, often servants and retainers, they face handicaps additional to those of other labourers. They are rarely able to use the potential strength of their large numbers unless they organise in clandestine groups. Aspiring to become cultivators also tends to attenuate their proletarian behaviour.

Legislation to protect this class and improve their position has had little effect. The potent "liberating" force has been the spread of capitalist production which impelled landowners to opt for "free" labour. Agrarian conflict itself, especially when combined with talk of agrarian reform, makes severance of traditional ties an urgent and prudent course of action for landowners to take.

Tenants and Sharecroppers
As already discussed this class presents a great variety within itself. Sharecropping tends to require closer contacts with and even supervision by the landlord. Fixed term tenancy is a looser relationship, more open to the capitalist approach to production. Capitalist tenants can, in fact, become a strong force and themselves dominate poor landlords.

What decides attitudes is the socio-economic position of the participants. As discussed earlier, in conditions of rural backwardness and population pressure, exploitation of tenants and sharecroppers can be very oppressive. Legislation has rarely been of any avail. The landlord class have a tremendous capacity to obstruct enactment of effective legislation and the enforcement of any law that has been passed; "soft" states have no power to enforce it and bureaucracies are unable, often unwilling, to cope.

As producers, sharecroppers and tenants tend to desire ownership of the land they cultivate; this desire often becomes a consuming dream, generating agitation for the distribution of large properties and for "Land to the Tiller". Forceful action, even revolutionary movements, have been bolstered up, if not actually started, by this class. The vast majority of agrarian reform measures have been in response to its pressure.

Ironically, the weaker the position of tenants and sharecroppers, i.e. the greater their need for agrarian reform, the lower their capacity to agitate.

Usually that section among them which is less insecure has been the spearhead and bulwark for stirring agrarian conflict and making reform possible.

Better-off tenants have supported agitation whenever they discerned an advantage and stood a chance of becoming the main beneficiaries of a likely reform or if they could get better terms in the resulting legislation.

Tenants of the state, especially in such colonial schemes as the Gezira in Sudan, can get well-organised and become a powerful political force.

Small-Scale Owner Cultivators

For present purposes this class comprises the mass of small-scale owner cultivators who do not stand out within their community or rural area by size of holding, volume of turnover, income, wealth or socio-political power. This makes it variable, especially for comparative purposes. Although the *actual* level of poverty is most important, *relative* poverty (and resulting powerlessness) can be equally important in less poor societies or in later stages of development of the same area.

Security of tenure and "being masters on their own land" are generally assumed for this class, but an indebted owner cultivator with mortgaged land is on the slippery road to insecurity and possible loss of land, while vertical integration of production with marketing or processing firms tends to diminish mastery of the land. Security of employment and income, albeit often at low levels, are also assumed, but the hazards of production and the market are a constant worry and source of insecurity and of fluctuating levels of living. Some owner cultivators are alternately overworked and unemployed in the course of the year, as are members of their household.

The main concerns of this class are land and credit. Infrastructure, production inputs and marketing at favourable terms are also essential and sought for. Passion for more land is paramount. Agrarian reform is an opportunity to obtain it and members of this class often benefit from reform measures. To them desirable measures tend to be ameliorating, rather than significantly structural, adding land to and/or consolidating holdings, thus raising the status and profitability of owner cultivators. Combined with other development measures, including improved technology, such public interventions have enabled many of those with land assets to advance strongly in the economic, social and political spheres. This, of course, applied largely to those landowners who stood out a little among the mass of owner cultivators. Owing to their position they were, or had become, important links with the public intervention authorities and policy makers.

Many critics of reform measures and of the style of development adopted have decried this "Kulakisation" process, which has fuelled the "Matthew effect" in many countries, from Poland to India and from Chile or Colombia to Kenya or Egypt. It has already been observed that small-scale owner cultivators object to land reforms that benefit agricultural workers. In fact they often take an ambivalent attitude to agrarian reform. They may be more lured by infrastructural and other development packages, cheap credit and subsidised prices for their produce rather than by structural measures.

Agrarian conflict for them may not go beyond agitation for handouts. Being numerous, often well organised and with secure assets, they can take such demonstrative measures as moving their tractors into the capital or their cows to a meeting of ministers. In India "The intermediate class of primarily family farmers is also a willing ally of rich farmers [mobilised and harnessed like the exploited poor peasants and agricultural wage labourers in large-scale rural movements]; it gains from lower irrigation and power rates, higher prices for farm products and subsidised credit and inputs, . . . even though the benefits go disproportionately to the rich farmers".[7]

The "Peasantry" and Agrarian Conflict

So far we have avoided use of the concept "peasantry", but since many studies and observations have been geared towards "peasants" (or *Campesinos*) as a class, a parenthesis may be of value. This class includes a variable ingredient. Some people exclude agricultural workers; others extend the class into the realm of rich peasants. In the present context it is best to concentrate on the lower strata of rural people connected with production from the land.

Progress towards a real grasp of the thought processes, conception of conditions, and aspirations for improved life chances on the part of the "peasantry" has been slow. Literature has also tended to stress that increased awareness of possibilities for change has come from contact with the urban world, which was often said to be the prerogative of the better-off. "The middle peasant . . . stays on the land and sends his children to work in town . This makes the middle peasant a transmitter also of urban unrest and political ideas."[8]

Empirical studies indicate that when malaise and even discontent is felt by those who believe themselves wronged, exploited and oppressed, these people react with force when they perceive a deteriorating situation, which further aggravates their conditions. A reaction to general malaise, servitude or usury suddenly erupts when an incident occurs; labour conditions have stirred forceful action when obduracy or bad faith was sensed among employers during contacts, if not in actual negotiations; the most violent outbreaks have occurred in land usurpation[9] or evictions of poor cultivators, or whole communities, from lands which they had been cultivating or to which they had traditional rights.

Much conceptual and theoretical discussion has centred on the capacity of the "peasantry" to act as a whole, and with the larger controversy of whether the "peasants" are a *class*. Discussion is often linked with the famous extract from Marx's *The Eighteenth Brumaire of Louis Bonaparte*, which strictly speaking referred to a particular category of a particular country in the 1850s.

Marx was describing[10] the category of small peasants (who, as he mentions in another work, "had been gratuitously freed from their feudal burdens by the revolution of 1789) which constituted well over half the French population of the time. The members of this mass lived in similar conditions but without entering into manifold relations with one another, their isolation being further enhanced by their own poverty and the bad means of communication. Each individual peasant family was almost self-sufficient and their scale of production admitted no division of labour. This pattern prevailed all over the French countryside, "an addition of homologous magnitudes". The question Marx raises is this:

> In so far as millions of families live under economic conditions of existence that divide their mode of life, their interests and their culture from those of the other classes, and put them in hostile contrast to the latter, they form a class. In so far as there is merely local interconnection among these small peasants, and the identity of their interests begets no unity, no national union and no political organisation, they do not form a class. They are consequently incapable of enforcing their class interest in their own name.

Marx traced[12] the deterioration of the position of the "free" peasants to urban usury, heavy mortgage indebtedness, and taxation. "The 'Napoleonic' form of property, which at the beginning of the nineteenth century was the condition for the liberation and enrichment of the French country folk, has developed in the course of this century as the law of their enslavement and pauperisation." He mentions risings in which a part of the French peasants protested, arms in hand. He observes further that peasants find their natural ally and leader in the *urban proletariat*, whose task is to overthrow the bourgeois order.

The "low classness" of the peasants has been hotly debated in recent years. Hobsbawm put[13] the debate in historical perspective and in a wider context (which will be discussed later). Dealing with peasant attributes, he distinguishes, as other writers following Marx have to a large extent done, between (a) their being a class "in itself", in the sense of a body of people who have the same kind of relation to the means of production as well as other common economic and social characteristics; as such this class is of "low classness" as compared, say, to the industrial working class; and (b) their being a "class for itself", a class conscious of itself.

Before the spread of capitalism peasants, even in today's industrial countries, formed the overwhelming majority of the population with the rest as untypical minorities. Peasants, however, were fully aware of their distinction from, inferiority in status to and oppression by, minorities of non-peasants, whom they did not like. This sense of a common separation from non-peasants in terms of inferior status, poverty, exploitation and oppression may have produced a vague "common consciousness". This peasant "class consciousness" is fully conceivable at the level of the community, the basic unit of traditional peasant life. Their unit of political action has in practice been the region. The greatest peasant movements all appear to be regional, or coalitions of regional movements.

The potential power of a traditional peasantry is enormous, but its actual power and influence much more limited. The normal strategy of the traditional peasantry is passivity, which utilises its major assets, namely, its numbers and the impossibility of making it do some things by force for any length of time. However, for them the problem is not whether to be normally passive or active, but when to pass from one state to the other. Broadly speaking, passivity is advisable when the structure of power, local or national, is firm, stable and "closed"; activity when it appears to be in some sense changing, shifting or "open".

This summary of the argument is intended to give what appears a valid picture applicable to a considerable extent to contemporary rural groups in a comparable position in developing countries. The spread of capitalism, and socialism for that matter, has changed the picture in much of the contemporary world and is fast changing it throughout. As Hobsbawm argues, at some point of economic differentiation "the peasantry" as a political concept disappears, because conflicts within the rural sector now outweigh what all peasants have in common against outsiders. The fundamental fact of peasant politics today is the decline of the traditional peasantry, and increasingly the relative numerical decline of any kind of peasantry.

Large-Scale Owner Cultivators
These economic peaks among the cultivators are (a) long-standing large landowning families with a tradition of dominance in the countryside; (b) large capitalist farming interests; and (c) foreign plantations and new agribusiness farm corporations.

Their stand on agrarian conflict reflects their interests and outlook. The old-style, traditional family systems leave little or no room for manoeuvre in relation to their dependent servants, tenants, sharecroppers, and semi-autonomous cultivators by institutional and other means (which have not excluded repression); through the manipulation of state power they resist any ideas or action to change agrarian relations. They may try tactical moves like settlement on public land to emasculate agitation. Only when agitation and action for change get beyond their control do they reluctantly opt for their own "expropriation" with secure and high compensation, promptly paid.

Modern capitalist cultivators tend to be on the scene in some force when differentiation within the lower rural strata is fairly well advanced and are important agents of this differentiation. As expansionist landowners, they act as cuckoos in the small landowners' nest, displacing the weak, unfortunate and indebted; as such they manage to obtain public land on sale, even in reform projects. As large purchasers and surplus producers, they influence and obtain terms from suppliers and from marketing; as enterprising and educated people they build links with public development authorities and technocrats, and reap benefits coming from that direction; as political operators, they associate with dominant political forces and institutions to influence decisions and action in their favour.

In agrarian conflict they will adopt an equally "pragmatic" but enterprising approach: they will judge where their interests lie. Their strong preference is for technical development, modernisation, infrastructure, services "for all". Any signs that the agitation is in favour of raising wages, lowering prices and especially in favour of redistribution of large properties will meet with their resistance. However, if agitation proves irrepressible, they will display "understanding" for a campaign provided it aims at redistributing underutilised, underdeveloped estates (not their own) as the "national interest" demands.

Many capitalist cultivators are in close touch, or integrated, with activities of foreign interests and concerns. This puts them in a position to mobilise support from abroad for their stand in the agrarian conflict. Plantations and agribusiness have had to face conflict for years. Because of their size and dominance in the economy of some developing countries and of their links with their home countries relations with these firms involve, directly, or indirectly, the leadership and its orientation at the highest political level in the developing world.[14]

Non-agricultural Classes in Rural Societies
In dealing with agrarian conflict it is worth looking at these in more detail.

Artisans and Technicians: Even the simplest rural economies develop the need for some special services which are the function of artisans and technicians: making and repairing agricultural implements and tools, digging wells and fitting them with draught mechanisms, building vehicles, and constructing and equipping storage and other facilities. As technology advances and agriculture develops, the activities of artisans and technicians become more complex and sophisticated and the services required by agriculture more varied and complex. The role of these specialists also becomes more important with the increasing dependence of farm work on equipment and machinery.

The composition of this class varies: originally they may be self-employed, with or without a workshop, with or without apprentices; in more advanced economies they become major maintenance and repair services and minor industries, i.e. capitalist enterprises with employed workers. Almost invariably in simple societies artisans and technicians are also cultivators or part of the farm population; in more advanced economies they may combine farming with their other activities; for instance, besides repair and maintenance, they may use their own machinery and equipment for customary work in agriculture.

Their outlook and stand in an agrarian conflict depends on their precise socio-economic position. If they are condemned to artisan jobs because of caste rules and practices, they can only stay aloof; if they are tenants or sharecroppers, they will be interested in the same way as their fellow tenants or sharecroppers; they may even be able to place themselves in the vanguard of pressure for change if they feel free and more aware of possibilities from additional contacts within their own community and beyond; if they are medium or large landowners they will join, and even be able to lead, those classes. On the other hand, if they have no direct links with agriculture, they will as a rule conservatively cultivate their main customers, the medium and large operators, who are also the power holders; in exceptional cases, if they are poor artisans, they find common ground with other workers, whom they join in their broad unions. The writer found artisans prominent in village unions and in workers' party branches.

Credit Providers: The small producers and those without land or other resources fall easy prey to extortion because of their precarious position and the hazards of agricultural life. While the picture of official or institutional credit as a saviour is true to some extent, in practice institutional, i.e. relatively cheap, credit is cornered by the better-off producers, in theory because they are credit-worthy, but mainly because they take over the institutions handling such credit. Furthermore, the vulnerable strata often need "non-productive" loans, for which they have to resort to the private lender, often a usurer. In backward agrarian conditions usurers tend to be the prosperous landowners; with the growth of towns and communications, they tend to be traders, professional classes, suppliers, and marketing middlemen. Through mortgages and the inevitable default of the small landowners these urban interests become landowners.

Thus their position in agrarian conflict is closely bound up with their main interests and situation and follows lines already discussed. One ultimate deterrent is beyond the individual credit provider – wholesale bankruptcy of the lower rural strata. Acute malaise and an open bankruptcy may make urban ruling élites panic at the potential for social unrest on a mass scale. Furthermore, political élites courting easy popularity have often found remission or reduction of debt an effective way to win votes or otherwise ensure legitimacy.

Rural Traders: Middlemen for agricultural produce, suppliers of elementary production inputs, traders in consumption goods, credit providers for family needs – these roles have been played in rural societies by the same persons, families, or ethnic groups, singly or in combination. Landlords on haciendas and other estates have usually performed or at least controlled these functions. In this way many a small producer has been "mortaged" to such traders.

As the economy advances, and production expands and is diversified, more sophisticated methods and organisation are needed to handle produce for sale, especially if processing or packaging are required; provision of supplies becomes a complex and diversified operation; consumption needs and services become greater and more diversified. The small trader is replaced by (or graduates into) a trading firm and may become a branch of, or even a full, urban enterprise. Rich rural interests join in or pioneer this development.

Small traders are also often small farmers or closely related to them.

Because of their economic position they often become influential in rural societies and in agrarian conflict tend to be defenders of the status quo. They have "middle class" preferences and capitalist inclinations, opting for technical developments and opportunities for enterprise.

Large traders are already "urbanised" and their outlook is that of urban élites, to whom they are subordinate and for whom they are sometimes literally the agents.

Rural Bureaucracy: This is a broad class of people employed by state, para-statal and other public institutions. It tends to be highly hierarchical and normally only the lower echelons live and work in rural areas. They man the public services of importance to rural people (agricultural administration, technical support and advisory units, tax and other financial situations), public corporations and other para-statal services (marketing, agricultural banks, co-operative activities) and carry out general administrative functions. They are not as close to the rural population as the people's needs require because they are stationed in centres (large villages or small towns) or in experimental farms.

Their education and selection ensure that they come from better-off farming or middle class urban backgrounds; they also tend to marry into such classes, are prone to associate with the landed interests which dominate their "parish", and are befriended by capitalist farming interests who wish to make use of technology and inputs available from public services.

By class origin, associations, and mentality the rural bureaucracy has proved to be at best ambivalent, and normally unsympathetic towards the aspirations of the lower rural strata for improvement of their position through complaints or organised pressure.

Perception and Articulation of Agrarian Conflict

The roots and causes of agrarian conflict and the potential role of primary actors, already examined, provide a range of possible scenarios. Socio-economic conditions do not, however, automatically imply class consciousness on the part of those involved and there is an important difference between feeling the consequences of a situation and perceiving its true nature.

Rural people with few or no assets are usually deprived of education and experience of the world outside their community. Their perception of the problems that afflict them is based on the symptoms and visible signs, as they view their poverty and deprivation from their lowly place in the rural social pyramid. They cannot escape perceiving its main cause, their absolute or relatively assetless position, and that production relations are key factors since they affect people so strikingly. In the circumstances the surface appears passive or quiescent; often it takes only an incident or special event to release pent-up resentment and the sense of injustice. The annals of agrarian history contain many outbursts of insubordination and even violence (styled "Jacqueries" in some literature) which the socio-political system can usually easily contain.

Co-ordinated and systematic action requires articulation, i.e. the translation of feelings of injustice, of vague longings and of resentful thought into an intelligible diagnosis of ills and prescription for remedies. Articulation helps enhance, deepen and spread awareness, and serves especially as a focus for orientation of thought and as a rallying ground for recruitment and mobilisation.

Sound diagnosis and viable prescription are invaluable tools for achieving progress by converting dormant resentment into purposeful energy. Mistaken diagnosis and faulty prescription are recipes for disaster, squandering energy or causing serious setbacks. Articulation is the gift of the few; it is a leadership quality. It can, however, be practised as a kind of midwifery, carried out by informal leaders or allies from the sidelines with action in the hands of active leaders.

The impulses generated by agrarian conflict have been articulated by a disparate range of people in a variety of conditions and circumstances and in several historical contexts. Successful articulators have been people with powers of observation and expression, of perception of solutions and of advocacy of their case. Sometimes these functions are divided: observation and diagnosis are carried out by one set, prescription and advocacy by another.

Articulation may take a long time to yield results, but its potential is undeniable. It can convert a large number of people into a mode of viewing their own conditions; this in turn opens possible avenues for action that will lead them out of their plight. It is an instrument of mobilisation. Articulation can also serve the opposite purpose. Comforting interpretations of conditions, a different gloss on causes, a pessimistic assessment of beguiling solutions, and a diversion into other (say non-materialistic) aspirations can serve to lull people's discontent and to demobilise them.

Poverty, deprivation and isolation are not conducive to endowing the mass of rural people with powers of articulation of their own condition and its causes. Among those who have figured prominently as articulators of agrarian conflict are returned emigrants, commuters or educated sons of rural people, i.e. persons or classes who have acquired experience and even additional assets by leaving the rural areas. The bulk, of course, of analysts and propagators of ideas concerning agrarian conditions and conflict have been intellectuals and educated élites.

The privileged strata, especially the landed interests, have always instinctively felt the risk to an established order or status quo posed by such subversive ideas. They have rarely been slow to mobilise cultural, social and political action to discredit, ban and punish such ideas and those who propagate them. Cultural institutions mobilise established bodies of beliefs and opinions to discourage people from lending an ear; social influence is used to isolate and pour scorn on these ideas and their propagators; political institutions are mobilised to ban, repress and punish such trespasses. Ideas are often suppressed, sometimes for a long time; they are rarely killed by such methods.

Translation of Articulation into Action

The rousing, orientation and mobilising functions of articulation create pools of usable energy that can set in motion vehicles for action, such as organisations and institutions. If ideas are resented, organisations promoting agrarian conflict are even more objected to and easier to eradicate. There is a long and depressing record of persecution, repression and even assassination of peasant organisation and workers' union leaders and presumed promoters. Many begin a clandestine life or have two lives, one clandestine and one public. Repression is common in all landlord-dominated societies, especially where landed interests feel their position seriously threatened.

Organisations are not only important instruments for self-defence by people with numerical strength on their side, albeit socially and politically powerless, but also media by which ideas can spread, orientation become purposeful, and common action be prepared even as a long-term goal. In short, they are proselytising media and mechanisms for translating awareness into action.

Like articulation, organisation is often pioneered by rural people who have had experience outside the narrow rural community – returned emigrants and educated sons.[15] Outsiders also take an active part and become an easily identifiable target for the opposing forces. In many cases persons who break ranks with their own class lend support to and even lead the formation of such organisations.

This discussion has been confined to the impulses generated by rural classes in pursuit of a change in their position. It concerns upwellings likely to occur or are suspected and feared by their opponents. The future of such upwellings, if they develop real momentum, depends on their not remaining local, obscure affairs. This in turn depends on circumstances and a wide range of variables. As Alavi puts it,[16] "Militancy or non-militancy are not absolute conditions, but, rather, they are contingent on changing conjunctures of social circumstances and movements."

Even if local action succeeds in solving a local problem, it is rarely a self-contained problem or isolated situation. Local action by discontented rural groups is viewed by its opponents as a symptom of a wider tendency to "destabilisation"; they therefore, take action to discourage similar happenings elsewhere. In an absolute sense localised agrarian problems do not normally exist. By the very nature of the problem, action and reaction become generalised. For this some rural forces at least are not completely unprepared.[17] The wider social forces and institutions which are relevant and essential must now be identified and their relations to agrarian conflict carefully investigated.

Notes

1. Martinez-Allier 1977 p. 52.
2. Mintz 1974 pp. 293–294.
3. Myrdal 1968 p. 1063.
4. Ibid.
5. Ibid. p. 1089. In Sri Lanka in the 1970s the standard joke was that nobody was too poor to have servants; even the servants were said to have servants who were poorer than themselves!
6. Ibid. p. 1067.
7. Bardhan 1984 pp. 47–48.
8. Wolf 1969 p. 292.
9. For Ethiopia see Bezzabeh 1980. One of the outstanding merits of this study is that it documents statements by many of the participants.
10. Marx 1945 Vol.II pp. 414–415.
11. Ibid. p. 280.
12. Ibid. pp. 417–419.
13. Hobsbawm 1973 pp. 3–22.
14. Vaitsos 1976 p. 119.
15. I was struck by the seemingly large proportion of returned emigrants (usually from France) among the leadership of various co-operative production units when I visited them in 1976 in the Alentejo of Portugal.
16. Alavi 1973 p. 28.
17. Gibbons, de Konnick and Ibrahim 1980 pp. 195–198, observe that the great majority of farmers in the two regions which they studied in Sumatra and Malaya, could not be said to be "parochial as far as the cognitive dimension of political culture is concerned". In general large farmers are better informed and feel more influential than do medium farmers; medium farmers in their turn score better than small.

8. Non-agrarian Forces and the Wider Context of Agrarian Conflict

Economic and Socio-political Forces in a Wider Context and their Role in Agrarian Conflict

The gap between rural and urban forces can be exaggerated. Many rural élites are urban residents, and many urban élites rural dwellers. The rural poor flock into urban areas in increasing numbers so that the shanty towns in which they live become extensions of the rural population. Thus urban and rural areas form one communicating system. At a further remove, the national system itself is not closed but communicates to varying degrees with the international system.

An analysis of classes and social groupings in a national socio-economy is often a snapshot of a particular "moment" in its evolution; each national socio-economic system has its own composition of social forces that reflects its economic and social endowment, historical evolution and the dynamic of its development. As a socio-economic system advances it becomes less agrarian as the structure of social and economic forces shifts away from agriculture and rural activities. The position of the various classes in the system and their role in its processes, more pertinently their relation to land and its future, are key elements in this present analysis.

The Commercial Class

Historically the commercial class is the first non-agrarian class to emerge and is always present. It has often provided capital for primary accumulation from which modern capitalism has developed. In its historical role it affected the whole world as the main force behind slavery, the colonisation of the New World, plantation agriculture, indentured labour and settler farming.

Resident in rural areas, often combining trade with agriculture, usury and services, are the lower echelons of this class, who may evolve into higher echelons. Sooner or later the area is penetrated by urban commercial interests who become dominant in rural towns and rural trade as well as in national commerce. Major fortunes have been made from serving as agents for foreign concerns and now especially for multinational companies.

Leading members of the commercial class go into banking or industrial production, a few beginning with processing agricultural produce. The latest developments, encouraged by policies of import-substitution, include the manufacture or assembly of industrial products under licence from foreign companies, increasingly multinational firms. The monopoly of economic life in many countries by a few families is based on this combination of land-owning, capitalist agriculture, commercial, banking, industrial, transport, and foreign agency activities. The Somoza family in Nicaragua was notorious. Similar conditions prevailed until recently in El Salvador. "For over a century, the social and economic life of the nation has been dominated by a small landed élite known popularly as 'the 14 families' (Los Catorce) . . . until recently they owned 60 per cent of the farmland, the entire banking system, and most of the nation's industry. Among them they received 50 per cent of the national income."[1] In Peru within the sugar sector the major 44 families controlled 23% of the cultivated land and in the 1960s 26 of these had interests in real estate, manufacturing and banking.[2]

In Pakistan the modernisation process provided many opportunities for large profits by relatively few families from business and industry.[3] These "fabled twenty-two families" of West Pakistan came from the rich landlord class.[4] Some members of the Nepalese hereditary aristocracy, a substantial landowning group, are heavily involved in important businesses, tourist agencies and other lucrative enterprises.[5] In Salazar's Portugal the famous "100 families" were landowners and forest owners who also controlled the country's main transport, shipping, international trade and industrial acti-vities.[6] As already observed, this concentration of economic activities into a few hands tends to take place under capitalism and is characteristic of its early stages. It finds a favourable environment in conservative absolutist regimes, or those under strong personalities, such as the Ivory Coast, Kenya (under Kenyatta) and Zaire.

These inter-connections influence the attitudes of commercial classes towards agrarian conflict. In general in a major conflict they will side with other privileged classes, especially the upper strata, who are also land-owners or have strong links with the landowning classes. In lesser conflicts the better-off, especially the enterprising sections of the commercial class, may *not* be averse to change, preferring capitalist agriculture with higher production and increased trade to unproductive latifundia.

The lower strata of this commercial class are in general averse to conflict and destabilisation, but sections of it may lead an agrarian conflict in expectation that they will pilot it in the direction of their own interests. This happened in Kenya where the Mau Mau movement found allies among the Kikuyu living in Nairobi; these petty-traders, together with other "marginal" groups, provided militant and sophisticated leaders.[7]

Financial Interests
These interests are rarely found as a "pure" class except in advanced countries with sophisticated banking and financial institutions. As already

seen, they often combine farming with landowning, commercial and business activities. This group is always influential, although rarely liked, as much of the literary tradition of many countries testifies, especially if financing is in the hands of an "alien" minority. The advance of capitalist agriculture has made financing an even more important element in agricultural production, together with processing and marketing. This has further strengthened the position of large producers, whose ability to pre-empt financial facilities from every source has taken much of the euphoria out of the "green revolution" which was at first thought of as "scale free", i.e. that both large and small farmers would benefit more or less without distinction.

The "green revolution" has accelerated a trend already well advanced, i.e. the incursion of foreign finance into the broad area of agricultural production, supply, and distribution. This includes financing by private and public international institutions (e.g. the World Bank and Funds set up by petroleum producing countries). The transnational banks are "the single most important global mobilizers of savings and allocators of finance" and the one motive common to all for their phenomenal expansion in the last two decades has been to service the internationalisation of production carried out by transnational corporations.[8]

The vast gradation and the gamut of interests involved naturally produce a varied stand on the issue of agrarian conflict. Those close to the land take advantage of their position to manipulate the issue and its handling, to improve their landowning or their connection with farming, or at least to contain and put down any threat to their interests. They tend to be conservative and suspicious of "subversive" ideas and tendencies. The "fabled families" even use their control over the state to repress any manifestation of "undermining the established order".[9]

The larger interests, especially those from urban areas, favour any safe change that promises increased demand for and profitability of investment (more technology in agriculture and other modernisation efforts, including land consolidation and opening up new land) but use their considerable influence to crush any "destabilisation", i.e. anything that will upset a favourable climate for investment and "development".

Industrial and Mining Interests

Industrial and mining activities are in some cases linked and may be carried out by the same interests. As an extractive activity mining may not benefit the area where it occurs because the raw material is transported elsewhere without generating additional local effects and beneficial activity. Mining can even be an enclave of alien techniques and managerial staff living in luxurious but artificial conditions,[10] and, as the result of mechanisation, employing fewer and fewer native workers, many of whom are migrants living in very poor conditions and receiving low wages. Such enterprises are owned by foreign companies.

Low paid workers flock to these areas out of necessity: in the past they were compelled to earn cash to pay poll tax; now they are driven by poverty and the hope of earning enough to return home and live better. In Lesotho, a large section of the labour force goes to South Africa leaving farming to the women in the family. This additional source of family income enables mining companies to pay lower wages than they would do otherwise.

Industrialisation is regarded as the longstanding recipe for economic development. This transformation, historically based on economic surpluses from agriculture, has never lost its appeal in the eyes of development policy makers and political leaders, especially since "economic miracles" have occurred in some countries. Developing countries have embarked on industrialisation with varied success, latecomers finding it difficult to make real headway.

The most advanced and rapid industrialisation has taken place with the support and even dominance of foreign concerns, e.g. in Brazil. Some large countries, like India, have industrialised with a fair degree of independence; some are even engaged in dominating others, e.g. India in Nepal where Indian capital and management are active in industrialising the Terai.[11] Many countries have used state control and initiative to advance industrialisation, for in a world of multinational company penetration and domination, the state is the only economic force strong enough to foster and sustain it.

Thus major industrial interests in developing countries, tend to be either agents of, or closely linked, with foreign interests, or a technocratic élitist state (or parastatal) techno-bureaucracy. In countries where economic power is concentrated in a few hands, such interests have, as seen earlier, landowning connections. Some may combine landowning and processing in a vertical integration of economic activities.

In general, industrialisation changes the structure of the economy, the hierarchy of interests and the outlook of social forces. Capitalist industrial development fosters, and even requires, capitalist development of agriculture to ensure provision of food for the industrial population and raw materials for industrial plants; labour transferred from agriculture provides manpower for this development. Where they do not pose a serious threat to the socio-economic system, technical agricultural reforms, including the reorganisation of production units,[12] may be favoured by industrial interests, unless their landowning is adversely affected. Middle level industrial interests may even manage to benefit directly from land tenure reforms, as in Kenya with the resettlement of the White Highlands. Infrastructural development is preferred to agrarian reform because it uses industrial products and helps industrial activity through better communications, hydro-electric and similar developments; these also help farming activities and raise land values, thus benefiting landowning and farming interests with industrial pursuits.

The Non-agricultural Working Class

The non-agricultural working class shows an even greater range of variation than that of workers in agriculture. The proportion of non-agricultural workers in the labour force reflects fairly faithfully a country's economic structure and social development. Figures given by Naiken[13] based on the 1950, 1960 and 1970 population censuses for 30 countries list the non-agricultural labour force as a percentage of the total labour force. Though not fully comparable, the data are of interest. At the lowest end is Mali with a percentage of 11.5 in 1960–61, at the upper the United States with 96.3 in 1970. The other low percentage, 15 in 1961, is that for Bangladesh. Turkey (1960) with 25.1 and India (1971) with 27.5 had at the time less than one-third of their labour force outside agriculture. Percentages ranging from 36.8 (Indonesia, 1971) to 50.2 (Peru, 1961) cover African, Asian and Latin American countries as well as some from Southern Europe. Thus Ghana has 38.4% (in 1960), Algeria 48.2 (1966), Pakistan 41 (1961), the Philippines 45.3 (1970), Sri Lanka 47.1 (1953), the Republic of Korea 49.1 (1970), Nicaragua 40.4 (1963), El Salvador 42.3 (1971), Romania 42.9 (1966) and Greece 46.1 (1961). Present day oil producing countries referred to include only Iran with 43.7 (1956), and Algeria and Indonesia already given.

Percentages between 52.9 (Poland, 1960) and the maximum of the United States include only one Latin American country (Chile, 72.3 in 1960), one African country (South Africa, 67.7 in 1960) and one Asian country (Japan, 80.7 in 1970); the remainder are European countries with the highest percentages those of the Federal Republic of Germany (90 in 1961) and Sweden (91.9 in 1970). The highest percentage for a socialist European country is that of Hungary with 75.5 in 1970.

Many non-agricultural workers are found in the informal sector, are casually employed with low wages and lack social security benefits. Most developing countries are undergoing a rapid rural/urban migration as the result of rural underdevelopment and high population growth and are thus fast building up a sizeable urban proletariat living in unhealthy housing conditions, often in shanty towns.

These mass concentrations of the urban proletariat, an extension and outflow of the rural proletariat, have attracted attention mainly by their potential for political and social "destabilisation", which is feared by authoritarian regimes. The floating population on city outskirts, in the north-east of Brazil, living in conditions where a wide social gap exists, was seen as a strong electoral base for the opposition and "local army authorities are less tolerant than they are elsewhere of political meetings and radical churchmen".[14] Generally speaking, however, because of their conditions of existence, this marginal mass of people has not shown a great propensity to organise. Their importance here lies in their origins, their links with rural areas and in the flow between the urban and rural areas.

Workers in steady employment have certain advantages, including the capacity for organisation, which they can use to improve their remuneration, conditions of work and general share of the product. Those working in large numbers, e.g. industrial workers in the same enterprise, have high class-ness, i.e. a concentrated, self-conscious force of the same class. As already mentioned, they are a heterogeneous category and growing stratification within the working class militates against its unity and effectiveness as an organised force. Intraclass and interindustry differences have been exploited more and more effectively by employers and other privileged classes, and by political élites. Such divisions are often reflected in the affiliations of workers' organisations and their loyalty to different parties.

This high classness has often been effective. Powerful workers' unions have not only managed to improve their bargaining position and conditions of work and employment but also to pioneer social change. Sponsorship by the organised non-agricultural working class of the agricultural workers' cause and the struggles of small cultivators in agrarian conflicts has often proved decisive in such conflict.

The power of organised labour is the only effective countervailing force in situations where economic, social and political power is concentrated in the hands of a minority who own the means of production, including land. Unity between workers and peasants has been the object of revolutionary strategists and the solid basis of many rural movements and revolutionary struggles.

The Professional Class
This includes people with a higher education who pursue a liberal trade based on special qualifications: doctors, lawyers, surveyors, architects, engineers, accountants, etc. They form a distinctly privileged class who, often enjoying a monopolistic position in their countries, achieve high earnings, status and prestige. If they do not come from landowning and other wealthy families, they can find their way into the upper classes through marriage and wealth. Many political élites come from this class, which plays an influential, even a key, role in the management of the political system.

Their attitude to the social and economic system is closely linked with their class origins, achievements and prospects. They are, or aspire to be, within the dominant élites. In special circumstances, or for tactical reasons, some professionals break ranks and join political forces opposed to the regime (and even to the status quo) and achieve leadership of opposition movements and parties. In agrarian conflict their attitudes are decided by their class connections, especially their landowning interests, so that they normally take the side of the landed interests; for political tactical considerations, however, some may decide to back demands by the underprivileged. Commentators on the historical experience of agrarian conflicts have often remarked how opportunistic is this backing, even if some famous leaders have come from this class.

The Bureaucracy: Administrative and Technical
As already noted, this class is of special importance and requires particular emphasis. Our concern here is with state and parastatal bureaucracy, though bureaucracies exist in large enterprises and in the service and financial

sectors, "the organisation men".[15] In developing countries state and parastatal bureaucracies tend to be the largest single occupational category outside agriculture. The following data give an idea of their numerical strength and economic power.

In Tanzania in 1970, parastatals (i.e. government-controlled corporations) accounted for 24% of total employment. In 1971 they accumulated 43% of gross domestic capital formation. In Zambia they accounted for an even larger share of each. In both countries, the parastatal sector employed far more people than did the Civil Service. In 1973 Nigeria had upwards of 250 parastatals; the Ministry of Agriculture in Kenya also controlled 100; Uganda had 14 major corporations and one Development Corporation with 53 subsidiaries; Tanzania by 1975 had over 200. Most were productive enterprises.[16]

Steadiness of employment, conditions of work, high salaries[17] and pensions (usually a colonial heritage), the prestige and power associated with the job, and its susceptibility to political patronage, explain why a post in the bureaucracy is so much pursued and why this class gets so swollen.[18]

The highest echelons in the Civil Service and the parastatals are not only well paid and prestigious, but also very powerful; their role has been enhanced and expanded in recent years so that many are more powerful and even better paid than ministers. Both directly and indirectly, they make most political decisions, originating or influencing all important matters of policy, while continuing to pay verbal homage to their "political masters" to whom they formally attribute their own decisions. In reality at best civil servants "advise ministers on the orders they should be given".[19]

The growth of power and influence of the upper echelons of the bureaucracy (or "technobureaucracy" as it is increasingly becoming) is linked with the nature of the state and the growth of its role: political patronage and the "soft" state provide opportunities for favours; unemployment of the educated and the semi-educated increases pressure for patronage; the state has assumed ownership of some of the means of production and developed new economic activities; considerable social security and other welfare services have been introduced.

The state's direct entry into production and distribution, or its indirect influence through parastatal corporations and institutions, has also changed the functions, composition and outlook of the bureaucracy. There has, for instance, always been high praise for the public administration inherited by ex-British colonial territories on independence. In India it helped the effective establishment of government authority in the first difficult years of independence and has exerted political influence as part of the governing élite. "But for the most part this has been a regulating and stabilising influence that has worked against radical departures from the *status quo* – in other words, a conservative force. . . . Indeed, one of the striking features of the administrative structure the British erected and the Indians inherited is its compatibility with the caste system."[20]

In an atmosphere of modernisation and development, the bureaucracy assumes new functions and receives an influx of technical and professional staff with scientific training and, in some cases, business experience. Dealings with international development agencies, negotiations with foreign investors, contractors and consulting firms, purchases and the assumption of responsibility for contracts involving many hundreds of millions of dollars, decisions concerning, and supervision of, major works, etc. bring the bureaucracy into direct contact with local and foreign interests, many of them multinational firms. In many situations there is a marked interpenetration of interests. "The state itself through the techno-bureaucracy increasingly assumes responsibilities for the continuation of the political, economic and social conditions undergirding the web of external-internal relationships."[21]

The responsibilities involved are illustrated in an article by Mark Webster[22] concerning the Ivory Coast State Sugar Company, Sodesucre, created in 1971 to build 12 sugar complexes for producing 500,000 tonnes a year, 75% for export. Six had been built for some US $1,300 million and produced a little over 100,000 tonnes. They were built by British, German, Belgian, Austrian, French and Dutch firms at a cost of US $1,000 million and financed by international banks from those countries and the USA and by the Ivory Coast Government. The project ran into many difficulties and was crippled by a huge debt servicing burden. According to the President of the Republic some managers have acted in a "scandalous fashion". The crop will be from plantations, two of them 6,200 ha each. It is not stated how Sodesucre acquired the land. Another State institution, however, the Rice Development Agency, Soderiz, "nationalised" the developed valley bottoms which belonged to village groups and allotted their use to volunteers chosen and directed by itself.[23] As Fieldhouse observed, "these agro-business parastatals became private fiefs of the managing élites comprised essentially of bureaucrats and party officials".[24]

This power derived from their exalted position involves many perquisites for the techno-bureaucracy, some of them not very legitimate.

> The temptation is considerable to use their positions in control of State machinery to advance their own status at the expense of efforts to restructure the economy . . . Foreign firms and domestic entrepreneurs have tried to influence critical decisions by government officials to win favour for their projects, regardless of the impact on national economic developments. The evidence indicates that not a few office-holders have succumbed to these temptations.[25]

Although this refers to Africa, such behaviour is found in all regions and is also noticeable in many developed countries.

The developed world has influenced the techno-bureaucracy in other ways. Nigerian élites are reported[26] to "have developed an imitation western-style enclave" and their "attitude to those outside the enclave [referred to by the élites as 'the natives'] is too often one of disdain". It is mentioned incidentally that money from rake-offs for contracts amounting to millions of pounds sterling is invested in property overseas. The second kind of influence is through the training of developing country personnel by international assistance agency experts. A trainee "picks up all of the negative behavioral, institutional, and professional norms and development strategies of the outside expert. He becomes, in short, co-opted in that international professional orbit. [He] is not likely to increase his identification with the poor and powerless people of his country".[27] The outcome is a readiness to seek identification with the foreign agency expert class. In Sri Lanka,

> many members of the Central Bank and the Planning Ministry privately express aspirations to join well paying agencies such as the World Bank, and in fact many have done so. . . . Invitations to foreign missions often stem from these foreign circuit local economists. It is in their interests to keep the system of intellectual dependence going, as they themselves benefit from it.[28]

Internally also the bureaucracy takes advantage of its position. There is evidence from many countries that one of their strong preferences is acquisition of land and entry into capitalist farming. We have seen already how Liberian politicians and government officials (and their relatives) are independent rubber farmers, how they depress wages on the plantations, including those of multinational companies, and how they practise involuntary labour recruitment under government auspices. In Malawi, all politicians, top civil servants and military officials are urged or even compelled to become large landowners.[29] Many cases of graft officially recognised in Zambia were connected with the Land Act[30] and I have given other examples from Africa elsewhere.[31]

As already seen, some top echelons of the bureaucracy come from the hereditary aristocracy and are already substantial landowners, e.g. in Nepal where, in addition, they belong to higher castes.[32] Land reforms do not always diminish the powers of the bureaucracy but may even enhance them. In Iran the reforms and post-reform modernisation efforts under the Shah, with emphasis on agribusiness, farm corporations and even co-operative development, increased and broadened the powers of the bureaucracy.[33] Monarchies and other personalised administrations tend to give exceptional powers to court or palace officials.

In agrarian conflict the conservative nature of the bureaucracy, their vested interests, especially their landowning, and their class affiliations make them very unsympathetic towards the weaker classes. This universally observed phenomenon is important because, as has been extensively discussed, of the bureaucracy's influence in the making of policy and above all in its execution. Many land reform measures have been obstructed at the policy-making stage and sentenced to a slow death in execution by an unsympathetic bureaucracy. It has thus become conventional wisdom that to put through a substantial reform programme requires an entirely new administration and government structure. One of the main reasons for the rapid execution of the first agrarian reform in Egypt in the 1950s was the creation of an entirely new authority, eventually a ministry, for handling it in a coherent and "sympathetic" fashion. In West Bengal the Government brought together 30 or 40 landless farm labourers and sharecroppers and 10–20 government officers in each of the reorientation camps set up; the former explained their plight and attitudes for the latter to gain an insight into, and develop empathy for, the need and justice of the reform.[34]

Another important aspect is class differentiation within the bureaucracy itself. As a member of the administration, the village worker is often overpowered and dominated by the local power structure. Faced with entrenched and aggressive local interests, a minor official is unable to offer resistance. If he gets into trouble, his superiors will not back him but dismiss him for incompetence. All too frequently he is treated by the higher grades of the Civil Service as a low grade peon. Thus the weaker rural strata can be freed from local oppression only by the upper levels of the administration, who have their own interests to protect.[35]

Against an unassailable local power structure and an unhelpful bureaucracy, as activities on the part of the state and parastatal authorities increase, the lower strata of the rural population survive by resorting to clientelistic practices and patronage.

State Security Forces

The power of the techno-bureaucracy is subtle and pervasive, that of the state security forces obvious and overpowering, if often kept in the background. The armed forces and the police represent the capacity of the state to enforce its authority. "The military organization is a fraternity and a community as well as an instrument of power and a bureaucracy."[36] The state security forces constitute a rigid hierarchical force geared towards executing orders of their superiors and are thus an instrument for ensuring conformity. Where the political system is liberal and open, relying on the citizens' willing acceptance of the laws and mores of society, the role of the police is one of regulation, that of the armed forces national security.

Rigidly stratified societies, widespread poverty and misery, deteriorating living conditions among large sections of society, a sense of extensive social injustice, the malfunctioning of public institutions, restlessness among organised underprivileged strata, government instability and social fragmentation create strains and stresses in society and a sense of insecurity among ruling élites. The latter often panic and call in the state security forces to restore order and stability. In the modern praetorian state these forces come uninvited to "save" the country. They find it easy to take over, but not to hand back power later.

The upper echelons of the security forces, especially the armed forces, are a privileged group, recruited normally from the upper classes or with affiliations to such classes. They have a caste mentality and a simplified view of socio-political issues, rate discipline very highly, and are imbued with a conservatism that combines a sense of mission with the defence of established order and the fatherland.[37]

The armed forces have been in power in some countries, especially in Latin America, for a long time. The "Salvadorean oligarchy has exercised political hegemony indirectly. The military has ruled El Salvador since 1931."[38] Other regimes last for a shorter time, but in some countries, e.g. Pakistan, Ghana or Nigeria they do not stay away from power for long. Some national liberation wars bring to power military men, who enjoy high prestige; elsewhere the armed forces may not wield power directly, but have enormous powers under martial law.

It has been observed that absolute rulers with martial law regimes have had to be careful with land reform measures in order not to alienate the officer class which has landowning interests or family connections with landowning classes. This applied to the Ayub Khan administration in Pakistan and the Marcos rule in the Philippines.

Although in general the armed forces tend to take over power to thwart reforms and social revolutions, even mild ones, as in Chile, Brazil, South Korea, Thailand and Ghana (in 1966), there have been military takeovers which instituted reforms, including agrarian reforms. Such reform-oriented military groups usually come from younger, less senior officers of middle-class origin, who rebel in protest against a serious national humiliation or social stagnation, government corruption and incompetence. Agrarian reforms are among the first measures to be proclaimed and are usually based on longstanding demands and agitation by the rural under-privileged. Often these demands have been articulated by clandestine intellectual or political groups. There are numerous examples: the Egyptian and Iraqi revolutions of the 1950s; the Peruvian of the late sixties; the Ethiopian and Portuguese of the 1970s.[39] Agrarian reforms aim at destroying the latifundist power structure and broadening the political base of the new regimes. The 1980s rebellion by non-commissioned officers in Liberia declared that they were acting on behalf of the humble strata from which they came.

The Political Class
The political class is composed of a core of professional or full-time politicians supplemented by outer layers of politically active persons and groups who engage in politics intermittently or for part of the time. The core consists of high party officials and political activists.

The role and influence of this class depend on the power which they can wield inside their political organisation and in the country, and with the closeness of their party to state power. At the stage when the political organisation is close to power the core of the political class take on major state roles or become kingmakers. The spoils of political office are numerous and important, and expand with the growth of the role of the state.

The stand of the political class in agrarian conflict reflects either class positions, i.e. strategic considerations, or tactical manoeuvring for immediate political gains. Some professional political figures such as full-time and whole-life revolutionaries have made a mark on events and achieved great prestige and a place in history.

The peripheral part of the political class consists of those who take charge of state and parastatal corporations, state-controlled banks, and public authorities; leaders of class organisations, such as farmers' unions, workers' organisations, and employers' federation; leaders of cultural and sectoral organisations, such as religious or ethnic groups, women's or students' movements, and officers' clubs; and regional and local bosses and power brokers. Many disclaim such a function, but all insist on being consulted and their voice heard. Some wield tremendous political power behind the scenes.

Agrarian Conflict and Socio-political Institutions

Class relations and cross-class interactions operate mainly through institutions, which carry out a large variety of public functions and are involved in a whole range of socio-political decision-making. In this section we examine some of the many and varied relevant, major institutions.

The State
The state is a composite institution comprising not only the government machinery but also other major components such as the legislature and judiciary and a varying number of state-controlled but formally semi-autonomous agencies.

As economic, social and political relations within society become increasingly complex and are constantly evolving, a regulatory apparatus is essential and this the state normally provides. The rules obeyed by the apparatus are ultimately sanctioned by those who control the productive capacity of society. It is the hallmark of every ruling class to safeguard its position, for preserving which both strategic firmness and tactical flexbility are essential. Such tactical flexibility imparts a semblance of impartiality to state actions.

Control is achieved through persuasion (the battle for people's minds in the service of which education, religion and culture are mobilised), through rewards and punishment, and as a last resort through direct repression. Persuasion is more effective if the semblance of equality of treatment (before the law, with open competition, broadened educational opportunities, etc.) is preserved and if electoral processes give the impression of popular choice. In all this the underprivileged lose heavily because, in the circumstances already examined, such opportunities are inaccessible to them and institutions do not work in their favour. In practice even much praised formal "freedom" has a very restricted range.

In some countries all important functions of the state are concentrated in the hands of a hereditary monarch through his court, e.g. Nepal, or in those of a traditional royal family, as in Saudi Arabia. Others are ruled by a junta (usually military) or by a strong personality and, whether formal institutions exist or not, his will is law and his preferences the norm, e.g. Malawi, the Ivory Coast and Gabon. Many countries have formal institutions with electoral systems and parliamentary procedures which are believed to ensure representation of the people.

In the final analysis, however, the state is controlled in complex ways by the dominant forces, usually those that are strong economically. This control is achieved through their hold on the productive capacity of society and thus on the life chances of the population. Sometimes that hold is in very few hands (*Los Catorce* in El Salvador, the Twenty-two Fabled Families of Pakistan, the Hundred Families of Portugal). The Saudi royal family not only holds the wealth but also carries out the functions of the state. Control of the state need not be direct or overt but is always present. The arrival in power of a junta of upstarts usually occurs because populist movements are seen as a real threat to the essential interests of those in control of productive resources.

On agrarian conflict and the political system I have written extensively elsewhere[40] and give only some essential points here. "A basic incompatibility exists between parliaments and land reform" says Huntington[41] bluntly. "The operation of the Western democratic processes meanwhile strengthened the power of conservative and even reactionary groups" in India writes[42] Myrdal, in a fabric of politics which was a "combination of radicalism in principle and conservatism in practice".[43]

The former Ethiopian regime was decribed[44] as "the conjunction of land and power [being] the fundamental basis of control in the country", and the system as "geared to perpetuating the rights of the landowners". For more than a decade before the revolution the imperial government maintained a Ministry of land reform, and received advice on land tenure problems from the United Nations system without result. In Brietzke's words[45] the government chose "to manipulate the symbols of agrarian reform without actually generating rural change".

Hobsbawm observes[46] that "democratic electoral politics do not work for peasants as a class", and that "peasants tend to be election fodder, except when they demand or inhibit certain specialised political measures". Baraona remarks[47] also that "the National Congress in Ecuador is looked upon by many as an organism to provide the means which allow the maintenance of local power or the local clientele of the landowners or of their political agents".

With electoral systems in countries where the balance of social forces is not overwhelmingly unequal, i.e. where changes in the economic structure bring to the fore a sizeable working class and a growing middle class, as happened in Chile, competition during electioneering tends to raise consciousness and elicit promises. It may then bring to power pro-reform or populist forces, as happened in both Chile and Brazil.[48] At this stage the ruling classes become frightened and a military takeover is seen as a strong antidote to such "dangerous" products of the electoral system. In El Salvador, however, the mildly reformist military government was made to retreat in 1980. Postponement of reforms, however, often makes matters worse, and this retreat brought about a protracted civil war. Ethiopia's manipulation of the symbols of agrarian reform was ended by the military takeover. In fact, agrarian conflict was the springboard for many radical revolutions, from Mexico and Cuba, China and Vietnam to Ethiopia and Mozambique.

Other Political Institutions

Political Parties: Openly permitted parties are overt political institutions. They have not always existed and have often been dispensed with or their number restricted to one. They proliferate under electoral systems, often amounting to very little more than groups surrounding political figures, which come to life at election time. Some parties are coalitions of disparate interests which rarely provide a firm base for effective action except in a conflict when they close ranks to fight an "external" enemy, usually an opposing class.

Agrarian or peasant parties, which appeared in some European and Latin American countries from time to time, have been coalitions with a relatively narrow focus. This has generally resulted in ineffectual performance and an ephemeral life. "Since the nature of the 'contract' . . . is concerned . . . with the flow of mundane pay-offs [and has] no ideological or programmatic content . . . peasant-based parties enjoy an amazing degree of flexibility [and] are able to accommodate . . . divergent view points . . . they are 'programmatic'."[49]

As already seen, Hobsbawm suggests that democratic electoral politics do not work for peasants as a class; he adds:[50] "Unlike 'the working class party', 'the peasant party' is not the regular projection of class consciousness into politics, but a historical freak phenomenon". As rural classes and class relations are more varied than is implied in the "peasant" concept, the class composition of political parties needs to be viewed more closely.

Those classes which, because of their possession of assets, have displayed tactical power, have proved politically effective especially when riding with the tide. The most impressive performance has been that of middle class farmers propelled by capitalist agriculture, fuelled by new technology, and helped by government modernisation policies. They have managed to pre-empt both new technology and government outlays and subsidies, and thus achieve political weight which in turn they have used to obtain further benefits and so raise their status.

There has, however, been very little autonomous political action from rural areas, even by such powerful groups as these modern middle class farmers. Here, a vicious circle comes into operation. Where the countryside is backward it tends to be dominated by large landowning interests who exercise overwhelming and oppressive control over political processes so that for the mass of rural people there is no easy escape from oppressive backwardness. Conversely, where the countryside is "liberated" by capitalist penetration and a section of the rural people makes impressive gains, at times as the result of land reform, the countryside finds itself more differentiated and stratified, while its relative weight in the economy is lessened because of greater advances elsewhere; in consequence, far stronger urban interests appear to make their mark and political power passes to new dominant élites. The inferior position of the rural classes has not changed, except qualitatively; dominance passes from the traditional landowning interests to the new urban élites. New rural interests have only local influence or at national level only through or in association with the urban élites.

Too much emphasis can be placed on class-based parties. Their importance lies in their claim to have a class point of reference. In practice parties are class coalitions, some emphasising an underprivileged, or assetless, class base, others their middle class character and tendencies. All tend to be run by middle class educated élites. Agricultural working class leaders rarely come to the fore and other working class leaders only less infrequently. There have been few political parties of pure working class pedigree. Even populist parties with a strong commitment to radical agrarian reform prove to be unable to preserve any cohesion in action for long because in essence they have no rural underprivileged or working class centre of gravity. Political parties tend to be in a hurry to get into power and thus cut as many corners as they can. Long marches are not their idea of travel.

Rural movements of the underprivileged have made more of a mark as clandestine, usually armed, resistance to oppressive regimes of landlords and local bosses and often weakened those local interests. They rarely evolve into generalised uprisings but have provided the fighting force for many a revolution.

Other Political Organisations: Writing of Bangladesh after the setting up of the new state Nurul Islam observes[51]:

> A few interest groups like the students and labour unions were organised politically; a few others such as the army and the bureaucracy were organised institutionally and bound together by a broad range of common attitudes and interests, while others like the surplus farmers or trading classes were not organised either politically or institutionally but had close links with the different groups within the party [i.e. the ruling Awami League] as well as within the bureaucracy and the army.

The vast majority of the population, the landless and the near-landless, seem to have been unorganised. This is not exceptional.

Students in many developing countries tend to become politically aware and to play an important role in pressures for fundamental changes in society; while in agrarian countries with oppressive land systems or acute rural poverty, they articulate agrarian discontent and stir up agrarian conflict. Student militant action led to land seizures in India, to agitation in Bangladesh and Ethiopia, to the first land reform law in Thailand, and to armed rebellion in Sri Lanka and in Nicaragua. Their organisation has not always been openly institutionalised, nor neatly fitted into the existing political structure.

More broadly based youth movements have been encouraged in most countries, either by forces supporting the status quo or by opposition and protest groups. There are two main aims: winning over future political forces to the side of the contesting groups, and using this powerful youthful force for their own goals. Many an authoritarian regime has developed its own youth movement, often run on military lines; one-party states develop the youth wing of the party as an organised force for state purposes; in multi-party systems practically every important party has a youth wing. In militant clandestine movements members tend to be young (e.g. Nicaragua) both because of the arduous and dangerous missions they have to undertake and because the young tend to become politically more committed.

Women's movements have always existed, usually with a less important role. The character of these movements has, however, changed in the last two decades, undergone profound politicisation and developed militancy in line with the struggle for equality with men and as a result of realising that their status tends to be worse than that of the rest of their family. In revolutionary movements like that of Nicaragua women have played a prominent role.

Class organisations are intended primarily for the defence of economic and social goals. In pressing their case they engage in political action in the sense of influencing political decisions and contesting the allocation of resources. The role and effectiveness of farmers' organisations, agricultural workers' unions, and tenants' associations have already been discussed. The class differentiation developing in rural areas, the emergence of aggressive capitalist groups, and the progressive decline in the relative position of agriculture in the economy have accentuated organisational weaknesses inherent in rural societies and enabled other political forces to divide the rural population not only along class lines but also within classes. Agricultural workers tend to have more than one union, each affiliated to a different party; farmers' organisations may be even more widely split.

Ideological differences, cultural divisions, ethnic grievances or aspirations, caste norms, and religious fanaticism are used by class enemies to split rural organisations and make them politically ineffectual. Church institutions and clerics working at family or village level are indirectly very effective political agents. Their stand on major issues is critical in many communities. A novel experience is the recent development by Catholic church organisations of grassroot activities among the rural underprivileged, championing human rights, and raising their level of consciousness, including political awareness, particularly in Latin America and the Philippines.

Notes

1. Leo Grande and Robbins 1980 pp. 1084–1085.
2. Angell 1984 p. 28.
3. See Papanek 1972 pp. 6–8.
4. See Sanderatne and Zaman 1973 p. 19.

5. See Blaikie, Cameron and Seddon 1980 p. 85.
6. Christodoulou 1976 p. 2.
7. See Furedi 1974 pp. 486–505.
8. Laidlaw 1980 pp. 10–11. The quotation is from a Report of the United Nations Centre on Transnational Corporations. Feder believes that the Foundations which set up the "miracle seed" research institutes in Mexico (CIMMYT) and the Philippines (Rice Research) helped to attach the Third World agriculture to rich country interests (seed producers, fertilizer, machinery and trading and processing concerns). See Feder 1976 pp. 57–86.
9. Alan Riding in the *New York Times* of 8 April 1977, already quoted, observes that the wealthy coffee and cotton growers, long the dominant political force in El Salvador, conducted a fierce campaign against the land reform of the government which came to power after the military coup, a reform encouraged by the Carter administration, and forced the Government to backpedal. Significantly he quotes a cotton plantation owner as remarking: "This was just the first project, then the whole country would have been affected, then there'd be nationalization of banks, industry and commerce – and then chaos." For the *Catorce* land reform seemed the start of a domino process.
10. Offered hospitality in a mining area near the Rwenzori Mountains in Uganda by the family of a senior technician, I was served German bread imported in foil and sealed in a tinned container.
11. Blaikie, Cameron and Seddon 1980 p. 56.
12. The 1964 Ecuador Agrarian Reform was designed to serve "the purposes of industrialisation . . . without generating major changes in land distribution and rural poverty". Vos 1985 p. 1130.
13. Naiken 1977 Table 1.
14. *Financial Times* 25 October 1977.
15. There are many theories about bureaucracy and controversy about its role. According to Mouzelis, Marx considered it a specific group, not a social class, serving as an instrument of domination by the dominant class, but also through its assumed autonomy acting as a smoke screen masking their domination. Its role varies with the social structure, political system and development stage and dynamics. For an evaluation of theories see Mouzelis 1970.
16. Seidman 1978 p. 258.
17. "Top parastatal officers [in Zambia in 1974] received $27,750 plus allowances; the lowest employees, $25 per year", Ibid. p. 403. President Senghor of Senegal is quoted as declaring that ". . . the annual income of an African civil servant is about 360,000 CFA francs: that of a wage earner in the private sector is 180,000 francs: whereas that of a peasant in the former French West Africa is 10,000 francs". Taken from Waterman 1975 p. 61.
"The *minimum* pay for a government labourer or clerk when I visited Upper Volta was ten times the average income of the farmer . . ." Harrison 1979 p. 424.
18. Myrdal 1968 p. 502 shows that the civil service in three South Asian countries trebled after independence.
19. Kellner and Crowther-Hunt 1980 p. 210.
20. See Myrdal 1968 p. 263.
21. Fagen 1978b p. 294. Dale L. Johnson argues that the overdevelopment of the state "compensates for the presence of weak classes of local capitalists. . . . States assume entrepreneurial functions, giving birth to technocratic managerial and technical groupings that do not owe their existence to private property. The bloating of the public bureaucracy is also due to systems of clientelism, often associated with graft and corruption (to the point of being almost unbelievable in countries like Nigeria and Mexico), most of whic' re modern patronage systems . . ." See Johnson 1985 p. 15.
22. *Financial Times* 9 December 1980.
23. Dumont and Mottin 1980 p. 216.
24. Fieldhouse 1986 pp. 193, 203.
25. Seidman 1974 p. 112.

26. Brian May writing in the *Guardian* of 14 December 1978. See also Edokpayi's article in Adedeji 1981 p. 366.

27. Hochschild 1978/3 p. 6.

28. Goonatilake 1975 pp. 6–7.

29. Mkandawire 1980 pp. 5 and 14.

30. Szeftel 1982 pp. 4–21.

31. Christodoulou 1977 pp. 4–6. It could be added that the rubber smallholder plantations developed in the Ivory Coast with state support are popular with civil servants and businessmen. See *Financial Times* 1 March 1985.

32. Blaikie, Cameron and Seddon 1980 p. 95.

33. This has been witnessed by the author. See also Katouzian 1974 pp. 222–239.

34. Bandyopadhyay 1981 p. 52.

35. These points are made *inter alia* by Myrdal 1968 pp. 887–891.

36. Perlmutter 1977 p. 6.

37. Colonel Gustavo Alvarez of the Honduran Public Security Forces said about the politicians during the November 1981 elections: "Their problem is that they promise people things will improve. That is how revolutions get started . . . people get ideas". The *Guardian* 1 December 1981.

38. Leo Grande and Robbins 1980 pp. 1084–85. In El Salvador "political power is in the hands of military personnel without scruples, and the only thing they know how to do is to repress the people and to favour the interests of the Salvadorean oligarchy". From the open letter to President Carter of the USA by Archbishop Oscar Arnulfo Romero dated 17 February 1980, i.e. 36 days before he was murdered while celebrating mass.

39. These have been called "revolutions from above." Land reforms "turned a political and nationalist coup into a social and economic revolution". Trimberger 1978 p. 147.

40. Christodoulou 1977.

41. Huntington 1968 p. 380.

42. Myrdal 1968 p. 280.

43. Ibid. p. 276.

44. Brietzke 1976 p. 639, quoting Patrick Gilkes in *The Dying Lion: Feudalism and Modernization in Ethiopia*, London, 1975, p. 84.

45. Ibid. p. 643.

46. Hobsbawm 1973 p. 19.

47. Baraona 1965 p. 82.

48. The military defeat of Tzarist Russia in 1905 and the internal turmoil that ensued led to constitutional concessions and in the Duma of 1906 the Constitutional Democrats (Kadets) were the majority. They had an agrarian programme aimed at expropriation with compensation to create holdings of acceptable sizes. In a climate of insubordination and repression and of rural violence against landlords' property the gentry moved to defeat the Kadets in rural Councils and eventually put an end to constitutional government.

49. Powell 1970 p. 422.

50. Hobsbawm 1973 p. 19.

51. Islam 1977 p. 32.

Part III: Tackling Agrarian Conflict

"To many millions let me furnish soil,
Though not secure, yet free to active toil;
And such a throng I fain would see,
Stand on free soil among a people free!"

Goethe: *Faust* Act V, Scene vi.

"Both the existing economic order and too many of the projects advanced for restructuring it break down through their neglect of the truism that, since even quite common men have souls, no increase in material wealth will compensate them for arrangements which insult their self-respect and impair their freedom."

R.H. Tawney *Religion and the Rise of Capitalism*, 1926.

"For us, the poor, there is no action,
But only to wait and to witness."
The Chorus in *Murder in the Cathedral* by T.S. Eliot.

9. "Fixing" The Conflict

Dealing with Agrarian Conflict

Enough has been said to indicate that, despite the capacity of the various socio-political systems to live with the agrarian conflict within their societies, pressures have to be dealt with in the best way circumstances permit. Four such ways can be identified:

The Nelson Approach
Governments rarely see "problems", unless they can be labelled "acts of God" or the result of "outside interference". Like Nelson they normally view difficult problems with the telescope to the blind eye. Agrarian conflict is perpetually taboo, exorcised by silence. Men of the world, the experienced politicians in power, do not wish to know it. In opposition, however, the same parties see nothing but "problems".

In truth the problem is rarely known in its entirety or true nature. Data are not collected, research not promoted, analysis avoided. Even professionals, especially foreign experts, assist in this; by drawing comfortable conclusions or by providing recipes for inaction, e.g. by "proving" that the situation may not be perfect but any proposed solutions will only make matters worse. In my long international career I was always surprised by the amount of competent analysis of essentially peripheral issues, by sophisticated mathematical treatment of dubious data, and by false analogies that have crowded the literature on land tenure and its reform.

Ignored, obscured by sophisticated analysis, or postponed by investigation, the problem rarely goes away but festers to persist as an endemic pathological condition. Time is not on the side of improved health. Sooner or later acute symptoms of crisis develop and have to be "managed".

The By-pass Approach
Analysts, particularly outside observers, often get a good grasp of the problem and even recognise the fundamental need for radical change. Myrdal's extensive and authoritative analyses of problems of South Asia fully recognise the importance of agrarian conflict. Nevertheless, he considered radical redistribution of land to the tillers unrealistic and afflicted

with practical defects; he appears to have opted for welfare capitalism, giving capitalist agriculture its rein and offering minor redistributional land reforms intended to give the landless a tiny plot with an individual title.[1]

More assertive voices were raised in the first flush of euphoria emanating from the "green revolution" when miracle seeds were publicised as capable also of working miracles in the socio-political field. The cautious declared that the green revolution postponed agrarian reform, the enthusiastic were certain that agrarian conflict had been resolved for good. A sophisticated explanation may be akin to Myrdal's observation[2] that orthodox economists view the problem of equality from the point of view of its effects on the volume of production. In other words once production is taken care of, no outstanding problems remain. The South Asian case *"may thus be one in which the promotion of social and economic equality is a pre-condition for attaining substantial long-term increases in production."*[3]

The attitude that recognizes the need for radical reconstruction of agrarian relations on the one hand and states, even regrets, that it is in practice unrealistic and unfeasible on the other is common and recurring. It char- acterises balancing views and is a generally practised compromise. The 1979 World Conference on Agrarian Reform and Rural Development declared "that agrarian reform is a critical component of rural development," and "that national progress based on growth with equity and participation re- quires a redistribution of economic and political power"; but in its Programme of Action the prescription is optional and mild: "Where these systems [of ownership of land and other productive resources] are judged to be constraints on rural development . . . governments should consider institutional . . . changes within the context of their national and rural development goals".[4]

The Fabian Approach
Fabius, the Roman dictator

> set forth to oppose Hannibal, not with intention to fight him, but with the purpose of wearing out and wasting the vigour of his arms by lapse of time . . . when they marched he followed them; when they encamped he did the same, but at such a distance as not to be compelled to an engagement, . . . by which means he gave them no rest, but kept them in continued alarm." (Plutarch)[5]

These dilatory tactics with the purpose of confusing and wearing down the opponent are the standard approach to agrarian conflict adopted by ruling élites in most countries. The methods range from rhetoric and promises, through manipulating symbols or protracted deliberations, to rarely imple- mented pseudo-reforms and even to reform mythology.

Rhetoric is so prevalent and easy that it has become the hallmark of politics. The surprising thing is that it works for so long. As the media become more widespread and sophisticated the effectiveness of this decep- tion increases. The more literate a society becomes and the greater its access to the media, the more it comes under the influence of this barrage of fabianism which creates what has been called "educated incapacity."

Literacy is not, of course, a one-sided weapon. The educational system and culture, however, are permeated by the ideology of the dominant classes, disguised and clothed in high principles, which serve as a sophisticated stabiliser of the socio-political system. The extended benefits of education serve to unify outlook and colour thinking, which is usually geared to the long-term interests of the ruling élites. The class alliances in the economic field between the national élites, or an important section of them, and foreign interests is paralleled by educational and cultural identification.

The influence, therefore, of the media and of education on the tactics adopted for dealing with agrarian conflict not only becomes more pervasive and widespread but increasingly also takes foreign-inspired and foreign-orientated motivations; the means and methods also become more sophisticated and mechanised, thus permitting the rhetoric of the dilatory approach to be rapidly and widely disseminated.

Manipulation of symbols is widespread and manifold. We have, already mentioned the Ministry of Land Reform of Ethiopia in the last decade of the empire. Feeble legislation and protracted campaigns and debates are the hallmark of numerous regimes with a vast range of tactics. In Brazil "In the seven-year period between 1953 and 1960, eight agrarian reform bills were introduced in Congress and shelved . . . vetoed by a Congress of which *coronelismo* was still a basis of power".[6]

The glorification of past achievements, including agrarian reform, for decades after its beneficial effects have been exhausted and deleterious developments set in, is another symbol manipulated to good effect. The best known case is that of Mexico where agrarian reform and its revolution have remained a glorified part of the mythology of a ruling party, which appropriately is called Institutional Revolutionary.

The Forceful Approach or "Solomonic Solution"
In many ways all these approaches lead to an eventual forceful outcome. A deterioration in agrarian conditions and the time and opportunity for opponents to organise can be determining factors. Or major events may supervene.

Mexico in the last year of the Echevarria administration felt stirrings in the countryside that signalled the need for at least promises of new agrarian reform. His successor tried to propitiate these forces, while the present President has launched a $5 billion "integrated rural development" programme, known as Pronadri.[7] Ethiopia could not avoid the upheaval. The military on takeover, with the impetus of student agitation, immediately embarked on drastic and far-reaching reforms.

The Portuguese Salazar regime and its immediate successor, bogged down in and weakened by colonial wars which they had no chance of winning, were overthrown in a military coup, the leaders of which were forced into a radical agrarian reform by the *fait accompli* of massive land occupations in the Alentejo.[8] The fortunes of Chile under the last four administrations show the fragility of regimes and their incapacity to deal conclusively with agrarian conflict.

Agrarian Reform Options

Agrarian reform does not happen naturally. It is yielded under pressure, and the minimum possible conceded. As the offspring of agrarian conflict, its parentage is rarely acknowledged. Often it is presented as a necessary, even desirable, humanitarian gesture towards "our" weaker brethren; or as an essential, even inescapable, step towards economic efficiency and modernisation. It is even advocated by global forces – the church preaching charity and social justice, or international aid agencies and donors stressing the technical need for modern production.

Charity and perceptiveness to propose "technical" changes are not forthcoming unless there is an evident conflict or at least the obvious potential for tension; without a serious challenge there is no response at all.

The connection between agrarian conflict and attempts to deal with it through reform is highly complex. Such a conflict, repeatedly ignored and not well understood or probed, cannot be easily solved by hostile, or at best reluctant, power holders, and attempts to do so are rarely appropriate or effective. The essential answer to questions like "Will the reform succeed?" will be "Not if those who decide have it their way".

It is well-known in the political game that difficult and unpopular measures are delayed so long that pressures mount up and situations disintegrate with the result that remedies, often left to successor regimes, are extremely difficult to achieve. If a violent overthrow of the system were to supervene, as it often does, even the best new rulers have to build on ruins and amid violent passions; with little knowledge or experience, and faced with no little resistance from the old elements and the overthrown order, they have to act in a hurry and under pressure internally and even externally.

Agrarian reform then becomes Hobson's choice. This is the essential and fundamental truth to keep in mind as a guiding principle. In previously surveying[9] the field of agrarian reform in retrospect I derived some tentative dynamic characteristics of this field. We must distinguish between gradual changes in agrarian conditions and production relations (some of which, cumulatively, are of a fundamental and even a revolutionary nature, such as the establishment of capitalism in agriculture) which do not constitute agrarian reform, and a definite, fairly drastic and planned public intervention, fixed in time and aimed at making the structure of access to land more in tune with the requirements of the associated productive and socio-political systems. This is how agrarian reform is viewed here.

Most agrarian reform measures are timid, reluctant gestures made in the direction of the problem or the prevailing malaise, more in anger or cunning than as genuine attempts to effect solutions; they are propitiating or exorcising measures. In fact, there have been far more pseudo-reforms in history than genuine ones.

The Genesis and Progression of Agrarian Reform

Since agrarian reform is the offspring of agrarian conflict, the origins and root causes of the one closely govern the genesis and progression of the other. The formulation of proposals for remedial action in the shape of agrarian reform makes explicit the presence of agrarian conflict or discontent. In other words it is an acknowledgement in retrospect.

The background, already sketched, and the actors and dynamics of situations already identified with reference to agrarian conflict remain valid and relevant for the genesis, growth and nurture of agrarian reform. Depending on circumstances, agrarian reform is initiated by a number of sources, internal and external to the parties to the conflict. Those who find themselves hurt by the land system, especially those condemned to poverty and lack of status through exploitative production relations, sense the injustice and resent it – but in most cases have no option but to resign themselves to – their fate.

We cannot underestimate the entrenchment of established systems and the innumerable ways by which they assert and perpetuate their existence, i.e. the seeming permanence of social, economic and political power structures. Certainly those who have been oppressed and excluded have learned from bitter experience not to take them lightly. One can illustrate this with two examples. In discussions with reform beneficiaries in Upper Egypt in 1963 I asked them when they first heard of agrarian reform as such. They replied that they heard whispered various vague ideas before the Nasser revolution, but could not believe or even take such murmuring seriously; after the revolution there was a good deal of talk and propaganda on agrarian reform but, they said, they did not believe it much; even for the first two years of their possession of the land, they could not quite convince themselves that the powerful *pasha*, their very large landlord and dominant figure, would not one day return to take the land back from them and punish them severely.

The other example comes from descriptions[10] of the indoctrination or stiffening of the resolve of prospective or actual beneficiaries of agrarian reform in China after the victory of the Communist Party and its armies. Nakagane distinguishes three stages in this process: (a) the prime impetus by such organisations as the Communist Party, the People's Liberation Army and the Peasant Association; these were used as a core among the people and a mechanism for forward motion; (b) attitudinal transformation mainly through the *suk'u*, or complaints over grievances on the part of the exploited and the ensuing *t'ampai*, or confession by the leaders of the preceding regime or system, which enabled peasants to develop a community of outlook and interest; and (c) demand fulfilment through participation in the land distribution.

Thus even a victorious regime, already tested in battle and possessing exceptional experience, had to consolidate its position systematically and further the advance of agrarian reform through meticulous and systematic work among its natural allies.

If there are problems in mobilising the mass of the underprivileged, and even greater difficulties in their self-mobilisation, there are frequently acute problems at the other extreme, connected with the impetuous and sometimes undisciplined factions of a movement or regime. Impatient with the slow pace of reform and the meagre early results (if any) for the under-privileged, such factions rapidly become disappointed that victory has not brought about realisation of their sometimes exaggerated expectations. Their frustration leads them to organise land occupations ahead of the reform and to agitate for more revolutionary measures. They are not always wrong and may be needed if the victorious regime is not to become com-placent. On the other hand, they too often destroy any chances of success the reform may have had by undisciplined, incoherent, and even theatrical, action. Examples of such impatient action were seen in Allende's Chile.

Agrarian reform can remain the intellectual interest of professionals in cities until a major event occurs, as in Egypt and Peru; or student and other youth groups can press it, often to the point of fruition as in Thailand, or of rebellion as in Sri Lanka, or to the point of revolution, as in Ethiopia; or it can get into the conventional propaganda of electoral systems.

The most significant agrarian reforms have usually been the outcome of sustained and hard-fought campaigns by broad-based movements with an effective rural component. The rise of such movements is rooted in the conditions and dynamic processes analysed earlier and in historical con-junctures of great variety and complexity. Similar considerations govern the progress of agrarian reform once it is born.

Movements, Conjunctures and Agrarian Reform

Movements and historical conjunctures relevant to agrarian reform have been studied only to some extent. In an earlier work I gave a thumb-nail sketch of many of them.[11] While some monographs and synthesising works are of interest, crucial facts and their linkages are not available in enough detail or quality for a real grasp of the true essence of movements – their role, fortunes and significance.

Such facts include: the quality, traits and class origins of the leadership and class composition of the membership; the class enemy; the conditions from which movements grow and the targets chosen for action; the strategies and tactics adopted; and relevant events that took place at the material time and their role in the outcome.

With the existing severe limitations only a few indications can usefully be given and illustrated with selected examples.

As has already been noted, the argument has consistently recurred that, since "peasants" are of "low classness", they are incapable of enforcing their class interests in their own name and cannot represent themselves; instead they must be represented by others. In some countries peasants are under extremely repressive control and forcibly prevented from organising. In most cases a chain of clientelistic relations are the only lifelines open to the underprivileged rural strata in their access to markets and state organs. It should also be recalled that present-day rural societies are increasingly differentiated and that their divisions are widened in proportion to their access to assets under conditions of capitalist development.

Most of the well-known and significant movements that propelled agrarian reform have been inspired, and often led, by educated, professional people, usually with urban connections and frequently of middle (and even upper) class origin. Important movements build on or incorporate local rural movements, some of which are in clandestine groups. Sometimes, as in Chile in the 1920s and 1930s, politically conscious working class cadres, urban or rural with urban connections, and with trade union or political organisational experience, are active in rural areas, promoting class consciousness and organisation among rural people. Thus cells are created and encouraged to mobilise classes of the population whose position in the agrarian conflict is favourable to their organisation. This activity is usually extremely risky. If clandestine, it may be discovered after being infiltrated; if open, it may be taken over or emasculated by the *caciques* or other political bosses. Tactical power and stamina in action are essential for sustained campaigns and in this groups with assets or secure employment enjoy an organisational advantage.

Concerning conjunctures it is difficult to generalise. They are best illustrated by actual examples.

Notes

1. Myrdal 1968 pp. 1375 and 1384.
2. Ibid. p. 1368.
3. Ibid. p. 1369; emphasis in the original.
4. World Conference on Agrarian Reform and Rural Development 1979 pp. 1, 2 and 6.
5. Plutarch 1959 p. 70.
6. Cehelsky 1972 p. 233 (fn.) The new civilian government of Brazil announced on 28 May 1985 an ambitious agrarian reform plan to give land to 7.1 million families by the year 2000. Land will be taken from unproductive estates. The reform will begin in the Northeast where there is a history of poverty and agrarian strife and one per cent of property owners control 44.5% of rural land. *Financial Times* 29 May 1985. This stirred a hornet's nest of protest and violence. Tens of thousands of squatter farmers started invading disputed land; the big landowners started taking on the hired gunmen traditionally used in Brazil to sort out land conflicts. The Government hastily backtracked. *Financial Times* 11 June 1985.
7. *Financial Times Survey: Mexico* 4 June 1985.
8. See Christodoulou 1976.
9. Christodoulou 1977.
10. See Nakagane 1976 pp. 306–311.
11. Christodoulou 1977.

10. Examples of Rural Movements and Circumstances

The Philippines

Agrarian unrest in the Philippines has been long-standing; in some periods it developed into armed resistance. One of its powerful rural-based movements, which showed fighting qualities, was the Huk Movement (full name Hukbalahap, an acronym for Tagalog words rendered as People's Army Against the Japanese). The foundations of the movement were laid by a socialist party leader, wealthy landlord and lawyer, Pedro Abad Santos, who in 1933 created the League of Poor Labourers (AMT), which gathered strength in the Pampanga area by organising strikes and protest demonstrations.[1] One of his most important collaborators was Luis Taruc, son of a peasant who had some education. Together they organised meetings in villages to explain the aims of the League. Taruc's approach was to focus on areas of action in which the League could effect victories, e.g. usury or a specific eviction. Their methods were non-violent and they would all go to prison if arrested. By 1938 the AMT had 70,000 members. An older and stronger organisation was the communist-led National Union of Peasants in the Philippines (KPMP). In 1938 the AMT and KPMP merged.

Myrdal describes the background. More than half of those engaged in agriculture were landless, their numbers increasing through a mounting burden of indebtedness to landlords and moneylenders.[2] The Catholic Church was a considerable power on the side of the landlords with whom they controlled the organisation of the rural people. Patronage and corruption were marked characteristics of the system. Central Luzon, where the Huk movement was active, not only had acute contrasts in wealth and poverty and strained relations between landlords and tenants but also experienced an expansion of sugar and copra plantations that exacerbated contrasts in wealth and disturbed traditional relations of production.[3]

In 1942 the AMT and KPMP set up the Hukbalahap to fight the Japanese, to cooperate with the allied armies and to establish, after independence, a democratic government with a programme of land reform, industrialisation and guarantees for a minimum standard of living. They managed to control whole areas of Central Luzon, taking over the lands of collaborator land-lords, while for the lands of those landlords who supported the Huk move-ment they only fixed the rent. After independence Huk leaders were elected governors in some provinces. In 1946, co-operating in the electoral system, their popular front's candidate for president failed to win, while their seven elected representatives were not allowed to take their seats in the National Assembly. Thus in spite of their important national liberation role their political fortunes did not prosper for many reasons. Their relations with the Americans were not happy and it took nearly a decade and American assistance to suppress by force the Huk rebellion which broke out. The new president started to persecute the Huks with the result that their support among the peasants increased; when their effective control of large parts of Central Luzon was seen as a serious threat to successive administrations, a more systematic approach was adopted with advice and support from the US Government. Magsaysay, the President, followed the twin approach of land reform and development through use of the army, and a military solution, using his own previous guerrilla experience in the war.

Land resettlement was also planned with financial support and advice from the US, including such non-official aid as that of the anti-communist Joint Sino-American Commission on Rural Reconstruction. Efforts by the official Bell Mission from the US for a more general agrarian reform met with strong opposition from the Philippine Congress which was dominated by powerful landed interests.[4] Thus eventually a more systematic Philippine-USA military approach, combined with divisions within the Huk movement,[5] reduced the Movement sufficiently to make it almost innocuous. Luis Taruc surrendered and was imprisoned in 1954.[6] For two decades nothing much happened, except pieces of legislation that remained largely dead letters. The same Congress class interests continued to obstruct, patronage thrived and even the "green revolution" made no difference to the mass of the rural people. In 1972 martial law was declared, and an agrarian reform decree issued and signed while being televised to the whole country. It took another decade to implement a decree which was literally *immediate*; begin-ning with large properties and progressively lowering the size bracket of land holdings subject to it. Foreign and local interests in large plantations remained intact.[7] By the end of the Marcos dictatorship in early 1986, of the nearly 7.5 per cent of the country's agricultural land liable to this limited reform only about one-third had passed legally to the beneficiaries, in essence the tenants.

The place of the Huk movement was gradually filled by other organisa-tions, loud in their bark but innocuous in their bite. Most in evidence, and best known abroad, has been the Federation of Free Farmers (FFF) set up in 1953 by Catholic laymen to fill the leadership vacuum, as often explained by its widely known leader, Jeremias Montemayor. Over the decades the FFF enjoyed the support of the administration, as I noted when visiting their headquarters. They also receive financial support from the Church.

The FFF is a mediating force and pressure group, effective in specific causes and concrete problems, which it takes up with the administration on its members' behalf. It is particularly good in defending tenants against landlords in court, and has also carried out varied and useful training activities. It has all the strengths and weaknesses of a sponsored and officially favoured movement, keeping within the set limits of action and advocacy.

A little more independence is shown by smaller, more grassroots Catholic groups, concentrating on local activities and on training, research and "conscience raising". Agrarian unrest has not ceased; local violence still exists; agrarian conflict feeds the widespread rebellion of new social movements. As a *Financial Times* editorial put it: "Some 90 per cent of land is owned by just 10 per cent of the people and these extremely wealthy landowners act as feudal landlords to impoverished tenant farmers".[8]

Mexico

The Mexican Revolution contains the most famous agrarian movement and leadership dedicated to the cause of the rural people; so much so that much is now viewed through the romance of legend. "In terms of the proportion of population lost, this was the most violent revolutionary struggle ever, [since] as many as one and a half million Mexicans lost their lives [out of a total population of only 14.5 million]."[9]

It is impossible to give a concise account of one of the most complex and eventful struggles in history, with so many simultaneously fighting fronts and colourful field commanders, leading mixed forces with so many mixed motives and aims arising out of a variety of root causes and aspirations.

"The popular movement of the Mexican Revolution . . . was an essentially rural phenomenon . . . The burden of the revolution – the long campaigns, the guerrilla wars, the pitched battles – was . . . borne by rural groups."[10]

The roots of the Revolution, which started in 1910, have been traced to colonial times, the humiliating loss of considerable Mexican territory to the USA and the expansion and deepening of US capital investment in Mexico.[11] In the second half of the nineteenth century the Mexican economy underwent considerable transformation, particularly under the dictatorial regime of Porfirio Díaz who ruled for more than thirty years after the military coup of 1876. Díaz favoured the large estate owners and foreign investment. The economic transformation that ensued brought with it or accentuated already existing social and regional differentiation. When the Revolution came the various fighting forces and their aims reflected a regionally and socially differentiated Mexico. The outcome was bound to benefit some and hurt others.

Foreign, essentially American, penetration of the Mexican economy was marked in the north by ownership of land, railways, mines, banks and industries. A minority of Mexicans also, did well but the situation "frustrated the economic ambitions of the northern Mexican bourgeoisie".[12] No wonder that "the revolutionary armies of the North included [the] élite component of men who were fighting to oust the narrow group of Mexican and foreign capitalists in whose hands economic and political power had concentrated."[13] On the other hand "the mass base of the Revolution in the North was formed by workers, miners, agricultural laborers, peasants, cowboys, shepherds, muleteers, and drifters".[14] It was led by Francisco Madero, a landowner.

On the northern front the army of the regime also clashed with the "Constitutional Army" of Venustiano Carranza, a large landowner who "armed the peons of his *hacienda* . . . and joined the fight on the side of Madero". This army was led by middle class liberals and its aim was to "replace the despotism of Díaz with a narrowly based 'constitutional democracy' ".[15] Two more revolutionary armies in the north should be mentioned – the so-called "Rich Man's Battalion" of General Alvaro Obregón, who gathered a group of 300 fellow ranchers into a fighting force whose ranks had the usual workers, peons, miners and cowboys; and the "Northern Division" of General Pancho Villa who eventually broke with the conservative northern generals to identify with the *zapatista* aims, even though in practice the large estates they seized by force tended to remain with Villista officers who thus became a new landed élite.[16]

Southern participation in the revolution was initiated by the invasion in 1915 of Yucatán by General Alvarado's revolutionary army, which eventually came up against opposition from Carranza, who had meanwhile achieved ascendancy over the Revolution and become President. Carranza was under pressure from Yucatán's wealthiest hacendados and the US government since the North American cordage manufacturers controlled 90% of Yucatán's henequen.[17]

The most famous force, however, was the Zapatista in south-central Mexico. Emiliano Zapata, born in a village in the state of Morelos, "was a horse trainer and trader, rather than a peasant farmer".[18] At the age of 30 he was elected president of a committee of his village to try to recover lost lands; his father, who had been a small farmer, had himself lost his land through encroachment by a neighbouring large estate; Emiliano had recently returned from a period of armed service and work with an hacendado in Mexico City – a punishment imposed on him for his rebellious attitude.[19]

Morelos was a densely populated state and a leading sugar producing centre, which also contained many independent small owner-cultivators. At the heart of the Revolution there was restoration of village lands, mainly communal lands to which villages had title from the period of Spanish conquest. The "Liberal Reforms" of the 1850s and 1860s, designed to transform peasants into yeoman farmers working individual family farms, opened the way for large commercial landowners to lay hands on the communal lands, thus legitimising massive land grabs, including those of small owner-cultivators and the peons, and spreading landlessness and destitution.[20] Independent owner-cultivators found themselves begging these commercial landowners for work as sharecroppers, peons or casual workers.

No wonder Zapata could gather an army of 70,000 landless men and women. Organised in small, highly mobile guerilla bands, they operated from the mountains and forests of Morelos. Thus the Morelos rural people began as petitioners for justice through their village committees; when that failed to produce results, the struggle took the form of desperate assaults on fences put round village communal lands by encroaching haciendas. When the élites of the north began military operations, the Morelos people under Zapata entered the war and fought as a fully mobilised population.

Unlike the others, the revolutionary forces of Morelos formed "a unified, ideologically coherent movement of landless peasants fighting under the leadership of men and women of peasant origin".[21] The personality of its leader was important. He "lived with the price on his head for ten years . . . he never asked or accepted any material benefits for himself". No wonder the loyalty of his troops was unique in the history of the Revolution.[22]

Their key principle was *Tierra y libertad* (Land and Liberty). They proved a very effective force not only because of their tenacity and dedicated leadership, but also because they were close enough to occupy the capital.[23] In fact they did march on Mexico City but could not hold it without easy access to their supply base. The movement produced its *Plan de Ayala*, an agrarian programme calling for the break-up of large estates and the restoration of land to the rural communities. In drawing up the *Plan* Zapata was helped by a group of urban and rural radical intellectuals – the only element to give him support outside his peasant followers.[24] The movement applied its agrarian principles by distributing land in the area under its control.

The overt and powerful support for agrarian revolution by the Zapatistas and the general undertone of the revolutionary ferment throughout the country compelled President Carranza to publish his own decree on 6 January 1915, thus anticipating the Zapatista Agrarian Law by a few months.[25] Although it bore little resemblance to the *Plan de Ayala*, the Carranza decree remained in practice a paper exercise. The fighting, sacrifices and hardships, the hopes, heroism and deaths of hundreds of thousands of poor rural people tragically proved to be in vain – at least for another two decades. The Mexican Revolution closely resembled a Greek or Shakespearian tragedy. "Betrayal followed betrayal, and most of the principal revolutionary leaders died at the hands of assassins and traitors."[26]

The ruling coalition which took over the Revolution and was formed round Carranza comprised "(a) the new élite of recently landed revolutionary generals, (b) industrialists and businessmen who had prospered during and immediately after the Revolution, and (c) members of the old land-owning oligarchy who [were able to carry on as before] by declaring their adherence to the new regime".[27] Not only was the new regime unsympathetic to the agrarista cause, to which they conceded as little as they safely could, but in some cases they caused a retrogression. Reoccupation of communal lands "was ruthlessly undone between 1916 and 1919 by federal troops . . . In order to receive title to land wrenched from their control by the *haciendas* before the Revolution, peasant communities were forced to become petitioners of the State".[28]

Zapata himself denounced what he saw as Carranza's betrayal of the peasantry in an open letter published in March 1919, shortly before his assassination. He said: "You have betrayed the agrarian reform and taken over the *haciendas* only to give the property and its proceeds to your favourite generals".[29] There was some land distribution under Carranza's agrarian law, but in essence it took place where local rural people were well-organised or had armed forces to defend them against the hacendados. Morelos was such a state; in Yucatán also the "campesinos organised resistance leagues [and achieved] more provisional grants than [any other state] except . . . Morelos".[30] For the underprivileged rural strata and the wronged communities, however, a bitterness remained, expressed in popular folk songs.[31] The symbols also remained; the ideas of the *Plan de Ayala* were incorporated into the 1917 Mexican Constitution, and the agrarianism of the Revolution raised into a national standard to be unfolded with pride on every possible occasion.

The spirit and purpose of the Revolution was realised only decades later – between 1934 and 1940 under the

administration of Lázaro Cárdenas during which more land was distributed . . . than at any time since the Revolution. A substantial part of it was expropriated from the richest farms . . . and delivered to agricultural labourers organised in collectively owned and operated enterprises known as "collective *ejidos*". [These] were a privileged and highly visible minority on whom most of the budget available for rural development was spent . . . a much larger group of beneficiaries was formed by other landless labourers or dependent cultivators associated with smaller and more isolated estates who received expropriated land in the form of non-collective *ejidos*.[32]

The poor state and performance of the non-collective *ejidos*, the plight of other small cultivators (increasingly semi-protelarianised in a growing differentiation of the rural population as the result of capitalist development and multinationalisation of agriculture) and rural unemployment constitute the main sources of rising pressures for a new agrarian revolution in Mexico. The only expropriations carried out in recent years were those of Luis Echevarría (1970–1976) which were on a very limited scale.[33] His successor López Portillo, announced the exhaustion of land for distribution and through legislation permitted *ejidatarios* to rent their land out to agricultural entrepreneurs, provided they were employed as agricultural labourers.

Kenya

In Kenya land reform refers to programmes of land settlement and land consolidation. White settlers began to colonise the Kenya Highlands at the beginning of the twentieth century with the completion of the "Uganda" railway to Lake Victoria, built with indentured labour from India. The area opened up was attractive to develop and live in: the railway interests welcomed settlement along the route for reasons of economic viability, while the settlers, mainly from the British Isles and South Africa but also from Australia and New Zealand, found fertile land to cultivate and a very agreeable climate.

Under customary rules the land was not unoccupied, but happened to be sparsely populated by Africans because in the Masai areas the ravages of rinderpest, and in the Kikuyu areas of famine, had reduced the population. The British Crown conveniently declared all "vacant" land to belong to itself. These "Crown" lands were "alienated", each settler being given c. 260 ha. at nominal prices (later raised to c. 400 ha.) After 16-years' occupation, and the setting up of a "homestead", the property became "freehold". For "pastoral leases" of 99 years' duration, holdings could be up to 3,000 ha., in exceptional cases as much as 40,000 ha., while company concessions exceeded even this.[34] By 1920 occupiers totalled 1,122 and holdings averaged 2,103, some acquiring more than one holding.

Concentrated settlement resulted in marked displacement of the indigenous population.[35] Friction was inevitable and the problem realised as early as 1904. Areas had been declared available for settlement in large blocks and the "logic" of the situation was to develop a policy of "native reserves", which were finally demarcated in 1926. Africans had other handicaps also. "The Coffee Plantations Ordinance of 1918 prevented Africans from growing coffee, while the Native Produce Ordinance of 1935 confined marketing, particularly wholesale trade, to Europeans and Asians. Taxes were introduced to force peasants into the money economy as wage-earners, and compulsory recruitment of labour was tolerated."[36]

A new wave of settlement occurred after the 1914–1918 war. "Fresh" areas were surveyed to meet the demand; free grants of land were ended but "pastoral leases" were given a 999-year duration. By 1960 there were 3,600 settlers, their numbers kept low because of the very large area given to the early settlers who were unwilling to divide their holdings to accommodate others.

Africans found on the land in the early days were welcomed to stay as squatters, while those living in the reserves were invited to come to the European farms, also as "squatters". The "squatter system" was a labour contract, whereby in return for at least 180 days work a year, a man was allowed to cultivate a small piece of land and graze his stock. Soon it became widespread in the Highlands and the terms worsened; the squatter was required to work for as many as 240 days a year. Within two decades 25% of the Kikuyu population were living on European farms as "squatters" and others became casual migrant workers.

Developing parallel with the white settlements in the Highlands was a plantation sector, based on coffee, sisal, tea and wattle, and operated by big plantation companies. By 1960 there were 498 such companies owning some 135,000 ha. Some companies owned more than one estate and employed both permanent workers and casual labour. By then, European-owned farms provided four-fifths of total agricultural output and 42% of total employment in the country.[37]

In spite of African customary tenure, an African landowning class practising commercial agriculture was also developing,[38] presumably outside the
Highlands, since under the Highlands Order in Council 1938–39, abrogated
only in 1960, all non-Europeans were effectively excluded from owning land
or farming there. This class had emerged from among officially appointed
chiefs and headmen, who took advantage of their influential position as
members or heads of land tribunals under African customary tenure, and
from a stratum of mission-educated Africans. This class differentiation on
the basis of land reached striking proportions and produced a backwash
effect of spreading landlessness.

With the growth of commercial agriculture in white settlements the settler/
squatter relationship had already become unsuitable by the 1920s.[39] Like
capitalist hacendados in Latin America, the settlers felt the need for a
relationship based on hired wage labour without other obligations, especially the use of small plots of land, and exerted pressure in that direction.
Feeling threatened, the "squatters" responded with increasing unionisation.
This uneasy situation lasted into the 1939–1945 war. Intensive production
for the war effort, promoted by the colonial government, and accelerated
mechanisation of settler agriculture further accentuated pressure to end the
squatter system.

The conjuncture of pressures to reduce the African labourer's land and
livestock, the drop in real wages for Africans, and the low prices received by
the Africans for their produce, which was marketed through the settlers, led
to serious impoverishment of a fast-growing African population. This took
place against the background of marked prosperity among the settlers, who
could recoup their whole labour bill from profits obtained from marketing
the Africans' produce alone.[40]

This situation led naturally to agitation on the part of the squatters for the
defence of what they considered their legitimate right to land in the for-
bidden White Highlands. By 1952 the squatter movement had developed a
distinct organisational structure, and under the leadership of young militants
engaged in protests against labour law provisions, in strikes, in mass migra-
tions and even in sabotage on the farms.[41] The government responded by
evicting squatters, a harsh treatment for those who had no land or links in
the native reserves and who were thus faced with unemployment, as well as
landlessness.

The squatter movement did not receive much support from the relatively
privileged, new middle class, i.e. the educated Africans, many in white
collar jobs, or from self-made businessmen, who grouped themselves in the
Kenyan African Union; they opted for constitutional change and were
opposed to the direct methods of the squatters.[42] The movement found
allies, however, among the Kikuyu living in Nairobi, from the ranks of petty
traders and other "marginal" groups, who provided militant and sophisticated leaders. These talented and ambitious people, resentful of their
marginal status, gravitated towards nationalist aspirations. Their economic
interests were linked with the purchasing power of the African population,

unlike the relatively privileged class whose interests lay with the colonial system.[43]

Furedi sums up[44] the strands of the Mau Mau Movement as follows: the mass of the movement was made up of the squatters; the activist wing came from the more skilled farm labourers, artisans and petty traders who were part of the squatter population and could provide the radical perspective; the militant and sophisticated leadership came from the Nairobi petty traders and "marginal" groups, the links being provided by the activist wing. Leys writes[45] that during the Emergency, squatters were deported *en masse* back to Kikuyu country without any prospect of finding land or employment there. Not surprisingly a number came to play a leading part in the forest fighting. Those who survived provided support for the Land Freedom Army formed in 1960, which posed the threat of forcible land seizure in the Highlands.

The British Colonial authorities adopted the classic method of dividing the nationalist front and hitting hard at the "extremists". The radicals attempted to gain control of the Kenyan African Union but were out-manoeuvred by Jomo Kenyatta in November 1951. In October 1952 the authorities declared a state of emergency. The war of liberation was launched in January 1953 and the Land Freedom armies began to assemble in the forests, mainly in settler and reserve areas. Their demands were for ex-propriation of the settlers' land, trade union rights and independence. The rebellion was lengthy and sustained. The authorities encouraged "moderate" trade unions; the Federation of Registered Trade Unions was formed in 1953. Under Tom Mboya it opposed the revolt and opted for constitutional nationalism. On the other hand, 100,000 Kikuyu squatters were resettled in the reserves, 3,500 rebels had their land confiscated, and the Land and Freedom Armies were pinned down in the forests. The Swynnerton Plan promised land and development reforms that appealed to the middle classes.[46]

In 1961, the Highlands were at last opened to Africans. Who benefited? The European landowners became very concerned and some began to leave. To relieve political pressure from the agitation by Africans for land, the British Government started programmes for the settlement of 6,000 "peasant" families. When the white settlers began to leave, in 1962 the programme was expanded into a resettlement programme, the Million Acres Scheme.

The purchase of farms by Africans was of necessity confined to those able to raise the money. Loans were available from the Land Bank, but "credit worthiness" on such a scale could not be expected of poor Africans. The farms were large and their total price high. Some Africans formed partner-ships. By 1967 when the Large Farm Census took place Africans owned nearly 400,000 ha in large farms or 11% of all land owned by Africans.[47] Asians made a significant number of purchases for speculative purposes. The European farms sold were mainly the settler farms; ranches and plan-tations remained so that the Europeans retained almost half their land.[48]

The sponsored transfer of land created two types of settlement: low density (i.e. large farm) settlement and high density (small farm) settlement. Financial sources comprised the British Government, the World Bank, the Commonwealth Development Corporation, and the Federal German Government. The high density settlement type accounted for 62% of the area; these were not very small farms (ranging from 4–6 ha. in high rainfall and high potential locations to 11–16 ha. in less favourable areas). The low density schemes were intended for the more educated farmers with some agricultural know-how and some capital, the average farm was 8–16 ha; these schemes incorporated the "Yeoman scheme" of earlier days with farms of 20 to 100 ha. There followed a succession of land settlement schemes, including a squatter settlement in 1965 and the Shirika scheme for the settlement of landless people in 1971, not always on economically viable land. The "reform" again left out both the fighters and the poor. It has turned a small class of Africans, many of whom were not even farmers, into prosperous landowners, and a slightly larger number into comfortable farmers.[49] They employ labour and some of the larger have activities outside agriculture. At the bottom of the farming scale the ILO Employment Mission[50] found some 620,000 small farmers who lack the ability to raise productivity; among them are at least some who do not have additional incomes, or are squatters on land which they do not own or are completely landless. This group comprises most of the people whom the Mission called the "rural working poor" and who account for most of Kenya's "employment problem." They have become a visible problem because, through migration, they are becoming an urban problem.

Sri Lanka

The movement for agrarian reform came from a surprising quarter, even if, in retrospect, this was perhaps predictable. Sri Lanka had enjoyed a general standard of living higher than that of most South Asian countries (the income per head was twice that of Pakistan in 1954–56[51]). The country was ahead of others in the region in welfare provisions and the view was expressed in 1965 that the standard of living of the mass of the population was rising faster, if only slightly faster, than the average.[52]

Observers have often remarked on the high numbers of educated among the population and their westernisation.

From schools founded and run by Christian missions – and in the British era more and more modelled on British lines – there emerged a thoroughly Anglicized upper class with generally conservative political leanings. These Ceylonese were so much like their colonial masters in outlook, manners, and social habits that they were often called "brown sahibs", and negotiations between them and the British were almost in the nature of dealings between gentlemen of the same club. . . . During the period of British rule Ceylonese leaders felt no inclination to make any radical or egalitarian appeals for public support and nationalism struck no roots among the masses.[53]

Sri Lanka did not lack politicians with radical labels and rhetoric to match. Myrdal refers[54] to a "few small leftist parties adhering to a 'Marxist' doctrine; [they] were led by upper class western-educated intellectuals who were at loggerheads with each other on ideological questions".

In a gentlemanly way Sri Lanka came to independence in 1948 with the main difficulties obscured under the cloak of an amicable and peaceful transfer of power. The ruling class may have been "brown sahibs" from the upper social echelons but had their own interests to look to in a society fissured vertically and horizontally. Vertical divisions comprise the two main ethnic groups – the Sinhalese majority and the Tamil minority, occupying mainly the central and south-eastern and the northern and eastern parts of the island respectively. There are also the Indian Tamil labourers on the plantations which the estate owners have imported from South India as cheap and unskilled indentured, or otherwise recruited, labour. They constitute a most underprivileged group[55] and are shunned by even the Ceylonese Tamils. In religious divisions, Buddhism, Hinduism and the Moslem religions predominate, while a small minority of Christians are strongly represented among the educated élite. Language divisions also exist and in addition to frictions, or because of them, knowledge of the lingua franca, English, is a distinct advantage. Furthermore, the indigenously educated find themselves at a disadvantage *vis-à-vis* those educated abroad, mainly in Britain and America.

Socio-economic divisions are less clearly delineated and not well documented. The upper class was formed by economic interests closely linked with the British colonial rulers. Under predominantly British interests also a plantation sector developed, which not only dominated agricultural production and export earnings but also processing and marketing. On the eve of independence this sector shared the agricultural land area almost equally with the peasant sector. As a result, Sri Lanka has been an importer of its main staple food, rice. The foreign ownership, management, finance, distribution, transport and processing activities connected with the plantation sector, not only deprived the country of the fruit of its productive resources and effort, but also cast its population in subordinate roles. However, as modern financial and commercial institutions had to be created, mainly to handle plantations and their export, some selected local educated personnel, usually from influential families, were associated with these enterprises.

The Ceylonese élites were building up their strength. "Many of the richest Low Country families have engaged in plantation agriculture particularly in rubber and coconut. Through the Low Country Products Association, founded in 1908, they built up considerable solidarity which was to be transmitted into political power."[56]

After independence in 1948, Sinhalese acquired many tea estates from some departing British, though the largest and best remained under British ownership. Furthermore, relatively small-scale traders and businessmen, professional people and civil servants were or became estate owners and together constituted the owning class in rural areas.[57]

The condition of the rural strata varied from one part of the island to another. The inhabitants of the central and southern provinces, who were the least westernised part of the population and claimed to be its core (as well as custodians of the country's historic and cultural traditions embodied in Kandy's monuments and functions) suffered from an acute land shortage which was aggravated by displacement from their lands by the plantations. Land hunger, therefore, and a sense of grievance characterised these areas. By a process of inheritance and subdivision, combined with emigration and marriage contracts, part of the land came into the hands of medium and small absentee, or other non-cultivating, landlords. Thus tenancy and sharecropping, poverty and landlessness, minute holdings and small land-lordships produced a situation of malaise, difficult to resolve – at least in paddy areas. In coconut areas there were even large to medium landlords and landless people.

The rural areas also contained a rural intelligentsia[58] of Sinhalese school teachers, notaries, and indigenous or *ayurvedic* physicians, who were over-whelmingly Buddhist and mainly or solely Sinhala-speaking. With increased facilities in education the numbers of educated people grew enormously; the civil service, which it was everyone's dream to enter, could not provide enough posts so that these educated people could find no employment and in addition felt acute competition from the English-educated group, which was also expanding fast.

The Tamil areas are drier and contain many major irrigation projects intended for the colonisation of the Dry Zone and decongestion of the Wet Zone. Some holdings in the settlement areas are quite prosperous and stratification has developed within the schemes. Attempts to settle youth in agriculture have not prospered. The worst problems were faced by Indian Tamil labour on the plantations, but these people were not the concern of the authorities and often faced the hostility of the population who were resentful of this foreign intrusion.

The country was rocked from time to time by language disputes and riots, communal strife and religious animosities. In 1962 the government claimed to have discovered a plot by high-ranking army and police officers to seize power; the conspirators contained a large proportion of Christian and western-orientated elements. Myrdal observes[59] that the Ceylonese officer corps has been so recruited that it seems to consist of men who are strangers to the common people, as are the higher ranks of the civil service.

The revolt that came nine years later was really serious and the army was relied on to put it down. Much has been made of the argument that Sri Lanka has no "feudal" landlords and that, at least in the crucial paddy areas, the landlords themselves are small-scale farmers or/and in middle class urban occupations. The tenants and sharecroppers, however, have been poor and exploited, especially because of their precarious tenure. Since the early 1950s, and especially with the 1958 Paddy Lands Act, efforts to control rents and prevent eviction proved ineffectual as seemingly in-nocuous landlords showed themselves more than a match for reforming ministers. Tenants fearing eviction were afraid even to register as such. In a country where it is said that nobody is too poor to have servants, a client/patron relationship often prevailed.

The April 1971 revolt can be seen in retrospect to have had a number of components: the frustration of the rural intelligentsia, the acute youth unemployment, and the plight of the poor rural cultivators, set against a background of rising expectations which stood less and less chance of being even remotely met. The rhetoric of the political class exacerbated frustrations when viewed against what they themselves were practising and how they lived.

The revolt took the form of a well-coordinated and well-prepared uprising in various parts by young people (mainly 15–25 years of age), organised in the People's Liberation Front (JVP). The leadership was well-educated and some belonged to well-known upper-class families; the response came from teachers and pupils of the high schools of country towns, in which English was an imperfectly taught second language.[60] Moreover, it was essentially the lower middle classes, peasants and labourers of the villages and small towns which contributed most to JVP strength.

The "ideology of the JVP, was totally eclectic" asserting "that the peasantry would be the backbone of the revolution", advocating "that tea plantations should cease to expand and that food should be grown on abandoned estates. Land tenure had become so unequal that the collectivisation was the only solution".[61] Clearly this body of youth had done a good deal of spade work in indoctrination and organisation.

The most determined fighting and prolonged occupation by JVP forces was in the Matara, Elpitiya and Kegalle districts. In those areas the rebels established collective cultivation. Other areas which supported the rebellion strongly included the Polonnaruwa rice settlement schemes and the Sinhalese slum ward of Colombo, Wanathamulla, where the JVP had its headquarters.

The three districts which put up determined resistance have in common "an overwhelming Sinhala Buddhist character, dense population, coconut and rubber cultivation through Sinhalese owned and worked estates, a Leftward but not always Marxist electoral allegiance and a history of caste tension".[62] The authorities were taken completely by surprise. The socialist programme of the rebels and the institution of land reform showed up the pretensions of a "progressive" government and embarrassed the "Marxist" members of the governing coalition. The revolt was eventually put down by the army and the presumed leaders tried and sentenced to imprisonment.[63]

The echoes of the revolt lasted a very long while and swift action followed. The ILO Employment Mission, which on arrival was caught up in the revolt, could not fail to emphasise in its Report either youth unemployment or land reform (the latter in nervous fashion and, without straying too far from the technocratic mould). In the wisdom following the event the facts came out. According to the Mission, in 1969–70 over 90% of those under 20 years of age who had passed the O-level GCE examination and were seeking work were unemployed, as were over two-thirds of the 20–24 age group.[64]

Particularly disadvantaged were those in areas of low urbanisation, high population density, a concentration of lower castes and weak influence of the English speaking culture.[65]

The new Constitution of 1972 pledged the realisation of the objectives of a socialist democracy. In the same year a Land Reform Law was enacted. In the debate of the Bill, which I attended as an official guest, the conservative opposition taunted the government that it did not go far enough and, especially, that it did not have the courage to expropriate the foreign plantations. The law imposed a ceiling of 20 ha. for holdings in the highlands and 10 ha. in paddy lands. As paddy land holdings rarely exceeded 10 ha., the poorer rural people could not benefit from the reform. That it was enacted and eventually implemented was due to the shock of the rebellion. Interestingly, the Common Programme of the coalition (the United Front) in power had not included land reform. Cabinet ministers were themselves large landowners and there was much heartburning about how their own interests would be affected. The Minister of Agriculture stood out as a courageous and capable minister who was committed to the task and saw it through. In 1975 he completed the task by seeing through the National State Assembly the law nationalising 232 Public Companies (87 foreign and 145 Ceylonese) which owned 396 estates of nearly 170,000 ha., thus bringing the plantation sector under national control.

Implementation of the reform was swift in its acts of expropriation, but, as I predicted in my advice to the government, wholly unprepared in those of allocation, which became a great muddle, utterly at the mercy of woolly ideologues and local politicians. Not surprisingly, the rural people remained totally unsatisfied; the whetted appetites of the educated, especially the young, were far from even partially quenched, and the politicians of the governing coalition were at loggerheads. This encouraged the expropriated classes and their allies in the entrepreneurial class to press home their advantage and, as the United National Party, win a landslide victory in the 1977 elections. The experimentation with farming cooperatives was halted, the system "reorganised", and within five years some 17,000 ha. of land acquired under the reform were released to "people who were politically victimised" by the previous government.[66]

Notes

1. Huizer 1975 pp. 34–35; also Huizer 1971.
2. Myrdal 1968 pp. 386–390.
3. Osborne 1970 p. 84.
4. For a summary of USA and Philippine inter-governmental dealings regarding agrarian reform see Wurfel 1959 pp. 469–472.
5. In October 1950 an informer enabled the Philippine Army and police to seize the Huk politburo headquarters in Manila, together with Huk plans and the majority of the movement's political leadership, a colossal blow to the Huks. Osborne 1970 p. 88.

6. I met him briefly in the Department of Agrarian Reform in 1973 when he was helping the government – a legend reduced to pathetic banality.

7. Their exclusion from the reform was ostensibly to safeguard production vital for export. Plantations and agribusiness became Marcos' base for "cronyism" – patronage for close business associates, mainly relatives and friends, prominent among them the "coconut king", Mr Cojuangco, and the "sugar baron", Mr Benedicto, both of whom had other major interests. *Financial Times* 20 February 1986.

8. 4 February 1987. Even after the "People's Revolution" in early 1986 and discussions with rebels, with land reform as a subject, prospects for social peace looked unpromising. The new President, Mrs Aquino, comes from a landowning family; she is a first cousin of Mr Cojuangco; her assassinated husband's family are also large landowners. Finally on 22 July 1987 President Aquino signed an executive order on land reform, leaving, however, to the tender mercies of the new Congress "the guts of the problem", especially when sugar lands (including plantations) will be affected and how much land owners will retain. Landlords have the right to assess the value of their lands. *Financial Times* 27 July 1987.

The land reform bill was approved by both houses of Congress on 8 June 1988, "seen by many as presenting the best opportunity yet to undermine the 19-year-old communist insurgency . . . if it can be implemented." *Financial Times*, 9 June 1988.

9. Hellman 1978 p. 1.

10. Knight, Alan "Peasant and Caudillo in Revolutionary Mexico 1910–17" in Brading 1980 pp. 20–21.

11. Garza 1979 pp. 281–306.

12. Hellman 1978 p. 2.

13. Ibid. p. 3.

14. Ibid. pp. 3–4.

15. Ibid. pp. 7–8.

16. Ibid. pp. 8–11.

17. Sanderson 1984 p. 31.

18. Hellman 1978 p. 6.

19. Huizer 1975 pp. 30–31.

20. Hellman 1978 pp. 4–5 and Garza 1979 pp. 298–299.

21. Hellman 1978 p. 4.

22. Ibid. p. 6.

23. Hobsbawm 1973 p. 10.

24. Hellman 1978 p. 7.

25. Sanderson 1984 p. 27.

26. Hellman 1978 p. 13.

27. Ibid. p. 15.

28. Hewitt de Alcántara 1980 p. 23.

29. Hellman 1978 p. 24.

30. Sanderson 1984 p. 31.

31. One, "Juan Sin Tierra" ("Landless John"), was the tale of a peasant who gave his all in the Revolution but had nothing to show for it; Juan will be too busy, the song concluded, planting the landlord's field, to heed the call for another Revolution. Hellman 1978 p. 173.

32. Hewitt de Alcántara 1980 p. 25.

33. Peasants marching from the south arrived at the Agrarian Reform Ministry in 1984 carrying banners representing Emiliano Zapata and demanding the break-up of large land holdings. The President, launching the "integral rural development programme", warned that "We are still a nation with a great potential for violence which derives . . . also from social inequality itself". And a historical irony: Zapata was the champion of the landless masses and gave his life for the struggle – yet his grandson Emiliano is a landless peasant. Taken from the *Financial Times Survey: Mexico.* 4 June 1985.

Thus today in the country of one of the most famous agrarian revolutions, where the official position is that there is no land for distribution, 70% of the irrigated land and of agricultural capital is owned by three per cent of the landowners, while half the landowners account for only three per cent of agricultural production. Baer 1986 p. 206. The *ejidos*, prosperous and disintegrating, are a basic unit in the pyramidal hierarchical structure of the National Peasant Confederation, i.e. one of the three main pillars of Mexico's ruling party (the PRI). Stavenhagen 1986 p. 266.

34. Factual information mainly from Odingo 1971.
35. See Furedi 1974 pp. 487–489.
36. Ake 1981 p. 188.
37. Wright 1982 p. 37.
38. Furedi 1974 p. 488.
39. Ibid. p. 490.
40. Ibid. p. 493.
41. Ibid. p. 495–497.
42. Ibid., The Kikuyu Central Association played an important part, but was banned. They tried to operate through the Kenyan African Union. They used oathing rituals, a Kikuyu tradition, to recruit for civil disobedience. Newsinger 1981 pp. 162–163.
43. Ibid. pp. 163–164, gives prominence also to the role of organised labour. The East African Trades Union Congress (EATUC) formed in 1949, started agitation culminating in the 1950 General Strike, which was defeated, leading to the collapse of the EATUC, its leadership then threw themselves into the Kenyan African Union oathing campaign.
44. Furedi, 1974 p. 504.
45. Leys 1975 p. 48.
46. Taken from Newsinger 1975 pp. 168–178.
47. Odingo 1971 p. 191.
48. Wright 1982 p. 37.
49. Wright mentions 1982 p. 37, that a recent survey showed that five per cent of the landowners held almost 70 per cent of useful agricultural land.
50. ILO 1972 p. 38.
51. Myrdal 1968 Table 12–1, p. 535.
52. Gamani Corea, quoted by Myrdal 1968 p. 571.
53. Ibid. p. 156.
54. Ibid. p. 347.
55. Over-exploited through low wages and poor working conditions. See "Introduction" in Gooneratne and Wesumperuna 1984 p. 3.
56. Jupp 1978 p. 41.
57. Ibid. p. 42.
58. Myrdal 1968 p. 349.
59. Ibid. p. 354.
60. Jupp 1978 p. 298.
61. Ibid. p. 305.
62. Ibid. pp. 299–300.
63. I was in Sri Lanka at the time of the trial but little could be made of the records of the trials as published in the press. I also visited the areas collectivised by the JVP during their occupation. In the mid-1980s JVP reappeared as an armed underground movement, so much so that in 1987 in the wake of the agreement with India on the "settlement" of the Tamil rebellion in the north, Sri Lankan security forces were moved to the south in strength to fight the presumed threat from the JVP. The JVP seems to have become an armed Sinhalese nationalist movement opposed to concessions to the Tamils in the north and east of the country.
64. See Thorbecke 1973 p. 399.
65. Jupp 1978 p. 300.
66. See Peiris 1984 p. 88; also Moore 1985 pp. 1087–1091.

11. Agrarian Reform: To Whom It May Concern

Agrarian Reform: Some Rules of Thumb

The examples of Chapter 9 illustrate the interplay between the organised reaction of rural people and a conjuncture of forces and events concerning agrarian conflict and reform. This reaction is always crucial but not invariably decisive; it does, however, condition the action or response of ruling élites who have long-term goals and basic interests to protect. Much of their action and reaction is, however, conveyed through the decisions of the executive group in power, who have narrow time horizons and whose first priority is their hold on political power.

Ruling élites vary in those attributes important in the formulation and progress of agrarian reform. From literature providing typological indications in this matter, I discussed the issues in earlier work[1], and constructed a table, reproduced here as Table 11.1, on the basis of the three hypotheses given by Hung-Chao Tai, that (a) in initiating land reform political élites are *decisively* influenced by the consideration to gain political legitimacy; (b) the manner in which political élites resolve conflicts related to land reform is determined primarily by the relation between those elites and the landed classes; and (c) political commitment to reform is of critical importance.

Though the criteria on which the Table is based are quite broad, they are not comprehensive enough, and there are many additional questions. A major omission is the vast territory (of countries, periods, and circumstances) in which a necessary agrarian reform, did not surface because it could not be attempted, or even contemplated. Instructive insights can also be gained from examining the reactions of beleaguered regimes or embattled political élites fighting to prevent agrarian reform or to contain it.

Of the many questions arising from the criteria used in compiling Table 11.1 the perception by political élites of what constitutes the "political legitimacy" essential for them to seek is an issue of key importance. The political élites' relation with the landed interests is of immediate importance, it is not simple or decisive.

Table 11.1
Classification of political élites in relation to agrarian reform
(developed from Hung-Chao Tai's model)

Political élites	Socio-political outlook and/or style of economic management	Class nexus with landed class	Attitude to landed class	Country example
1. Non-indigenous				
a) Temporary involvement	Capitalist	Unrelated	Unsympathetic	Japan, S. Korea, S. Vietnam
b) Quasi-permanently settled	Capitalist/Etatiste	Unrelated	Unsympathetic	Taiwan
c) Colonial domination	Capitalist laissez-faire	Unrelated	Ambivalent but generally sympathetic	Asian & African countries before independence
2. Status-quo oriented				
a) Dominant industrial financial interests in developed countries	Capitalist	Tenuous class links	Dominating	Europe, North America, Australia
b) Dominant commercial industrial interests in developing countries (with links to outside interests)	Capitalist	Class links	Cooperative	Venezuela, Colombia, Philippines Chile (Frei period)
c) Monarchy	Capitalist/Etatiste	Class links	Unsympathetic	Iran
3. Constitutionalist Radical Reformist	Etatiste/Socialist	Unrelated	Hostile	Chile (Allende period) Tanzania
4. Revolutionary				
a) Military; middle rank officers	Capitalist/Etatiste	Mostly unrelated	Hostile	Egypt, Peru, Burma, Portugal
b) Anti-colonial; middle class elite with peasant links	Etatiste/Socialist	Unrelated	Hostile	Algeria, Guinea, Congo
c) Anti-colonial; professional revolutionary élite with peasant/worker support	Socialist	Unrelated	Hostile	Vietnam, N. Korea, China, Cuba, Mozambique, Angola
d) Insurrectionist; professional revolutionary élite with work/soldier support	Socialist	Unrelated	Hostile	USSR

These questions take us back to the central issues already considered, namely the analysis of production relations, vertical socio-cultural divisions, general socio-economic structures, the role of institutions and the class nexus (internal and external), which we have already examined as essential ingredients in the drama as conditioning, even activating, factors in agrarian conflict.

These considerations assume different importance on each major occasion depending on the conjuncture of events and moves. The plots of the drama actually performed are many, few are known. Four were sketched in the preceding chapter. Plots never performed are a matter of conjecture and imagination. Smothered or fobbed-off agrarian reforms may be considered at this point.

"Los Catorce" of El Salvador, the erstwhile Somoza regime in Nicaragua and Stroessner regime in Paraguay, the vanished Salazar regime of Portugal – are well known polities controlled by rigid military and police methods backed by absolute powers vested mainly in a dictator or a junta and in effect sustained by an oligarchy of wealthy and extremely conservative interests in what is often called a custodial system; such a policy ensures the continuance and prosperity of the oligarchy. Usually the system is frozen into near-immobility by fear that change may undermine it. In the long-run it cannot seal itself off completely and is eventually undermined by capitalist developments generated inside and fostered by attractions from outside.

The interest of the ruling élites is for peaceful change in order to expand opportunities for investment, an aim which, as already discussed, is not always possible. Somoza and the Salazar regime were overthrown by progressive forces and military action; in Chile in 1974 the reverse happened; El Salvador is still in agony; the Paraguay regime seems solid.

Experiences from countries and circumstances in which considerable mobility and even far-reaching action have occurred are best treated through a number of examples.

Ruling Élites and Agrarian Reform: Some Examples

Chile: Political Competition and Reformism
Within the 1960s and 1970s four successive administrations in Chile had to take decisive action in agrarian problems. This was a novel political necessity of long gestation. Tables 4.1 and 4.2 show that in 1955 family-sized farms formed less than 15% of the whole and sub-family units about five per cent; on the other hand three per cent of agricultural families accounted for 79% of the country's agricultural land. The traditional nature of the haciendas was changing so that by the mid 1960s "landlords had *almost* completed the transformation of their estates into capitalist enterprises".[2]

Agriculture was diminishing in importance in the economy and contributed less than 10% of the national product. The vast majority of the population was urban. Unionism started early. A country with important mining activity and growing industrialisation and urbanisation also had a record of militancy. Organised labour in the 1920s "began to penetrate the countryside, challenging the hegemony of the hacendados".[3] This also helped stiffen the rural people's resistance to pressure. Workers returning from the nitrate fields were marked out early as a "bad" element, since as far back as 1921 landowners in some areas rejected them even during the harvest season.[4] Thus "the process of liberation of the campesino has been a long, uneven struggle which was always a part of a larger politico-ideological challenge to the existing system of property in Chile".[5]

In this challenge the large landowning class – urban class with extensive interests in agriculture – proved more than a match until at least the 1960s. They could wield "a trump card-veto power in Congress over rural unionization and agrarian reform legislation. Manipulation of elections in the countryside was an important source of the landowners' national political power".[6] Divisions, at times fratricidal conflict, among the political groups and movements supporting the rural people's struggle for a better deal also helped the landowners.

The *Liga Nacional de Defesa de Campesinos Pobres*, founded in 1935 under the leadership of Emilio Zapata Díaz, a political activist and at various times a deputy, was the first national organisation of rural people. Active rural groups were also incorporated in the Chilean Workers' Confederation. The Catholic-oriented rural organisation, the *Federación Sindical Cristiana de la Tierra*, was formed later, in 1952.[7]

The changes in the countryside also had a profound influence on the political process. The capitalist transformation of agriculture had raised the proportion of wage labour in the rural labour force, enhancing their capacity for unionisation and militancy, and making them an important voting and political force by the late 1950s. Moreover, no sooner had the conservative government of Jorge Alessandri come to power than the international climate was transformed. Fidel Castro won in Cuba and the new Kennedy administration responded to this challenge by promoting the Alliance for Progress for Latin America. Chile agonised. Agrarian reform was inescapable, for both internal and external reasons.

In 1962 Parliament approved the first agrarian reform law; the view prevailed in the Alessandri administration that given the rural unrest, the establishment of a new group of owners of land would constitute a middle class of campesinos indispensable for greater social stability.[8] The reform came to very little because of the half-heartedness of the ruling group. The election of 1964 was won by the Christian Democratic Party in a brisk competition with the Left Forces, under a programme styled "Revolution in Liberty", in which agrarian reform featured prominently. There are numerous accounts of reform under the Christian Democrats and the Popular Unity which succeeded them.[9]

The divided Christian Democratic Party took three years to enact an agrarian reform law and in the remaining time managed to implement only a fraction of its programme. In the 1970 elections Popular Unity was returned to power as the largest single group but as a minority government. Using the existing agrarian reform legislation, within the first year the new administration expropriated as many properties as the previous one had done in its six years of office; by the time it was overthrown in 1973 it had expropriated 4,490 properties or 6.6 m.ha. It also adopted the cooperative use of expropriated land by the beneficiaries which had been initiated by the previous administration and on which the Christian Democrats were divided.

Chonchol sums up the Popular Unity achievements in agrarian reform as (a) abolition of the traditional latifundio, (b) introduction of new systems of organisation better suited to the development of a society based on greater equality and solidarity, and (c) more dignity regained by the rural people. As failures he lists the food shortages that arose mainly from increased demand as the result of better pay, and the lack of a cohesive policy towards small farmers.

The Popular Unity administration was brutally overthrown in the 1973 coup. The extremely conservative military government flaunted an economic philosophy based on the Chicago School of liberal economics. As it was, the state which the military seized was the legal owner of nearly two-thirds of irrigated land and one-third of dry-farmed land.[10] The military junta promptly returned the expropriated land to its previous owners if they could be found; the rest they parcelled out as viable farms for entrepreneurial farmers. The liberation of the rural people, above all of the underprivileged, suffered a sharp relapse.

The poor working people paid the price for the intended economic miracle which was essentially founded on very low wages and poor working conditions for an oppressed and voiceless mass in both rural and urban areas.[11]

Colombia: Fabianism and Pseudo-reformism
For half a century Colombia has been legislating for agrarian reform but implemented little. Law 200 of 1936 was intended to deal effectively with the precarious conditions of squatters, sharecroppers and minor tenants, within 10 years. There have been at least six more such major legislation enactments. In the 1959–60 Census of Agriculture about half the holdings were less than 3 ha. and accounted for 2.5 per cent of the area in farms. In addition to these 600,000 holders, another 500,000 rural families, had no land of their own. Some two-thirds of the farm area was in holdings of 100 ha. or more, and accounted for 3.5 per cent of all holdings. An inventory of landholdings larger than 2,000 ha. carried out by the Colombian Agrarian Reform Agency (INCORA) in 1962–63 showed that 874 holdings contained almost 30% of Colombia's land in farms; 12 of these units were larger than 100,000 ha.[12]

Between 1960 and 1970 the situation became even more acute with land concentrated in fewer hands. The main problems of land tenure were: concentration of the good agricultural land in the hands of relatively few people (mostly absentee landowners, usually professionals and politicians) and the numerous non-owner tenure arrangements combined with lack of sufficient additional land for the bulk of the cultivators, who were thus condemned to lack of bargaining power and alternative economic opportunities.[13] Bloody riots and land invasions have occurred intermittently since the 1920s.[14] The agitation that shook the country and left 100,000 to 300,000 people dead between 1945 and 1965 came to be known as "La Violencia".[15]

Colombian political élites have successfully evaded agrarian reform through tough measures, including military dictatorship, and a proliferation of legislation and other promises, as brands of conservatism alternated in power.

> The dominance of a rather selected élite of land holders in Colombia in all economic, social and political matters has rendered their power structure a formidable weapon. Furthermore, it has become intermingled with other economic interests due to the intrusion of entrepreneurs into commercial and industrial farming. The new amalgamated power structure looks for the perpetuation of the overall system, mainly for the benefit of the power élite. Many a member of this élite has also entered into very close agreements with commercial interests in the industrialised countries whose interests they have come to serve more than those of Colombia itself.[16]

Ethiopia: When the Symbols would no longer do

The imperial system of Ethiopia was earlier defined as the conjunction of land and power to form the fundamental basis of control in the country. In an agrarian economy with feudal traits and an ancient church, which actively supported the system, the main population consisted of poor cultivators with few rights and no voice, who bore their lot with patience over the centuries. The feudal relationships of subordination and patron/client dealings were loosening with the development of commercial agriculture and being gradually replaced by capitalist forms of production relations.

In 1960 the regime suffered a coup which nearly toppled the emperor while he was out of the country. During its brief life this 1960 palace coup (or fight among political favourites) included agrarian reform among its aims. The coup was easily put down but it made the emperor look for a broader political base, especially since political activity in the country was stirring.

The Emperor began to manipulate the symbols of agrarian reform. In 1961 he established the Land Reform Committee. On its recommendation an Authority was set up, to become the Ministry of Land Reform and Administration in 1966. I got to know personally all Ministers of Land Reform and the policies they tried to pursue. A long period of studies, sketches of legislation and much debate in Parliament ensued, but no concrete results. The policy on University admission was widened, enabling less wealthy students to attend. This was to have far reaching repercussions.

The spectacle of students in Ethiopia demonstrating in the streets of Addis Ababa in 1965, campaigning for land reform with the slogan of "land to the tiller" was a portent of things to come, as was the introduction in 1966 by the government of a one-year programme of field work for all Ethiopian university students.

The tempo quickened as landlords, often led by the imperial court and nobility, turned themselves into entrepreneurs. Multinational interests both for their own account and in support of notable landlords developed plantations. The government, also encouraged modernisation with capital provided by the Agro-Industrial Bank. Tenants and dependent labour with traditional ties to the landowner began to feel the pinch as evictions, and reduced employment due to mechanisation became important. In Chilalo, for instance, the tenant population was reduced from 40% to 12% among the holders within four years; one landlord with 1,300 tenants decided to mechanise because he found the tenants "incompetent".[17]

Outbreaks of insurrection, including assassination, answered with repression, became more frequent in various parts of the country. Peasant armed resistance was triggered off by the eviction of 1,000 tenants in Yeju by two landowners intent on farming with tractors; this led to organised guerilla action.[18]

The fateful year of 1974 saw an intensification and generalisation of rural discontent and of acts of rebellion with land invasions and takeovers, assassinations, destruction of machinery and the agricultural infrastructure, numerous acts of insubordination and strikes. This alarmed the landed interests in Parliament,[19] and the government reacted with more repression. A new prime minister was appointed, a member of the powerful landed aristocracy; a Security Commission was appointed with very wide powers to bring in repressive measures. Meanwhile the situation was approaching its climax. The Ethiopian Workers' Union Confederation called a four-day general strike which deprived the government of the capacity to enforce repression effectively. The Confederation demanded *inter alia* immediate land reform, a demand echoed by those regiments of the army who made common cause with the striking workers.

The government announced its intention of implementing measures of ceilings on holdings, tenancy regulation, abolition of obsolete tenures and the distribution of government lands to tenants. This proved to be too little and too late. The emperor was deposed in September 1974, the situation gradually became more radical under military rule and nationalisation of land was declared in 1975. A radical agrarian reform was implemented, probably under pressures from student and peasant militancy, in order to secure the new regime by ousting the landowning oligarchy.[20]

Rural land was nationalised, leaving the cultivators only usufructuary rights. Within 10 years about two-thirds of peasant households were organised in some 20,000 peasant associations with functions such as periodic redistribution of land, administration of public property, promotion of producer or service cooperatives and settling disputes. Ghose found that under Ethiopian conditions cooperative farming could be regarded as superior to peasant farming in that it can better mobilise surplus labour for capital construction.[21]

Guatemala: No Nonsense Tolerated Here

Guatemala is perhaps the most striking example of the continued iron grip on economic and political life and development by a landed oligarchy in alliance with a military establishment and the use of ruthless paramilitary groups who use terror and repression to maintain control. The oligarchy belongs to the "white" élite which dominates and exploits the "Indios", the Indian speaking majority, of Mayan origin. The sharp contrast between the two is very striking, in a country which is one of the least developed and most poverty-stricken in Latin America.

There is a far greater concentration of land ownership than in any country of the Region. Table 2.2 shows that 29% of the rural labour force were landless, another 59% near-landless, giving a total of 88% with no land from which to earn a living in rural areas. Table 4.2 indicates that 0.1 per cent of agricultural families accounted for 40% of all the country's agricultural land, which they ran as large multi-family farm units employing more than 12 people. Family-sized farms were run by only 6.6 per cent of agricultural families.

Gardner[22] mentions that less than three per cent of the population own 65% of the land in giant coffee, sugar and cotton estates which rely on impoverished peasant labour (typically paid just under US\$1 a day during harvest) to keep up with falling commodity prices. He considers it the most feudal land tenure system in Central America.

A reforming government which emerged from the overthrow of the dictatorship in 1944 abolished forced, unpaid labour on the estates for two weeks every year. The nearest the country came, however, to having an agrarian reform programme was when President Jacobo Arbenz was democratically elected in 1951. His Decree 900, Land Reform 1953/54, intended a relatively mild reform but was enough to incur the hostility of the estate oligarchy and of the United Fruit Company which had extensive banana plantations. Echoes of today's claim by US Government officials of "international communism" in Nicaragua rang in those days for Guatemala. Gardner recalls the "CIA-organised coup" which overthrew Arbenz in 1954[23] and adds that the political heirs to the coup are the National Liberation Movement (MLN), the overtly fascist party, described by its leader, Mario Sandoval Alarcón, as "the party of organised violence". This party, with the backing of the landed oligarchy, organised a formidable paramilitary base, and, as the country's largest party, has always been close to power without actually holding it. Like the fearsome *Orden* of El Salvador, these para-military networks became the precursors of the death squads of the 1970s and 1980s. So-called counter insurgency operations adopted a "scorched earth" policy in 1982–83 which laid waste much of the Mayan Indian-populated highlands, with up to 15,000 people dead. It is reckoned that human rights abuses have cost more than 100,000 lives since 1970.

This was too much for the Carter Administration which cut off military aid in 1977. Other aid was, however, forthcoming. The World Bank/FAO credit programme, for instance, was criticised for advancing "full one-half of its credit to the top three per cent of all landowners" i.e. to those with more than 45 ha.[24]

By the mid-1980s there was a new climate in Central America which amounted to the military retaining firm control of security while a plausibly centrist government talked about reform. In this climate elections were held and the least illiberal of the candidates elected as President. He is Vinicio Cerezo, leader of the centre-right Christian Democrats. In a pre-election policy pronouncement he stated: "We have not wished to talk about agrarian reform, which in Guatemala causes great confusion and has emotional connotations".

The Christian Democrats could achieve an election victory only by giving an undertaking to the military and the private sector that their power and privileges would not be interfered with. General Guillermo Echevarría, Guatemala's most senior officer, says that the army will defend its economic and political power and will expect to be consulted on issues ranging from land reform to foreign policy. Gardner adds that "senior officers have come to own large enterprises and landed holdings as well as run the economy".

Thus with this US-inspired prototype of democracy safely installed and safeguarded there are hopes that lavish US aid will flow in. Prospects of confusion through agrarian reform are remote indeed.

Agrarian Reform: Some Special Dynamic Issues

The bulk of the voluminous literature on agrarian reform based on a technocratic outlook, has concentrated on technical issues. To a large extent the aversion of ruling elites to stirring up socio-political issues in a sensitive area of policy accounts for this. Researchers and other professionals reveal a determination to stay within their field of competence, while much of the work has been done by advisers whose purpose is to analyse and prescribe action in a specialised part of the programme. In agrarian reform, therefore, more and more is known about less and less. Since the present work reverses this emphasis, some of the issues and problems involved must be briefly examined.

Technical and operational issues are far from being of lesser importance. They ensure that a programme is implemented to achieve expected results, without which the whole effort remains at best a paper exercise or becomes a disaster. The essential point is that technical and operational effectiveness and preparedness are not independent variables; they are part and outcome of the total decision-making capacity, which in the final analysis is controlled by the power structure.

Technical preparedness begins with the level and quality of information necessary for decision, planning and action. As already noted, information on land ownership is almost universally unavailable; usually what there is tends to be of poor quality and even apt to mislead. Besides the real difficulties of gathering such information and of maintaining it up to date, there is the special concern of landed interests for protection which lies in secretiveness. Any talk of agrarian reform or taxation and the land owner takes defensive action.

> When the Communist Party came into power in Kerala in 1957, big landlords rightly apprehended that their feudal interests on land would be at stake. This fear paved the way for large scale land transfers in the State even before the Agrarian Relations Act of 1960 was adumbrated. The passing of the Agrarian Relations Act in 1960 and the Kerala Land Reform Act in 1963 also prompted some hectic sales and transfers around those years.[25]

That is a common and universal reaction. Where information is inadequate and confused, land owners gain the initiative and even get away with fictitious transfers.

Legislation and other policy instruments essential for bringing about agrarian reform are also the concern of professional workers and critics. Again their existence, quality, nature and content, and their potential for implementation reflect political commitment and capacity which in turn are the expression of the socio-political power structure and of the perceptions of political elites. Parliaments controlled by landed interests or by their class allies will not legislate away those interests, as is illustrated in various parts of this work. At best they will concede weak legislation and innocuous policy instruments. In other circumstances legislation is hastily put through, often by a radical regime, because the government came to power suddenly and no preparatory work had been made or was possible. This is not meant to deny occasional incompetence in designing a law, or faulty drafting, or incapacity to implement, all of which are not uncommon.

Financing agrarian reform goes to the heart of the political content of the problem. It is not simply "technical" in the sense of finding money in the budget, and preparing for its disbursement. Of fundamental importance is whether to pay compensation and on what basis; of major importance also is who will bear the cost of compensation and of the rest of the implementation of agrarian reform and on what terms. Some compensation is paid or promised by practically all regimes, save some radical revolutionary groups who come to power after a victorious armed conflict, e.g. the USSR, the Cárdenas administration in Mexico, China, Cuba and Ethiopia. At the other extreme, some conservative regimes pay such high compensation that landlords *press* the authorities to "expropriate" them – in a very attractive real estate transaction. Strictly, such "expropriation" is not a reform because it implies no redistribution of economic, social or political power; it simply makes those with real estate more secure in their wealth by enabling them to convert it into more safe forms and thus into a more profitable investment.[26]

The attention of technical advisers and critics is also concentrated on planning and administration, which are, of course, critical for success, and expertise and skill in these are rare and valuable. There are inherent problems here because the planner and manager should have the imagination and capacity to deal with the requirements of the given reform on the basis of its real dynamic: therefore a grasp of its critical elements and of their whole context is essential; this requires sensitive political insights as well as technical competence.

A key to failures in planning and implementation is to be found in (a) the class orientation of planners and administrators; and (b) the socio-political position of ruling élites. Planners tend to come from the upper classes or, through their professional success, they have joined the privileged minorities, and may have even higher aspirations. Their vision and sympathies are limited; very rarely can they see issues from the point of view of the underprivileged; on the rare occasions when they do so they tend to lack the courage to stand up for that point of view out of consideration for their careers or for fear of the "bosses". Civil servants, as already discussed, have almost always proved unsympathetic to agrarian reform. They also lack the ability to tackle something novel and tough because routine and formality are the keynote of their work and habits of thought.

The power of ruling élites to sabotage, or frustrate, agrarian reform, which has been wrenched from them, includes obstructing planning and implementation. In Colombia INCORA, the government's main instrument for implementing agrarian reform, was rarely given a clear mandate, sufficient powers, adequate finance, enough personnel or other encouragement to carry out tasks which would have been difficult even if all the backing were available. Ruling élites that come to power unexpectedly, e.g. in a coup or after military victory, are both unprepared and in a hurry. They are also anxious to undermine the power of their opponents by taking away their land. Expropriation is embarked upon rapidly; allocation becomes slow and erratic, e.g. Iraq and Syria in the 1950s.

These are some of the issues raised by the dynamics of agrarian reform. Advisers and critics concentrate on the micro-aspects and draw conclusions or proffer advice out of the conditioning context. In my experience, it is all too often assumed that all a government needs is convincing and good advice and it will do "the right thing".

Notes

1. Christodoulou 1977 pp. 14–15 and Table 2. The cue for that Table was given by Hung-Chao Tai 1972 pp. 295–305. de Janvry 1981 gives a typology of land reforms in Latin America (Figure 6.1, p. 205 and on pp. 204–205) based on (a) the impact of land reforms on the land tenure system and (b) the social class that has hegemonic control over the state.
2. Kay 1981 p. 495.
3. Loveman 1976 p. 134.
4. Ibid. p. 191.

5. Ibid. p. 133.

6. Ibid. p. 200.

7. Loveman in Chapters 5 and 6 describes and documents the various affiliations and political allegiances as well as the strife which at times crippled the capacity for rural resistance when landowners retaliated with force.

8. Ibid. p. 225.

9. Jacques Chonchol, a prominent architect of agrarian reform in the two administrations of Frei and Allende, wrote a well-documented account. See Chonchol 1976 pp. 599–623.

10. Loveman 1976 p. 305.

11. This model was also tried in Brazil by the military a few years earlier and resulted in income concentration. With strikes banned and wage arrangements regulated by a wage formula dictated by the government real wages were held down but the lid was off at the top. See Taylor, Bacha, Cardoso and Lysy 1980 pp. 6, 22 and 305. "The military regime nationalised labour and hired it out to private capital at a price which the regime deemed expedient," a commentator described the arrangement to the writer about Brazil.

12. Data from Adams 1966 p. 48 and Table 1.

13. Ibid. pp. 47 and 50.

14. Ibid., p. 46.

15. Sanchez 1985 p. 792.

16. Posada, Antonio J, paper presented to the International Seminar on Agrarian Reform, University of Wisconsin, July 1977.

17. Solomon Gashaw reporting to the International Seminar on Agrarian Reform at Madison, Wisconsin, in July 1977.

18. Bezzabeh 1980 pp. 25–27.

19. See Note 15, p. 17.

20. See Halliday and Molyneux 1981 p. 105.

21. Ghose 1985 p. 145. See also Griffin and Hay 1985 pp. 53–55.

22. David Gardner in the *Financial Times* 1 November and 12 December 1985 from where much of the information given here is taken.

23. For the social and political background to the coup, see Handy 1986 pp. 390–391.

24. Kinley, Collins and Moore Lappe 1979 p. 3.

25. Kerala, Bureau of Economics and Statistics, "Land Reform Survey, 1966–1967; Report" Chap. X. Quoted in United Nations 1975 p. 62.

26. "The primary beneficiaries of the settlement schemes [in Kenya] were the former European owners, who were able to extricate their capital (and capital gains) through a market sustained by state action." Young 1982 pp. 209–210.

12. Agrarian Reform: Solution, Holding Operation, or A Trojan Horse?

Dilemmas of Agrarian Reform

Agrarian reform is introduced to meet a difficult situation – agrarian conflict. It is never applied to anticipate problems. In other words, benign, advance generosity or visionary zeal, or even wise providence, never enter the equation. This is a realistic assessment. In my long international career I have met, and even been consulted by, generous landlords who contemplated distributing their estates to their tenants; it must be said in all fairness that the strains and stresses of conflict and the fear of being engulfed by a revolution were becoming unbearable;[1] some felt like denying agitators the satisfaction of taking over the land either legally or illegally. They themselves wanted to pass it on to people of their own choice.

Whether agrarian reform will prove a solution or remedy is an immense problem about which experienced planners and qualified observers are careful:

> We have a better appreciation now of the evolution of modern capitalist institutions and their hold on political decision-making and hence we are more aware that the very pattern and organisation of production itself indicates a pattern of consumption and distribution which is politically very difficult to change.[2]

That, of course, is being wise after the event. Policy-makers and planners want to know in advance. The insistent fundamental question is whether there are golden rules to success. A good deal of the literature looks at the issue from the common sources or causes of failure. The examples of Chapter 10 reveal the formidable obstacles to even contemplating reform. The following examples consider the reform itself and in some cases go beyond it.

India: Two States, Two Experiences
India is a vast subcontinent with great regional variations and local differences, where radical rhetoric has accompanied conservative practice. In

the final analysis the upper-class status of the élites that came to power with independence has ensured the survival of privileged groups; this was aided by the adoption of Western electoral processes, which "strengthened the power of conservative and even reactionary groups".[3] That land as a political responsibility was left to the states, as distinct from the central government,[4] did not prevent frustrations in reform originating from that government. At one time or another practically every state has adopted land reform measures. Generalisation is difficult, but there are overall patterns. "The real beneficiaries, [of land reform] were indeed the intermediate classes."[5] Furthermore, "it led, in effect, to large-scale transfer of land to a class of rural merchants and money-lenders, who had both the financial means to pay such compensation and had, in many cases, already established . . . rights . . . above the actual tiller".[6] Technology reinforced these beneficiaries and boosted commercial tenancy. The advance of this aggressive and acquisitively capitalist class has depressed the status of small cultivators and badly affected precarious tenants. Under the policies most likely to be pursued, i.e. approximately those pursued in recent decades, land distribution may not become further concentrated but there will be a greater increase in the concentration of assets and income among the bigger farmers,[7] while the political voice of this new class will become more difficult to ignore.

At state level the experiences of Kerala and West Bengal provide an interesting contrast in implementing agrarian reform. The Kerala reform was, in fact, rated the most radical, comprehensive and far-reaching in South Asia.[8]

Kerala: Kerala has the most productive land in India. Its background is of agrarian conflict and open strife that can be traced to the early nineteenth century. An important distinction is that between the Kudiyirippu, i.e. tenants who are landless and dependent on landlords even for house sites, and owner-cum-tenants. Both categories included rural rich in respective percentages of 1.2 and 33.2. There existed a vigorous and militant agrarian movement.[9] The 1957 election was won by the Communist Party and the government programme promised comprehensive agrarian reform with the aim of abolishing feudalism and generating capitalist relations in agriculture.[10] The Agrarian Relations Bill, enacted in 1961, i.e. after the Central Government had imposed Presidential Rule, was significantly watered down to accommodate landed interests.[11] Real agrarian reform was implemented by the second Communist government's 1969 legislation; this vested all landlords' rights in the government, which in turn was to transfer them to cultivating tenants. By 1980 the reform was practically implemented and some 40% of the operated farm area transferred. Compensation was rather low and, combined with inflation, made the transfer a good bargain for the beneficiaries. Since transfers were to cultivating tenants, many of whom were not poor, the privileged groups possibly benefited disproportionately. Labourers were not given land; in response to organised labour's strikes and agitation, however, employment and wages were to be protected and improved by legislation which in the circumstances could at times do very little.[12]

The administrative problems of implementation, the painstaking drafting of legislation, the watering down and earlier delays by Congress-controlled ministries and emasculation of the law by the courts gave ample chance to landed interests to protect themselves. The High Court also weakened the 1969 Act.[13]

West Bengal: To some extent the West Bengal experience of agrarian reform parallels that of Kerala. In both states the Communist Party split in two in 1964; the Congress Party was dabbling in milder forms of land reform for electoral purposes, but in effect shifting away from the radical position it adopted in the struggle for Independence. In those days, as a reaction to landlord support for British rule, on the eve of Independence the Congress Party committed itself to reform. After Independence, it was increasingly linked with the interests of the landowning classes.[14] Mitter analyses in detail the differentiation among rural classes, especially with the development of capitalism, which forced choices on the parties, mainly for electoral reasons. Even the two Communist Parties became differently inclined, one sponsoring mainly the sharecroppers, the other the agricultural workers.

The state had been an area of agrarian strife with sharecroppers agitating for many decades, climaxing in the 1946–7 harvest.[15] All Parties favoured reform, some more radically than others. The difficulties encountered in its implementation prompted the Land Reform Commissioner of West Bengal, D. Bandyopadhyay,[16] to observe that even with resolute and unambiguous political will at the top, there were formidable inbuilt road-blocks in the path of land reform in a pluralistic society and in a constitutional frame as found in India, even when such reforms aimed at no more drastic measures than a slight rearrangement of property relationships.

The slow process and limited scope of the reform was bound to exasperate more radical groups and this may explain the outbreak of the Naxalite rebellion. The Naxalbari subdivision of Darjeeling District, in the foothills of the Himalayas, from which it derives its name, comprises some 60 villages and about 45,000 population. It is an area of tea estates with a plantation economy using migratory and day-wage labour. Approximately one-third of the land belonging to a plantation is used; the rest remains fallow for agricultural reasons or is used by plantation workers in return for services rendered.[17]

The area is inhabited by tribal people of indigenous Dravidian origin (58.6% of the population) and by scheduled (untouchable) castes (22%). For many years there had been agitation for land owing to overcrowding.[18] The landless resented and coveted the uncultivated land of the plantations and staked claims to it in the courts. Added to this were the activities of moneylenders and land speculators and a divided political leadership; hence the emergence of a local agrarian reform movement led by the underprivileged.

A Convention of the Naxalbari branch of the Kisan Sabha (Peasant Association) in March 1967 decided on direct action and launched a massive campaign to take back lands, "illegally occupied by vested interests". Action was by organised bands of tribal followers numbering 20–500 each. They occupied land, seized food in storage and harvested paddy in the field. The armed guards of a tea estate clashed with squatters on estate land. The police intervened. Landlords' gangs also joined battle. There were casualties on both sides.[19]

The strongest backing for the Naxalites came from the tribal and low caste people with virtually no support from the cities.[20] They thus lacked a socio-economic constituency.[21] They failed to establish a major base among the students; the tribals in the movement were a small percentage; the Catholic Church and Muslim community had given the underprivileged a semblance of self-respect and hope. To this day Naxalite groups in fragments survive in spite of official repression, active not in armed struggle, but in organising oppressed sections of tribal and ex-untouchable people.[22]

Peru: Revolution from Above and Thereafter
The experience of West Bengal in agrarian reform with the epiphenomenon of the Naxalite rebellion is to some extent matched by Peru with its agrarian reform and the Shining Path revolt.

Peru has a long history of agrarian conflict and the reform introduced by the junta of progressive officers who seized power in 1968 was hailed internationally, especially since it came into conflict with giant multinational companies and their supporting governments.

Until practically the 1960s Peru's economy was dominated by two powerful groups: the internal "oligarquía" or forty-four families (including the presidential families of Prado and Belaúnde) with a strong base in financial activities, and, allied with the "oligarquía", foreign corporations (which tended to become multinational and eventually the major partners in the economy).

Large landowners (the "gamonales") dominated the rural economy and political life.[23] In 1961 there were 1091 holdings of over 2,500 ha. accounting for 0.1. per cent of the area in holdings.[24] The "oligarquía", with the sugar hacendados as its most powerful wing, "exercised control over the policy of both civilian and military governments almost uninterrupted until General Velasco took power in 1968".[25]

Differences within the agrarian structure, regional contrasts, and associated production relations, have influenced agrarian conflict, reform measures, and benefits. In general: the giant capitalist enterprises were on the coast, as were most of the other commercial farms; both types used permanent labour and seasonal (*eventuales*) workers. Traditional estates were mostly in the mountainous part and mainly used tied labour (*colonos*) and sharecroppers (*yanaconas,* or *huacchilleros* – sheep tenants); there were also the Indian communities, mainly in the highland areas, who *inter alia* provided labour for the coast.[26]

A record of strife, including grievances and action on the part of communities for loss of their lands, had affected all large units, especially in the 1950s. In 1962, the army seized power, decreed the Law of Foundations of the Agrarian Reform, but failed to quell rural insurgency. President Belaúnde was elected in 1963 on a reformist platform and in the face of mobilised rural militancy got an Agrarian Reform Law enacted; its implementation was frustrated by Congressional opposition who allocated severely limited funds.[27]

It took a revolution from above to make headway. Led by Juan Velasco,[28] the officers who overthrew the government in 1968, with no links with the landed upper class whose power they wanted to destroy, "established a stable authoritarian regime, sought national economic autonomy and initiated basic social and economic change".[29]

The first move was the expropriation of large enterprises, including farms and processing plants, e.g. sugar mills, some of which were foreign-owned. About 40% of the land was eventually taken over and allocated. The large commercial enterprises turned into workers' self-management cooperatives (Cooperativas Agrarias de Producción or CAP), accounted for 53% of the adjudicated land.[30] In the highlands, the livestock estates especially were turned into the Sociedades Agrícolas de Interés Social or SAIS, cooperatives that also embraced a number of neighbouring rural communities. Little land was adjudicated outside the cooperative sector.

The benefits of reform were distributed unevenly. Naturally, only those with a stake already in land benefited. The most to benefit were the permanent employees of the large estates, the members of the cooperatives. The seasonal labour were not made members, with the result that they "work more hours per day, do most of the irksome tasks and receive considerably lower wages".[31] Those who benefited least were the Indian communities in the highlands; although they formed 31% of the beneficiaries, they received eight per cent of the adjudicated land.[32]

The disappointment of the highland communities, where even SAIS had to be dismembered, and the general plight of the Indios have been used by a radical group to launch a new organised rebellion.

The group was formed in 1970 as a splinter group from the Peruvian Communist Party. Under the leadership of Abimael Guzman, a teacher of philosophy at the University of Ayacucho, that University, especially its teacher training department, became the main centre of cadre formation. Guzman went underground in 1978 and, through those rural teachers, spread the ideas and organisation widely into the rural areas of the Sierra. In 1980 a movement started in Ayacucho with the name "Sendero Luminoso" (Shining Path), a phrase taken from the writings of the well-known Peruvian writer, journalist, and activist, José Carlos Mariátegui, who believed that Marxism-Leninism would open "the shining path to revolution".

Sendero called for armed struggle as the only way to resolve Peru's development problems. In its eight theses the peasantry is considered the main revolutionary force and the countryside the site of the principal contradiction. The social base of the revolution is worker-peasant alliance, but the peasants are the principal motor force while the proletariat is being formed and developing into a leading class. "The people's war is a peasant war or it is nothing."[33]

Reid considers Sendero a movement with fundamentalist Maoist ideological roots that evolved into a home-grown revolutionary one of the Sierra and drew on ancestral traditions of indigenous rebellions against oppressive outsiders.[34]

The movement's base of operation is the poorest department in Peru, with Ayacucho as its capital, although acts of sabotage have been claimed in other parts of the country. Little is known about it although world public opinion is disturbed by news of atrocities committed both by the army, which tries to suppress it, and by the movement itself. Graham described it as "hermetic, contemptuous of publicity and xenophobic, advocating a primitive form of rural Luddism".[35]

The movement shuns cooperation with other radical groups whom they appear to despise as tainted by "Parliamentary cretinism and revisionism". Their approach seems to be for the country to take over the towns, after the destruction of government and infrastructure. Graham suggests that the movement has been exploiting the neglect of the region by the central government and the vacuum created in authority after the removal of the big landowners.

Reid adds[36] to the longstanding resentment of the indigenous rural populations of the poorest and most neglected region the disaffection of Indian and mestizo youth whose education made them increasingly impatient with landlessness and unemployment. They formed the rank and file of the guerrillas, with women playing an unusually prominent role in the movement. In 1984 full-time guerrillas numbered some 3,000.

Reid also mentions that the movement relies on intimate knowledge of the Sierra terrain. They strike but have hitherto made no effort to defend, let alone hold, territory. The guerrillas seem to be peasants working the land during the day and mobilised for action by night. They have had their setbacks, including a massacre in prison in which many of the leaders were killed, but they are by no means out of action.

Tanzania: Reform Intentions and Reform Outcome

Tanzania, a large and varied country with the population unevenly distributed, is also one of the poorest. Development efforts have varied. As a Protectorate, it received only intermittent attention. Plantations by outside interests and other foreign activities gradually gave the economy an export-oriented colonial character with a narrow base. Food production development was mainly for similar purposes, as was dramatically illustrated by the notorious "Groundnut Scheme", intended to serve the edible oil needs of a war-ravaged metropolitan country.

In the early post-independence years this pattern continued, with advice from the World Bank and emphasis on major and modern agricultural schemes, including large settlement. Adoption of the *Arusha Declaration* in 1967 marked a major change in ideology and policy. The aim was to develop socialism geared to Tanzanian conditions. The ideology was based on the President's view that land was a free gift from God to all living things.[37] Tanzania had earlier declared land public property but access to it was only gradually regulated.

The aim was now to utilise land on an *ujamaa* (literally familihood) basis, with emphasis on collective work in production, and the concentration of scattered dwellings into compact villages, which would be provided with social amenities. The undoubted enlightenment, skill and goodwill of Tanzania's President Nyerere were the inspiration behind these innovations, but as he said himself, "Governments by themselves cannot achieve rural development".[38] This is particularly true of governments lacking resources. Of importance also is the precise socio-economic environment into which the reforms are introduced and the forces encountered there. Ismani, in the Iringa Region, has been studied in detail and illustrates some of the problems.[39]

Land tenure in Ismani was by the customary system of group ownership. The traditional land authority (Jumbe) was bound by rules, which allowed "borrowing" by "strangers" (called "pledging", i.e. a sort of "renting" by outsiders) who came "begging" land from it. As long as land and population kept in balance the system worked. Encouragement to grow more food and earn more cash in World War II triggered off immigration and settlement which accelerated during the post-war years. Heavy immigration, heavy demand for land and the capacity to farm larger areas led to customary arrangements being all but set aside. Migrants were not only agricultural people, but also lorry drivers, former sisal or mining workers, shopkeepers and bicycle repairers, who farmed commercially and most of whom needed labour. Mechanisation increased the capacity of people, who did not even live there, to farm large areas in speculative cropping on a temporary basis. Since they were not interested in land ownership, the legality or otherwise of renting was no deterrent.

At this stage there were four classes of cultivators: (a) rich capitalist farmers; cultivating 16 ha. or more (some exceeding 140 ha.) and with other business in Iringa; although only nine per cent of the households, they held 53% of the land under cultivation; they exercised enormous influence, penetrating government and parastatal institutions and the cooperative movement; even the Party was not immune; (b) petty capitalist farmers: cultivating a range of 7–16 ha. and constituting 23% of the households, they accounted for 28% of cropped land; some engaged in petty trade; they did not sell their labour and only those with the larger acreages hired labour; (c) poor farmers and part-time workers; cultivating holdings of less than 7 ha., they constituted 68% of households and accounted for 20% of the cropped area, not all their own; to sustain themselves they sold their labour. Awiti considers them the bastion of revolutionary forces living permanently in the area; and (d) hired labour: (i) those paid daily who were mostly local poor farmers; and (ii) the semi-permanent workers, generally migrants from outside, who were paid at the end of the season.

Not surprisingly, agitation for *ujamaa* came from the poor farmers and workers, while the rich landholders opposed it. Many of those interested in joining *ujamaa* owned no land at all. On a visit to the area in 1971, the President asserted that the land belonged to the people of the area as a whole, and that those with land within the mapped area would have to belong to the *ujamaa*. In the event, the rich farmers in their majority did not join; others joined but did not themselves work on the *ujamaa* land; instead, they paid money in lieu or sent paid labour to do their share of work for them. The middle strata had divided opinions about *ujamaa*, even though they provided the majority of the leadership. Their ambivalence could not possibly help *ujamaa* forward.

This case is not necessarily typical. There has been criticism that *ujamaa* was often established by rich peasant leaders who wanted government assistance given preferentially to *ujamaa* villages because they could thus add government funds to their sources of patronage.[40]

This spotlight on local situations gives some insight into the real problems likely to be encountered at local level, no matter how committed is the central policy direction. Tanzania's problems have encouraged criticism, largely on ideological grounds, from both right and left, as appears in the vast literature on the subject.[41]

The main lesson seems to be that a colonial heritage and acute poverty, implying *inter alia* a very primitive infrastructure, both physically and in human terms, are not solid foundations on which to build rapid, effective and egalitarian development. As Nyerere put it "Our mistakes made an impossible situation worse: they do not account for the situation".[42] Such an undertaking is difficult even in better endowed countries. Objective evaluation of the Tanzania reforms will illuminate issues useful for the future.

Nepal and Iran: Two Monarchies, Two Reform Approaches

Nepal is a monarchy that has managed to avert agrarian reform and is showing signs of longevity, while Iran was a monarchy which tried agrarian reform in a white revolution to prevent a feared red revolution but was overthrown by an Islamic revolution.

Nepal: We have already referred to Nepal's land tenure and class structures and to the key role of the Palace in controlling political processes. The ruling class of landlords and employers of labour have sustained the king in thwarting any advance towards a more open political and social process. "The Nepali Congress government of 1959–60 was committed to a significant land reform programme, and this was almost certainly one of the factors which led to the support of the conservative landowners for the king's coup in 1960."[43] Foreign aid donors brought pressure to bear on the Nepalese ruling class to implement some land reform and in 1964 a Land Act was passed with minimal effect; by 1972 only about 21,000 ha. had been distributed.[44]

In rural areas

> it is the "middle peasant", who neither employs nor sells labour as a commodity, that characterizes the peasantry as a class. Rich peasants have much in common with the small commodity producers of the urban petty bourgeoisie. The poor peasant is often virtually indistinguishable, except by the land he owns, from those almost totally dependent for their livelihood on working for others . . . The rural proletariat . . . is relatively limited in size.[45]

For the present the ruling class maintains overall control through the state apparatus and through patronage on a massive scale.[46]

It is ironic that the Land Reform Law of 1964 had the opposite effect to what the foreign aid donors expected. "Under the law, secure tenancy rights are guaranteed to tenants who had cultivated the land for a full year or more. Therefore, landlords now look for ways to manage their land without tenants and previous tenants are forced to become landless agricultural wage labourers."[47] Many migrated to the Terai and became squatters.

Iran: Iran emerged from oriental despotism through the early twentieth century constitutional revolution led by urban elements with no independent peasant participation. This laid the foundation of property, strengthening private ownership of land,[48] and the agrarian reform measures of the 1960s, assisted by oil revenues, consolidated total bureaucratic power over all social classes.

The main drive came from a monarchy with illusions of grandeur which wanted to speed the pace of modernisation while ignoring the high social cost and confident that oil revenues could take care of the economic cost. Powers were concentrated in the hands of the monarch. In rural areas the successive reform measures of the 1960s reduced the power of large landlords, each of whom owned a number of villages, and created landowning classes as the spearhead of both small and large capitalist farming. The first phase of the reform and the preceding period provided the opportunity for properties to be transferred, thus evading redistribution. Even a token mechanisation enabled others to escape. The reform benefited tenants or sharecroppers on the basis of previously operated holdings. The poorest, estimated to be 47.5% of the rural population,[49] i.e. labourers (usually seasonal) were left out.

The drive for modernisation followed two directions: (a) the setting up of Farm Corporations, a compulsory grouping of agrarian reform beneficiaries under state bureaucratic control with technocratic goals. In visiting them I was struck by the passive role of the farmers themselves (styled "members" and believed to be making the decisions) and by the fact that, with mechanisation, about two-thirds of their available labour was becoming redundant; I reported at the time that, if the Corporations succeeded, they might manage to maintain a fair income for the members – as rentiers; and (b) agribusiness based on a partnership between the state and foreign interests, which involved large enterprises (in many cases removing whole villages and resiting them elsewhere) producing with ultramodern methods and the intensive use of advanced capital.

For the rest of the agricultural sector there was much propaganda and some action in cooperative development. A barrage of official pronouncements and comings and goings left the rural people confused. This malaise was reflected in heavy rural/urban migration, the abandonment of agriculture in general, and even of artisan and craft work.

The Islamic revolution that took over in 1979 only reached a settled policy on land by 1985. At first the revolution took over the land of the rich who had left, that of those who escaped the reform through bogus mechanisation and that of those who borrowed from the banks to develop their farms. This land was distributed to small farmers, landless peasants, and agricultural school graduates. These beneficiaries had not had their tenure confirmed by 1985, when talk of more comprehensive reform was finally disposed of and the situation as it then existed allowed to remain. All state-owned agribusiness projects were retained, foreign shareholdings taken over by the government, while private Iranian ones not in the category of those taken over, remained as they were. Farm corporations were dissolved by decision of the members, the land returning to the previous owners (beneficiaries of the Shah reform). Of the 39 rural production cooperatives, 19 were dissolved in this way.[50]

Egypt: Revolution from Above but Skin Deep

Egypt's agrarian reform dominated the literature of the 1950s and 1960s.[51] Introduced by the Nasser revolution from above and glorified for more than a decade, it has recently aroused more criticism than praise. At the 1977 International Seminar at Wisconsin an authoritative Egyptian voice made the point that there were then already far more landless and poor farmers in Egypt than before the reform, the inference being that such a reform was not a solution then (and none was required now). The underlying argument is, of course, valid. The reform itself benefited about one-third of the farming population who became small owners' thus raising their status and for a short time their income. Landholdings below 0.42 ha. nearly doubled between 1950 and 1975; those of 0.84 to 1.26 ha. remained roughly the same proportion of total landholdings but trebled their proportion of the land; the proportion of holdings of 1.26 to 4.2 ha. dropped by some 40% but their share of the land increased by a third. Larger holdings decreased considerably.[52] Regulation of tenancy was not a success because its rent control provisions were seldom put into effect; the strong pressure for land and the domination of land reform institutions by large landowners made it easy to evade regulation and to squeeze tenants.[53]

The main outcome of the reform and post-reform policies was the capitalist development of agriculture. The middle class (some of them urban) landowners not affected by the reform took advantage of the services and infrastructure (intended for reform beneficiaries or small farmers) to make a considerable advance and become a dominant force in rural areas; with their other activities and links, they are now economically and politically influential. The practice of cheap labour, the displacement of weak agricultural producers, and the high rates of population increase in a country with limited agricultural land have accelerated the proletarianisation process and rural/urban migration. The Sadat government's "open door" policy opened the rural economy to agribusiness and other foreign interest activities and further advanced the fortunes of Egyptian capitalist interests, especially those allied with foreign interests. Pauperisation and marginalisation of the rural population, and the rapid increase in urbanisation and unemployment, accelerated. Agricultural production has been geared to export and the satisfaction of middle class demand. In the 1980s Egypt imported annually US$ 2,000m. worth of food and yet there were food riots – an alarm bell that has not rung for the last time. The situation has worsened by the return of large numbers of workers with the decline of activity in Arab oil-rich countries from 1985 onwards. In fact the acute situation building up in the early 1970s was relieved by the availability of such work abroad. Rural distress can be gauged from the figure of 60.7% of people living below the poverty line. By 1984 up to 20% of the agricultural labour force was working abroad. The considerable remittances – some 1 billion US dollars a year – have not, however, been invested in agriculture,[54] and returned labourers are seeking non-agricultural employment.

Algeria: Liberation, Reform and Rehabilitation

Algeria was the epic story of the 1950s, with its destructive, seven-year war of national liberation dominating world news. Considered part of metropolitan France, with 130 odd years of colonial rule, Algeria had 24,000 French settlers, the *colons*, on some 3 m. ha. of the best land, which they developed into capitalist farm enterprises on a medium to large scale with irrigated citrus, vineyards, orchards and other high value crops for export, mainly to France. The *colons* also rented land from native owners to increase the size of their operations and employed both permanent and casual native labour, believed to have numbered 200,000 and 450,000 respectively.

Native farmers were largely consigned to less fertile, mountain or semi-arid and unirrigated, areas, known as the traditional sector, where, with backward means and methods, some 1.5 m. cultivators, one-third of them small farmers, practised predominantly subsistence agriculture. These areas saw most of the fighting and destruction and were subject to harassment, surveillance and resettlement by the French army.

In the intense war those classes actively engaged suffered hardship and sacrifices. The victorious National Liberation Front (FLN) officially recognised that the fight was led by workers and peasants. The workers were really the vast numbers of people displaced from the war zones and crowded into native quarters and shanty towns within or on the periphery of major cities. The least militant, or those with least opportunity to engage in active resistance, were those who worked with or for the *colons* and the civil service, the professional class, and the wealthy merchants, small industrialists and real estate owners who had close ties with the colonial government and the metropolitan interests.

The war ended dramatically and abruptly in the summer of 1962 when the *colons* and other French economic entrepreneurs were holidaying in France, leaving a vacuum in the *colon* farms and French-owned industrial and other large enterprises. Workers, therefore, took over the farms and other major enterprises, encouraged by the Workers' Union (UGTA).

The FLN leadership, who as directorate and government-in-being, were out of the country, later endorsed this takeover and management of the farms and enterprises, which, in the absence of the owners, had to be continued by the workers, was styled self-management (auto-gestion) and eventually raised to the status of an important element in the economic policy of the new Algeria. Theoretical and ideological clothes to dress this policy were later borrowed from Yugoslavia. In this vacuum of power events moved fast. The FLN was a coalition of class interests and ideologies, of outlooks and personal pursuits, forged together in the stress and requirements of a tough war of liberation. Sooner or later differences were bound to appear. A general assessment[55] of developments, some of which I studied at first hand in 1965, gives the following picture of agrarian problems:

On the ground the essential force in ex-colon farms, now the self-management sector, was made up by the permanent workers, usually under the leadership of specialist staff; the discontented, and disinherited, were largely casual workers and mostly excluded from the self-management set-up. Only in 1969 were some admitted on the basis of work-days performed. The control of the self-management sector became a battleground for many years between those of socialist inclinations centred round the UGTA, on the one hand, and the FLN apparatus managers on the other; the latter eventually won and gradually installed a form of state enterprise regime. Close control and many of the decisions were in the hands of the state bureaucracy, many of whom carried on from the colonial civil service. The theory of self-management (and the formal position) was that decision-making rested in the assembly of workers with execution by an elected council. In reality these functions were performed by the state bureaucracy and appointed technical managers, some of whom, as I myself saw, were at first French. There were two main reforms of the self-management sector in 1968 and 1975 respectively. In the latter a determined effort seems to have been made to reduce control from above and from outside, by passing responsibility to where it formally belonged – the "popular assemblies" of members.

In the new circumstances and trade conditions there were acute problems of rehabilitating, managing and re-orienting farm production. Looked upon as a means of sustaining heavy industrialisation, the self-management sector was expected to play a key role.

Meanwhile, the traditional sector was increasingly shown to be in acute straits with the occasional assistance offered not proving even an effective palliative. Migration to the towns and abroad brought the problem to the notice of the élites. Essential progress needed basic structural reforms which the landlord class had managed to thwart. Figures presented by Bennoune gave the following picture of the traditional sector in 1972: those with land and those without land were more or less equal in numbers; over 70% of the land holders had 10 ha. or less; nearly a third had 10–50 ha.; three per cent had 50–100 ha.; 1.5 per cent had over 100, while some 600 landholders had more than 500 ha. each.

The structural reforms of the traditional sector were embodied in the Charter of the Agrarian Revolution promulgated in November 1971. In its own words it did not aim to abolish private ownership of land but to eliminate exploitation of man. The Charter was to be implemented by local authorities, the peasants organised into a pyramidal structure of unions and a cooperative structure built.

Expropriation under this Charter would affect lands over a ceiling, with compensation in cash, leaving sufficient land to the landowner to yield an income three times the wage of a permanent agricultural worker in the self-management sector. The land of absentee landlords was liable to nationalisation. By the end of 1974, according to Bennoune, 788,000 ha. were allocated and by May 1977 another 400,000 ha. Progress was slow because of the need to establish all necessary institutions and survey the lands. Bennoune argued that from the beginning there was strong resistance on the part of landlords, the urban mercantile-industrial class and their allies in the government; the bulk of FLN Party leadership came from an upper class background. The techno-bureaucracy appeared to support the reform because their own interests were not affected; the left of the FLN cadres, the workers, students, and independent revolutionary intellectuals and writers, strongly supported the reform. The impoverished and landless peasants were unreservedly enthusiastic about its coming implementation.

After President Boumedienne's death in 1978, agrarian revolution was toned down and the name abandoned.[56] The emphasis shifted to enhancement of production and productivity, since Algeria spent increasingly vast amounts on agricultural imports. This new emphasis on agriculture was reflected in the new National Charter, ratified in January 1986.

Portugal: Revolution, Reform and Regrets

Portugal presented many unusual features in its agrarian reform.[57] When the April 1974 Revolution took place, agricultural workers carried out *de facto* reform by occupying large estates. The revolutionary government afterwards institutionalised what had already taken place; in addition, the state set out rules for further expropriations and provided assistance to the units created. The constitution gave this formal approval and a legal base. A year later reform was abruptly halted when the military defeated a coup attempt by more radical officers.

The dynamic of agrarian reform came from organised labour who showed initiative, drive and ability. Considering their inexperience (they emerged from a clandestine existence) and the complexity of the task, they made considerable progress in rehabilitating the farm units (run down and even sabotaged by landlords or their agents), organised production on cooperative or collective lines, began important infrastructural works, and managed at first to increase overall production. As they had no resources to sustain themselves, a good deal of credit (including government credit) was used to pay wages and not enough was available for operation and development. As the reform areas were contiguous, they formed an extensive and compact area which enabled its beneficiaries to withstand siege and onslaughts to which within two years of the reform successive governments subjected them.

After the coup attempt, the governments moved sharply to the right, but provided no firm or coherent policy on agrarian problems. The important fact is that Portugal's reform areas were an island in a sea of unreformed structure made up of large estates and well-developed capitalist farms (some specialist and very important, e.g. wine making in the Douro area) and an extensive sector of small fragmented farms, forming the bulk of rural Portugal, especially in the North. This backward and depressed small farm sector, much of it left by migrant workers to wives and old people to manage, was mobilised, under slogans more to do with ideology than economics, by interests opposed to agrarian reform and public ownership of the means of production (mostly former owners) to attack the reform sector.

Holding the political upper hand, these conservative interests have been trying to undo the reform in the south, under the guise of remedying the abuses of land invasions, of enforcing the law, and of "encouraging" co-operative units to dissolve into private farms for "reasons of efficiency". That the reform sector needs tidying up and has lacked credit and technical assistance to yield the expected results cannot be denied. That it should be extended and the reform completed, as the law provides, has tended to be forgotten. And that the Constitution in force is in favour of the reform is resented and efforts are being made to change it. Finally, no reform has been mentioned concerning the small-farm sector.

As a radical socialist path for a European country in Portugal's position, the revolution had very little scope from the start because of the network of ties and conditioning processes that enmeshed the socio-political system. The armed forces, integrated into the North Atlantic Treaty Organisation, with their equipment, training and basic outlook provided by the Alliance, could not expect to pursue an independent course of action. The economic ties with and high degree of dependence on international capitalism, especially the multinational companies, make it highly unrealistic to expect an easy detachment for a small and poor country, where the economic and socio-political forces remained largely intact.

Writing in the *Financial Times* of 14 November 1978, Jimmy Burns, mentioned the clashes between communist-led peasants and riot police which took place following attempts by the Government for over a year to return some of the collectives to private ownership in implementation of the land reform review legislation, the enactment of which was "looked at benevolently by EEC officials". The existing Portuguese constitution, observes Burns correctly, recognises the legitimacy of the collectives and the chief Portuguese EEC negotiator denied that there existed any contradiction between Portugal's present institutional framework and its future role as a member of the Community. Now that Portugal has been admitted as a member, the EEC will find that the problem is not the reform sector, to which it objects on ideological grounds, but the small farm, unreformed sector, which will become a heavy social and economic burden.[58]

The Short Answer

These and earlier examples provide some insights into the variety and complexity of conditions, actors, interactions and dynamic influences affecting the genesis, progression and outcome of agrarian reform. To the question whether agrarian reform is a solution, a holding operation or a Trojan horse there is no simple answer.

The origins of agrarian reform are to be found in a complex and acute conflict. Contestants use reform variably as ammunition, a defensive/ offensive position, or a subterfuge. It is probably more often brought into the battle for irrelevant reasons – essentially to defeat or weaken opponents – than as a positive and well-cared-for undertaking. It is, of course, a complex and composite operation, which requires unusual skills and experience if it is to be applied successfully.

The short answer, therefore, must be that it is rarely a solution because it is rarely given a chance. A further question can thus be asked: solution for what? The pressures that bring about reform are so disparate and the forced path through which it passes in the circumstances so rough and so mined that in the end the essence of the whole exercise is lost sight of, if it ever received much systematic attention. The end is messy and not susceptible to systematic, reasoned and substantiated analysis.

That reform has too often been a holding operation is obvious and common; in practice, it is more used as an anodyne promise than as concrete action; it is especially the sport of electoral systems, in which parties are at times compelled to act on their promises. They then try to get as much political benefit from reform with as little cost as possible, thus providing the strongest anodyne available. Some committed regimes find the path bristling with difficulties as enemies lurk on both flanks.

In this contest fear that agrarian reform may be a Trojan horse has affected both camps: the privileged classes and the custodians of their interests fear it as a corroding influence or thin edge of the wedge; their radical opponents that it may prove an anodyne or diversion from the necessity for more profound transformation. From time to time agrarian reform has confirmed both fears, while its inconclusive outcome sets back the appetite for it for a very long time.

Notes

1. It is interesting to recall what the Tsar's close counsellor, D. F. Trepov, said in the years of reform following the 1905 defeat by the Japanese, "I would be glad to relinquish half my land if I were convinced that this would allow me to keep the rest". Quoted by John Keep in *The Times Literary Supplement*, 27 May 1983 p. 532.
2. Ul Haq 1971 pp. 11–12.
3. Myrdal 1968 p. 280.
4. The Constitution of India considers the right to property as fundamental and, therefore, guaranteed; compensation to landowners, as a multiple of annual rent, has to be paid; and this is binding on all state governments.
5. Joshi 1974 p. 333.
6. Bhaduri 1981 p. 44.
7. Rudra 1978 p. 404.
8. Nossiter 1982 p. 292.
9. Information taken from the summary by the author in Herring 1980 pp. 1–8. A more detailed analysis, including the history of agrarian conflict in Kerala, can be found in Jose 1984 pp. 48–61.
10. Nossiter 1982 p. 150. Nossiter describes in detail the political changes and alliances and the actions taken by governments in Kerala, including their attitudes and action in agrarian reform.
11. Ibid. p. 150.
12. In a fuller account and analysis Raj and Tharakan reached the conclusions that there was a reduction in the concentration of landownership, particularly in the two extremes, but the medium-size owners generally strengthened their position. Agricultural labourers did fairly well thanks to their mobilisation and unionisation, partly due to policies of the government connected with land reform. Raj and Tharakan 1983 p. 91.
13. Nossiter 1982 pp. 292–296.
14. Mitter 1977.
15. Cooper 1983 pp. 226–255.
16. Bandyopadhyay 1981 p. 51.
17. Franda 1971 p. 153.
18. Das Gupta 1974 pp. 2–3 refers to resentment by the tribal people, who practised shifting cultivation, for eviction from lands which they had cleared and tilled. The Communist Party of India since the mid-1950s was active in organising them.
19. Franda 1971 pp. 159–160. See also Appa 1970 pp. 34–41, and Das Gupta 1974 pp. 2–3.
20. Appa 1970 pp. 37–38.
21. Nossiter 1982 p. 359.
22. Omvedt 1985 pp. 173 and 178.
23. Fitzgerald 1979 pp. 48, 52 and 320.
24. Ibid. p. 106.
25. Reid 1985 p. 25.
26. Kay 1982 pp. 142–144.
27. Ibid. pp. 148–149.
28. "A charismatic mestizo from a provincial lower middle class background . . ." Reid 1985 p. 43.
29. Trimberger 1978 p. 147.
30. Kay 1982 p. 153.
31. Ibid. p. 156. For the performance and problems of the CAPs, the privileges and attitudes of members and the reasons for, and conditions of, employment of casual labour, see Caballero 1983 pp. 169–175.
32. Kay 1982 p. 153, also Stein 1980 p. 62.
33. Petras, Morris and Havens 1983 pp. 49–50.
34. Reid 1985 p. 106.
35. Robert Graham in the *Financial Times*, 4 November 1984. See also the *Financial Times*, 13 January 1984.

36. Reid 1985 pp. 106–109.
37. Feldman 1971.
38. Nyerere 1979 p. 8.
39. Besides Feldman, already cited, and other work by the same author, investigations have been carried by Awiti and his 1974 paper is used here.
40. See, e.g. Putterman 1985 p. 184.
41. Nobody has been more aware and open about the problems, and even errors, than President Nyerere himself. He was reported by the BBC World Service on 24 May 1985 to have acknowledged that centralisation of decision-making on numerous rural problems was a critical error; he was still of the opinion that *ujamaa* was useful in that it distributed the few opportunities available more equitably; and he insisted that *ujamaa* was a voluntary cooperative use of land and agricultural resources and not a compulsory collectivisation; hence, he stressed, the uneven pattern in the country, with collective farms in some places, looser cooperatives in others and none at all in many parts of Tanzania.
42. Nyerere 1986 p. 388.
43. Blaikie, Cameron and Seddon 1980 p. 59.
44. Ibid. p. 60.
45. Ibid. pp. 88–89.
46. Ibid. p. 89.
47. Kaplan and Shrestha 1982 p. 77.
48. Katouzian 1974 pp. 221–222.
49. Halliday 1979 p. 117.
50. From *Financial Times Survey* on Iran, 1 April 1985.
51. For a concise and comprehensive fairly recent evaluation see Radwan 1977.
52. Adams 1985 Table 6, p. 712.
53. Radwan 1977 pp. 29–30.
54. Adams 1985 Table (p. 707) and pp. 716–717.
55. See for instance Clegg 1971 and Bennoune 1977.
56. Expropriated land was said to have been returned to its former owners. Francis Chiles in the *Financial Times* 9 April 1986.
57. Christodoulou 1977.
58. Since this was written the *Financial Times* (9 May 1986) writes about the sector's "trouble adapting to the sophistication of the Common Agricultural Policy"; those large farmers who had their land returned to them are reckoned to do very well indeed. Earlier on 12 March 1986 the same paper wrote about the bleak outlook for Portuguese farming with its tiny plots.

Part IV: International Dimensions of Agrarian Conflict and Reform

"What are we waiting for, assembled in the public square?
                    The barbarians are to arrive today.
                    Why such inaction in the Senate?
                    Why do the Senators sit and pass no laws?
                    Because the barbarians are to arrive today.
                    What further laws can the Senators pass?
                    When the barbarians come they will make the laws.
                                    ....
            Why have our two consuls and the praetors come out
                    today in their red, embroidered togas;
                    Why do they wear amethyst-studded bracelets,
                    and rings with brilliant glittering emeralds;
                    Why are they carrying costly canes today,
                    superbly carved with silver and gold?
            Because the barbarians are to arrive today,
                    and such things dazzle the barbarians."
                                    C.P. Cavafy
                            (Translation by Rae Dalven)

"113. And again they say that from them that have it shall be redistributed
                    by the United Nations.
114. And yet again that the landlord be shorn of his land and give it to them
that have none. But I say, the land hath been improved by the United
Cashcrop Company, thou shall not covet thy neighbour's plantations.
                                    ....
125. Nay, I say unto you, blessed are the strong, for they have inherited the
                    earth. This is the law and the profits."
                    From "The Gospel according to the New Right."
                    The Economist, 29 September 1984.

"... right, as the world goes, is only in question between equals in power,
while the strong do what they can and the weak suffer what they must."
            The Athenians to the Melians, 418 B.C. Thucydides, Book V
                    89. (Translation by R. Crawley)

13.   Outside Countries in the Conflict

Rationale and Setting

Our world is already exceedingly interdependent and grows more so daily. The international aspects of agrarian conflict and reform are extremely important, at times more important than internal factors, if one can separate and assess such inextricably linked reciprocal influences. Yet for no apparent reason, this vital dimension has remained almost totally unexplored at all comprehensively. Here this wide-ranging, complex and critical component can be treated only tentatively as an integral part of this study in its aim of giving a rounded view of a problem with so many strands and such an agglomeration of complex patterns.

The outside influences felt by a country depend on many variables: its size, location and endowment; the size and nature of its economy; the social and political conditions; the share of foreigners in such important economic factors as land and water, agricultural production, marketing and processing, supply of inputs, rural infrastructure (especially communications), finance for agriculture and related activities, and transmission of information, knowledge and technology; political, economic and financial dependency through political influence, if not control, by outsiders; military cooperation with, if not dominance by, another country; and indebtedness or other financial obligations to other countries or institutions influenced by them; trade and aid relations; and general ideological and interest links between the country's élites and those of other countries.

A second important set of variables, which provides the impetus for, and control over, the operation of the above elements, is the competence of the ruling élites of the country, their orientation, perception of their interests, the ways and direction chosen for the pursuit of those interests and the role they have assigned to their supporters or allies outside the country. The interests of the mass of the rural people are only subordinate.

Alliances with foreign interests, and patronage by them, must of course serve the purposes of those interests. Patron/client relationships, whether voluntary or constrained, always unequal, give ample scope to the patron's interests, including essentially the main initiative. Even aid is no exception. As far back as 1964 Chenery described the main objective of US aid as with "other tools of foreign policy, is to produce the kind of political and economic environment in the world in which the United States can best pursue its own social goals."[1] In other words ". . . aid-receiving between nations would always be a matter of optimisation of mutual interests of the governments involved; serving the cause of the poor . . . has *per se* nothing to do with it".[2]

We have already referred to the penetration by multinational companies of the economy of practically every country in the world. Hitherto multinational ventures in developing countries have been exclusively in the hands of major enterprises from a very few *developed* countries. But since the early 1970s new developments have taken place in the form of "joint ventures", which make use of capital from oil-producing and exporting countries and of land and labour in less well-endowed developing countries. Examples include: the Africa Plantation Company, established in 1971 by an investment corporation of Kuwait and Sudanese investors; the Indo-Malaysian venture, 1972, by public interests, for 60,000 tons of refined sugar and sugar plantations; the Thai-Malaysian Company for Poultry Development, 1974, by State Malaysian interests and private Thai ones; the Arab Livestock Company, owned by 10 countries, to produce and process livestock and fodder, with $165 m. equity; the Arab-Brazilian Development Corporation, 1975, owned by Brazilian and Kuwaiti financial corporations; and the Colombia-Venezuela venture to develop 780,000 ha. of sugar cane near their border and to process it.[3] A recent venture is a combined enterprise by the Jamaican Government and an Israeli entrepreneur and associates, who pooled $30 m. to use Jamaican labour and Israeli Kibbutz specialists and experience, to develop large scale specialised farm and livestock production for export.[4] The venture was reported to have failed, in one case because of the choice of poor soils for winter vegetables.[5]

These ventures combine agricultural and agro-industrial development on modern lines. The most ambitious was the Basic Programme for Agricultural Development in the Sudan, 1976–1985, by 13 Arab states, with $500 m., comprising infrastructure and a small farmer development, from which not much profit was to be expected, and modern large-scale agricultural enterprise from which the commercial profit could give overall profitability to the venture. The aim was to provide investment opportunities for Arab capital and to utilise excess supply of labour and land in the Sudan. The venture hoped to increase food supplies for participating countries, increase utilisation of industrial capacity in the countries involved and extend industrial development into agricultural inputs, such as fertilisers and machinery.[6] Viewed against the famine that engulfed large parts of Sudan in 1984–85, this throws light on both the complexities of the problem and the development priorities of the élites involved. In early 1987 in Khartoum there were "continuous traffic jams . . . new buildings, plenty of good bread, video libraries and a reasonable selection of imported goods . . . to keep the townspeople happy . . . [fruits also of assistance by] Western and conservative Arab countries . . . to keep [Sudan] free of Marxism, Islamic fundamentalism . . ."[7]

Problematic Elements Bearing On Agrarian Conflict and Reform

We may divide problem elements into those that concern the general setting and environment and those more closely related to the genesis and progress of agrarian reform.

General Conditions

The size and location of a country influence its general economic weight and links with other countries. Economic weight is a key to influence. Monopoly, or even oligopoly, over any key economic factors confers considerable potential influence. Potential weight is not, however, the same as actual weight.

Historical links, some of them involving dependency, condition many a country's economic structure and prospects for development. The most obvious examples are former colonial dependencies, some of whose patterns of economic development and relations, even decades after independence, have remained largely unchanged.

In this context the world economy is viewed as a bi-modal system, comprising the core (or centre) and the periphery. Roughly speaking, the core is formed by the few advanced industrialised countries, while the rest, mainly developing countries, are peripheral. On grounds of products, and levels of wages and profits some theorists[8] insert between these categories a third, the semi-peripheral countries. There are, of course, the further "complications" of the recent OPEC ascendancy to *financial* influence. In reality there is a hierarchy of centrality and periphericity in "an interaction between the autonomous expansion of an international capitalist division of labour and the power of individual nation-states in securing unequal shares of the distribution of resources within this world system".[9]

This approach is often linked with dependency theory which divides countries into dominant and dependent ones. Dominant countries "expand through self-propulsion" and "are endowed with technological, commercial, capital and socio-political predominance over dependent countries . . . and can therefore exploit them, and extract part of the locally produced surplus". Dependent countries "can only expand as a reflection of the expansion of the dominant countries".[10]

Often a parallel is drawn between national and international processes of surplus appropriation.

> Institutionally the appropriation of wealth generated in the satellite takes place directly through capital transfers by landowners (often absentees) to metropolitan centres (national or international) or directly through the terms of trade . . . and through metropolitan control of the commercial and financial centres.[11]

A further important point is that

> the peculiar virtue of private foreign enterprise, namely that it brings a "package" of capital enterprise, management and know-how, is also its peculiar defect: it means that monopoly rents and profits accruing to

those factors go abroad, and that only the reward of unskilled or semi-skilled labour, in highly inelastic supply and with little bargaining power, goes to the host country.[12]

Again, we note "that anti-trust action and restrictive practices tend to be outlawed for domestic activity but permitted in international ones".[13]

Increasingly and in the final analysis, advanced countries derive their dominance not only from their stage of development but also from overwhelming preponderance in research and technology and in financial institutions. The dominance of a few strong countries is now mostly exercised through large multinational companies, many of whose individual economic power far exceeds that of many small countries and an even greater number of governments.[14]

Ultimately, of course, the dominant economies have the power of coercion:

> In the longer-run [confrontation between developed and developing countries] is bound to stimulate defensive and harmful responses from governments and peoples of the developed world. The developed countries who have the military, political and economic power can only be persuaded by appeals to mutual interest.[15]

The vast majority of today's "independent" countries, therefore, have varied, but generally limited, room for truly independent decisions on issues affecting the interests of powerful economic (and military) powers; to a lesser extent this also applies to those affecting the interests of indigenous groups within dependent countries, who are allied to foreign interests. This is particularly true of agrarian reform; it is not uncommon for indigenous interests to appeal to foreign backers for support. When the foreign interests' own resources, or activities likely to be materially affected by agrarian reform, are threatened, the alliance becomes quite explicit. "United States support of land reform in Japan and Taiwan appears to have been unique. In neither case was US-owned land involved."[16] At the 1970 Spring Review of Land Reform Ernest Stern, Assistant Administrator for Program and Policy Coordination, in his Concluding Remarks on "An AID Policy for Land Reform", said that in "the past the US has been notably reluctant to become involved in any aspect of land reform and its attitude has sometimes actually prevented progress" but the US policy was "moving from apathetic neglect to benign interest and a willingness to share in the effort".[17] In reality attitudes are far more complex and action has varied over time and from country to country, according to how the US perceived its own interests.

Foreign Ownership of Land
Ownership by non-nationals of land within a country, while not uncommon, is not well-documented. Nationals of the metropolitan powers, and of other favoured countries, acquired much of the land during the colonial period. Some of these non-indigenous people were encouraged to settle and

develop farming enterprises. The larger holdings were (some still are) owned by major commercial interests who developed plantation enterprises. Others purchased land for investment or for enterprises, including plantations, in many countries.[18] Even when legislation limits or forbids foreign ownership, there are ways and means of acquiring land, for instance, through the use of "national" companies or with nationals serving as a "front". A government report in 1971 stated that "Ceylonization has meant principally that Ceylonese Agents became available to look after non-national interests" in estate (plantation) land.[19]

Foreign concerns not only own land, but also engage in agricultural production, processing and trade, and manage rural infrastructure, especially transport and processing. In some countries their total share in land ownership is significant within agricultural production; combined with marketing and processing, it can exercise a strategic hold on key aspects of the economy.

If they do not actually invite in foreign interests, many countries' ruling élites welcome their presence because they share the benefits and derive support from such an alliance for the achievement or preservation of their status. The situation, however, is generally unstable. Before they came to power, ruling élites often campaigned on a nationalist ticket and their opponents can exploit the force of nationalism. That wealthy foreigners have a large share of the better lands in places where acute landlessness and poverty exist is an obvious "provocation" leading to conflict, while a large share, if not a monopoly, in the export trade (and in the imports of inputs) and in key processing lines becomes a focus of discontent on the part of suffering small producers tinged with nationalist fervour. The charge of "collaborationism", i.e. collusion between indigenous landed interests and colonial rule or oppressive foreign interests in pre-independence times, also arouses nationalist stirrings. This unstable situation can provoke a number of adverse reactions.

Where multinational companies have penetrated developing countries, the rising middle classes and élites (especially the aristocracy, the political class, the bureaucracy and the officer class) have in recent years increasingly taken advantage of the new technology and multinational approach to production to enter capitalist farming, at times on a large scale. They have thus developed an interest in both large landownership and close relations with the multinationals which supply inputs or act as processors or exporters of produce.

Foreign ownership of land is thus of critical importance in many countries, but precise and detailed information does not exist and a good deal of reticence surrounds the subject.

Plantations: Information on this form of agricultural enterprise exists, but there is very little quantitative material. The most comprehensive treatment, that of Beckford,[20] applies the term plantation economy "to those countries . . . where the internal and external dimensions of the plantation system dominate the country's economic, social and political structure and its relations to the rest of the world". The countries listed are: Cuba, Jamaica, Haiti, Dominican Republic, Puerto Rico, Antigua, St. Kitts, Guadeloupe, Martinique, Dominica, St. Lucia, St. Vincent, Grenada, Barbados, Trinidad, Guyana, Brazil, British Honduras, Liberia, Portuguese Guinea, Rio Muni, Cameroon, Zaire, Angola, Mozambique, Mauritius, Reunion, Comoro Islands, Sri Lanka, Malaya, Indonesia, Philippines and Fiji. To these he added countries containing only, or also, plantation sub-economies (defined as part of larger national economies with which economic relationship is very much akin to that between plantation economies and their metropolitan counterparts) as follows: N.E. Brazil, the Caribbean Lowlands of Honduras, Guatemala, Costa Rica, Panama, the US South and Hawaii. Other countries with plantation sectors not listed include: Peru, Tanzania, Ethiopia, Ivory Coast, Malawi, Kenya, Somalia, India and New Caledonia.

Many of these plantations have been expropriated and passed into national ownership (private or state), as in Cuba, Guyana, Peru, Tanzania, Ethiopia, Angola, Mozambique and Cameroon. The opposite happened in Ghana, where, after the 1966 military coup, Firestone Rubber purchased the rubber estates originally established as state farms. Thus the trend is mixed. Some plantations pass to indigenous élites; some foreign ones expand, e.g. in Malaysia, Indonesia and Belize; most development is now in joint ventures.

The plantation sector has varied in size: in Guyana,[21] at the time of nationalisation, one multinational company, Booker McConnel, controlled 80% of the area under sugar, while another 10% was in the hands of Jessels Securities. The sugar area averaged 50,000 ha., and the area controlled by these two companies was "the best drained and irrigated, the most fertile, and the most accessible agricultural land in Guyana". Over 50% of the land used by Booker McConnel was rented from the state "at peppercorn rental". The peasant sector harvested 12% of the area but had to sell its cane to the estate to which each peasant was attached. These attached peasant holdings had to conform to other controls by the plantations which included housing and production operations. In Cameroon it was estimated[22] that plantations of foreign origin in the South, now nationalised, covered 2–3 per cent of the cultivated area, provided employment to 1–2 per cent of the active population and contributed 10% of export produce. In Sri Lanka[23] in 1974 the plantation sector, then foreign-owned, accounted for 16% of the GNP, 25% of employment and 72% of foreign exchange earnings. Foreign owned plantations in 1970 numbered 182 (tea) and 96 (rubber). The area taken over in 1975, and vested in the Land Reform Commission, totalled nearly 80,000 ha.

In Liberia[24] six foreign firms operate rubber plantations totalling 60,000 ha. the largest being Firestone. Timber concessions cover 1.6 m. ha. In Kenya[25] in 1977 there were 675 plantations, mostly coffee, tea and sugar cane estates, covering 40,000 ha. Kenyanisation increasingly takes the form of Kenyans buying shares in tea companies. Since 1972 the Kenya government have prevented Brooke Bond Liebig from buying more land; some élites and the government bought shares in it; and some indigenous capitalists, including senior officers of the Kenya Tea Development Authority and several government ministers, proceeded to develop tea cultivation outside the smallholder system.[26]

Areas listed in a report by Panama[27] include: 42,392 ha. owned by the Chiriqui Land Co.; 3,992 ha. owned by Chiriqui Citrus (American Company); and 50,000 ha. of the Amsterdam S.A.

In Brazil, Jari S.A owns a ranch of 1,500,000 ha., Mitsubishi and Volkswagen possess respectively 300,000 ha. and 200,000 ha., Robin McGlohn 400,000 ha., and Toyomenka 300,000 ha., helping to make the country the leading beef producer. The government offers subsidies for these developments. In fruit production, Castle and Cook have a plantation of 100,000 ha.[28] Esman[29] gives figures of the estimated percentage of plantation workers in the rural labour force. Mauritius with 32.8 ha. by far the highest; Liberia 6.3; Ivory Coast 7.2; Kenya 4.5; Tanzania 4.4; Cameroon 2.9; Ghana 2.2; Uganda 1.8; and Nigeria 0.2.

There is considerable mobility in pursuit of capital gains, profits or safe operations. Ecuador has an "unblemished record of relations with foreign companies", yet US companies left in the 1960s, perhaps because of whiffs of agrarian reform, to go to Central America; they have now returned to begin production.[30] Gulf and Western of the USA sold its properties in 1984, including the world's largest sugar-producing unit *La Central Romana* in the Dominican Republic, making the future of 22,000 workers uncertain. The buyers were two Cuban American entrepreneurs. That firm was the second largest employer in the country, after the government.[31]

Medium-sized Farms in Considerable Number. If data on plantations are scanty, information on the considerable number of foreign-owned and operated medium-sized farms is practically non-existent. Information only appears when independence or a change of regime takes place on a nationalist tide, especially if armed conflict is involved.[32]

We have already discussed the well-known cases of Kenya and Algeria. Mozambique and Angola fought wars of liberation to reclaim their lands; but Zimbabwe has to wait even after liberation. "Freedom from Deprivation of Property", a clause entrenched in the 1980 Lancaster House Independence Constitution remains unalterable for a decade. The victorious ZANU PF Party campaigned in the liberation war on a platform of land reform, for its distribution and labour conditions were unfair to Africans. Two years after independence 5,500 large scale white farmers still owned 36% of the land, produced 68% of agricultural output, employed 35% of African labour and accounted for over 90% of marketed produce and for 56% of agricultural exports. African farmers have been crowded into the native reserves, known as communal land and number 675,000. This is a colonial heritage which confined 35% of the population on marginal lands while a minority (some 2,600) of large-scale white settlers occupy over three-quarters of the country's best land.[33] The Independence Government announced an intensive resettlement programme, aiming to buy 1.1 m. ha. for that purpose, but, until the Constitution is amended land can effectively be purchased only on a willing buyer-willing seller basis. The cost is prohibitive, because land prices went up and landowners were willing to sell poor land. The estimated 375,000 "excess" families on the reserves and the government may have to wait.[34] Under the provisions of the Lancaster House Constitution, if land is acquired under a compulsory purchase order, it must be paid for in foreign exchange.[35]

In the notorious regime of South Africa (and Namibia), monopoly of land and territorial separation are pillars of the racist systems. Conflicts are mounting and repression increasing. Conflicts also persist in varying degrees in Botswana, Zambia, Malawi, Ivory Coast, Zaire, Gabon, Swaziland, Lesotho and Niger. A study of Botswana[36] gives the following data: of blocks of concessions by the colonial authorities to European farmers of generally more fertile land, totalling 29,000 sq. km.; those farmers are still a dominant economic factor in an independent country, in 1971 contributing 55% of all cattle exports and in 1969/70 producing 68% of the country's maize. A recent Labour Inspection report described the position of natives employed in these areas as "voluntary slavery". The irony is that all development efforts by the government, and other changes, tend to favour these few privileged farmers and to strengthen their position, rather than to benefit the native rural majority.

Foreign control of agriculture is a serious factor in that, cumulatively, a vast amount of land and agricultural production is in the hands of a considerable number of medium capitalist foreign producers who are encouraged, or permitted, by the countries' authorities to invest and expand their activities. The justification is that they benefit the country with higher production, productivity, employment and contribution to exports. Often such operations are hidden behind a façade of native enterprise and "participation."[37] We need much more light on this important problem and more substantiated analysis.

Control of Important Areas of Production and Distribution

Ownership of a large proportion of agricultural land creates problems for the foreign interests concerned so that shrewder sections seek other, more trouble-free, modes of operation.

With government participation or encouragement plantation firms, and other agribusiness interests, commonly cooperate with small producers in "nuclear or core plantation" developments. Essentially this comprises a foreign-owned and/or run processing activity within a central estate (the nucleus), and the neighbouring small producers of the same crop, e.g. sisal or sugar cane, working on their own account.[38] The plantation or agribusiness firm provides technical assistance to small producers on their farms and processes their produce in its plant; it also employs some of them (and others) on its own nucleus estate and in processing. The long-term idea is often for the whole enterprise to be taken over from the foreign firm by the producers jointly (or by the government). Meanwhile the foreign concern has a period of secure and profitable activity (10 to 20 years) and time to consolidate its export-import marketing position. It also retains the good will of the government and of the interested producers.

Multinational, plantation and other major foreign agricultural producers willingly sell their surplus land and even their developed farms at good prices and concentrate on processing and marketing, in which they build up a monopoly, while achieving great flexibility by operating in more than one country.[39] They derive, of course, strength from their entrenched and specialised position in the international, and especially their home, market. The United Fruit Company in Central America has maintained "the great white fleet" and control of marketing in the USA after it disengaged from its plantations in some Latin American countries. Such a land sale strengthens the position of foreign interests, gives a good image to a friendly political leadership and ensures the entrenchment of cooperating local élites who succeed them in land ownership.

Multinational firms and other major agribusiness interests change over to or enter more profitable and flexible economic activities in which they can build a monopoly or key position. Thus seed production, livestock development and forestry exploitation become important areas of activity in developing countries, usually under licence and often in partnership with local interests or with state institutions.[40] They opt for flexible (in that disengagement[41] is less difficult) and profitable opportunities for use of their technological and organisational (including management) superiority. Of the 87 agri-food companies on which data were compiled in 1972 (and of which 69 were multinational), 44 diversified their activities upstream into production. Such integration is limited by the risks involved in agricultural production. Companies with production components include Castle and Cook with 100,000 ha. in the Pacific Islands for pineapples, CPC International with seed for grains and Ralston Purina and Central Soya with integrated stock breeding.[42] Belize, "an uncut jewel waiting to be exploited" according to the country's most prominent businessman, is offering state-owned forest land for agribusiness. Coca Cola has started on a development of citrus cultivation of up to 40,000 ha. for orange concentrate exports.[43]

Because in developing countries the share of state or parastatal institutions in development activities tends to be very large, foreign concerns enter into partnership with such institutions in a number of activities: land clearance, plantations, ranching, special farming operations, forest exploitation, processing, fertiliser production, input supply or production, and so on.[44] Often these state or parastatal institutions serve as no more than "sleeping partners." Some are only supervisors of concessions. Partnerships are sought also with local private concerns, which at times provide only the name and the façade.

The Ivory Coast concessions to multinational companies have raised the country to the rank of the largest wood exporter in Africa and the fifth in the world – but at a very high price. The dense tropical forests, which in 1960 covered 10 m. ha. shrank within 20 years to only 3 m. ha. and, many experts feel, are doomed to disappear within a matter of years, since they are shrinking at the rate of 0.5 m. ha. annually. The rape of the country's forests has been not only a matter of wholesale destruction by timber companies; the latter have also scoured huge areas for the most valuable species. With loans from the World Bank the Government has launched reafforestation projects, which, if successful, will enable 20,000 ha. to be replanted over five years.[45]

A love-hate relationship prevails between multinationals and local élites, some welcoming them and sharing in the spoils, others fearing them but using them. In this climate there is a good deal of blowing hot and cold because the dominant élites are divided or have different political perceptions. Multinational companies can look after themselves, since by their own nature they can escape such outside (i.e. local) control. They operate integrated systems of production, processing and marketing and have privileged access to finance. They own patents and have numerous lines of activity as well as a high degree of integration. Thus in Central America, United Brands acquires 86% of its bananas from company-owned land; Castle and Cook 62% and Del Monte 58%. Multinational companies increasingly concentrate on brand foods. Cross-border intra-firm transactions give them the opportunity to decide where they will declare their profits, pay taxes, hold working capital, reinvest earnings; thus they hold the upper hand when it comes to monitoring efforts by any national authority.[46] Their control of trade can be truly overwhelming. For instance, one company, Gill and Duffus controls 40% of cocoa on the world market, Unilever totally dominates the world trade in palm oil, Brooke Bond Liebig and Finlays dominate the world tea trade, General Foods (Maxwell House) dominate the coffee trade and a Tate and Lyle subsidiary controls 40% of the world molasses trade.[47]

Even the combined efforts of several governments can be defeated by the might of multinational corporations.

> In early 1974 seven Central and South American states formed a Union of Banana Exporting Countries (UBEC) and proceeded to raise export taxes against the opposition of the major US fruit companies. The companies retaliated by [*inter alia*] cutting production in and purchases from the countries concerned, eventually forcing UBEC states to reduce or entirely remove the new taxes.[48]

In a wider context the United Nations Centre for Transnational Corporations confirms that

> increased ownership and control of production by host countries have not significantly reduced their dependence on transnational corporations as regards access to technology, market and the distribution channels. It is estimated that in the late 1970s approximately 80 per cent of the exports of agricultural commodities from developing countries remained under the control of such corporations.[49]

Their strong point is marketing, which in some commodities, above all in bananas, coffee, tobacco and cotton, is highly concentrated in very few corporations. Furthermore, such corporations can exert strong indirect influence on production through contract production, consulting services to national enterprises or patents of new varieties. Progress in the genetic revolution will give them added power.

Zorn sums it all up:

> Even where ownership and control of production is in the hands of small producers or of the State itself, TNC control at the processing, transportation and marketing levels, as well as TNC influence in the international price-setting mechanisms for agricultural products, can significantly affect the ultimate return to producers and host country treasuries . . . Direct access by producer countries to markets in developed countries continues to be difficult.[50]

Foreign Interests and Agrarian Reform: Perceptions and Reactions

Agrarian reform may be part of any policy inspired by nationalist aspirations. Militant nationalist élites, even if merely seeking political legitimacy, will not "tolerate" such "provocations" as monopoly over the best land by wealthy foreigners; the large income from lands developed and operated with low-paid indigenous or imported (indentured) labour; the control – often viewed as a stranglehold – over agricultural production, processing and trade; or the general dominance by "exploiting" foreigners of the country's economic and social life. Support for such élites is easier to gain if nationalist feeling is also directed against internal political enemies who collude with the foreign interests.

Ownership of large estates or farming enterprises was an early, at times the only, target for agrarian reform programmes: Algeria, Kenya, Tunisia and Morocco. Revolution from above had similar tendencies: Egypt, Peru, Panama, Ethiopia; the Islamic Revolution in Iran. Some countries have hesitated: the Philippines specifically excluded foreign-owned plantations from its 1972 agrarian reform decrees; Sri Lanka nationalised foreign plantations 2–3 years after its major reform of indigenously owned land. Uganda in a widespread anti-foreign campaign took over many farms, including a large tea estate of 2,000 ha. belonging to Mitchell Cotts. Finally, Cuba, Mozambique and Angola took over foreign-owned land without compensation.

Foreign interests directly affected are primarily in landowning. Agrarian reform also includes linked processing and trade activities included in expropriation by the government, processing as part of nationalisation of industries, trade through transfer to official marketing boards or cooperatives. These linkages may deter reform because multinationals have a trump card which they can use to make it a Pyrrhic victory.

> Agribusiness multinationals . . . with long history of foreign involvement in agriculture [normally] the plantation-based companies – United Fruit and Tate and Lyle – are generally vertically integrated, have a fairly wide geographic compass, and have a cushion of political influence . . . They are in a position to play different countries off against each other, particularly since they tend to operate in small countries that are largely dependent upon a single plantation crop.[51]

In these circumstances agrarian reform faces not only external strength, but also internal opposition, since it will usually involve heavy "sacrifices" by at least some powerful indigenous élites. Only a regime capable of fighting successfully on both fronts can bring about nationalisation.[52]

Some plantation and other dependent economies rely so much for employment, income, capital investment, production and trade on a few firms, sometimes only one or two, that the government of such a country is a very poor and weak institution against the power of foreign firms. This powerful presence of economic giants even qualifies the sovereignty of many developing countries to the extent that some writers[53] consider the trend to be against the nation-state and in favour of multinational companies. Thus an agrarian reform that challenges powerful interests such as these requires backing from a strong state, i.e. one with impregnable internal support and powerful allies abroad.

In the rare instance of a determined government nationalising such foreign interests, powerful weapons are deployed against the action. They will mobilise internal allies – strong indigenous interests (partners, agents, bureaucratic and political supporters), their (privileged) employees and the middle class; they will use the media to undermine faith in the state's capacity to manage the enterprises and to cast doubt on the motives behind the expropriation; they will give "friendly" warnings as to what will happen in the marketing field and to the financial benefits which the "country" has enjoyed; and they will employ the best indigenous and foreign lawyers to challenge the legislation in the local courts.[54]

External marketing outlets can be inhibited, if not closed, foreign financial institutions alerted and mobilised to deny the "offending" country credit, since the country has "violated established norms" and developed a "climate hostile to foreign investments."

Finally, the political might of the mother country will be mobilised to exert pressure on the developing country to desist if it is contemplating expropriation or to think again if it has carried one out; otherwise the government of the mother country will not be able to secure aid for the developing country or may have to cancel aid because parliament or congress are "angry" at this breach of faith. Sometimes even the use of force may be vaguely implied. Certainly "fair" compensation will be expected. The lobbies in parliament or congress of the mother country will be more vociferous and threatening. The press of the mother country and the mass media, including the major international ones, will provide a wide-ranging campaign, reproduced by the internal media.

Faced with such powerful and orchestrated hostility expropriation of major foreign agricultural interests can take place "normally" only when there is a radical change in the regime, often after an armed struggle to overthrow the previous regime, especially in a liberation war. Cuba is an example of such struggle to overthrow the previous regime; Peru of a takeover by armed forces after a *coup d'état*; Vietnam, Algeria, Mozambique and Angola of protracted liberation wars resulting also in the flight of foreign owners; Chile under Allende acted in the wake of an electoral victory; and Sri Lanka in the aftermath of a rebellion by young radicals.

At times mild takeovers occur only after a protracted "softening" period. This provides the opportunity for foreign interests to slow down and even cease investment; they "decapitalize" their enterprises in the country, develop alternative economic activities and strengthen their position else-where; in short, they prepare new and better defensive positions and/or cut their losses. In a parallel internal process powerful interests save what they can.

Both the central protagonists – foreign interests and their indigenous allies on the one hand and the country's ruling élites on the other – often ignore conflict at the grassroots. Yet, when battlelines are drawn, the rural people involved are the primary actors. The overcrowded, poverty-ridden, and marginalised neighbours of the prosperous foreign concerns may develop or acquire a leadership to guide their agitation, as in the Naxalite movement or the 1950s Malayan rebellion. The Castro armed struggle had support from such sources since Oriente Province where he operated for three years had more than four-fifths of the country's squatters and some of the largest sugar-cane farms.[55]

While labour employed by foreign interests is in a better position to organise because of similar conditions of work, i.e. in large groups, its organisations may choose to defend sectional or corporate interests, i.e. to protect their own relatively privileged positions. In this they are aided and abetted by "enlightened" foreign employers and even by the government. Foreign employers may, however, accentuate the militancy of their organised employees by unenlightened policies such as high-handed anti-union be-haviour and by a superior attitude. This may unite organised labour with the mass of the rural people, especially in a protracted labour dispute, and lay the foundations for a formidable struggle. Support may then be mobilised from national labour unions or other labour sectors. With multinational companies, the support of international trade union federations may also be provided; but hitherto this has not been common or effective.

The two aspects of this problem, the wealth, income and social contrasts,[56] inherent in the situation and the "foreign-ness" of the interests involved, i.e. the combination of a call for social justice with a patriotic appeal, can mobilise wide support in the country, and sooner or later some political élites will use it.

Usually powerful foreign interests are able to cope with situations but at times they invoke support from the home country,[57] and other sympathetic countries. This powerful card can be played very effectively. Some countries, notably the USA, have legislation and strong lobbies ready to deal with any country that expropriates property of their own nationals.[58] Punishment takes various forms: the cutting of aid (including investments and credit) trade war, financial and banking penalisation, and political proscription.

Fomenting agitation and strain within the country is achieved through agents and by influence within the native armed forces, some of whom may have been trained in the foreign country concerned; they may be equipped with arms from that country and have established a camaraderie with their counterparts. Threats of military intervention have often been alternately used and denied as a war of nerves.

The climate is changing, at least at the ideological level, as a result of the proclamation by the United Nations General Assembly of the principles of the New International Economic Order, including that concerning the sovereignty of the country over its own natural resources. Not all countries fully subscribe to this principle, especially those with legislation and lobbies against expropriation by the governments of the host countries of properties belonging to their nationals.

To date the debate on the New International Economic Order and the North/South Dialogue has had very meagre results. The power of those who monopolise the benefits of the existing system is overwhelming and the Dialogue too unequal for effective progress. Part of the weakness lies in the fact that

> the majority of élites speaking in the name of the South *have from the outset* been the spokesmen for, and in some cases the direct agents of, national and international, class interests quite satisfied with the existing world economic system if not actually with their share of the pie.[59]

The international dimensions of agrarian reform extend even wider. The issue is seen as an important part in the contest between forces threatening wider economic and political interests, including "security". Agrarian reform thus becomes a symptom and symbol of, and therefore a target for, that wider contest.

In the mass media it is often presented as a battle of the military blocks into which the world is divided. It also helps justify foreign intervention or invitation to intervention and the activities of secret services. The ultimate deterrent and real obstacle to agrarian reform, which seriously affects the power structure, lies, however, in the dependency of most countries, a dependency at times bordering on helplessness.

Notes

1. Quoted in Nafziger 1979 p. 35.
2. Mitra 1976 p. 42.
3. United Nations 1977.

4. *The Economist* 22 September 1984 and the *Financial Times* 3 January 1985.
5. *Financial Times* 12 September 1986.
6. United Nations 1977; the Programme was to have cost $6 billion and to raise Sudan's agricultural production growth to six per cent a year. Doubts and difficulties made the parties start in 1981 on smaller projects. O'Neil 1983 pp. 60–61.
7. *Financial Times* 16 January 1987. All this against a background of civil war, famine and heavy indebtedness.
8. See e.g. Wallerstein 1974 pp. 3–7.
9. Holton 1985 p. 208.
10. Dos Santos 1973 pp. 76–77.
11. Cockcroft, Frank and Johnson quoted in Long 1977 p. 76.
12. Streeten 1973 p. 9.
13. Streeten 1980 p. 19.
14. In 1978, Unilevers, the world's biggest food business, had a turnover of $10,000 m. which was roughly equivalent to the combined gross national products of 25 African countries (including Angola, Mozambique and Gabon). See Hines and Dinham 1981 p. 5. "The value added by each of the top ten multinational corporations in 1971 was . . . greater than the gross national product of over 80 countries," United Nations 1973 p. 13.
15. Gardner, Okita and Udink 1974 pp. 19–20, quoted in Fagen 1978a p. 167.
16. Adams 1973 p. 137n.
17. Carter 1970 p. 30.
18. Sometimes when they leave a country as soon as it becomes independent they move to another which is still a colonial dependency or welcomes colonists of this kind. New Caledonia was favoured by such *colons*. Similarly French interests in the 1950s left South-east Asia and moved to African countries such as the Ivory Coast.
19. Quoted in Peiris 1984 p. 39.
20. Beckford 1973 pp. 12, 19, 16 respectively.
21. Information from Thomas 1979 pp. 204–231.
22. FAO 1978 p. 16.
23. Country Review Paper 1978a p. 11. Table 8.1, and Appendix XII. In 1950 foreign ownership of plantation land was almost three times the acreage at nationalisation in 1975, amounting to 69.1% of tea, 37.6% of rubber and 11.9% of coconut plantation acreage. Peiris 1984, Table 4, p. 38.
24. Country Review Paper 1979 p. 12. See also the *Financial Times* 11 May 1983. In 1983 Firestone produced half the rubber exported and is the largest employer after the government. *Financial Times*, 21 November 1985.
25. Country Review 1978b p. 12 and Table 7.
26. Swainson 1980 pp. 262–263.
27. Republica de Panamá 1978 p. 86.
28. Data from Fabre 1978 pp. 84–85.
29. Esman 1978 Table IV, pp. 505–506.
30. *Financial Times* 26 June 1985.
31. *Financial Times* 15 July 1986.
32. New Caledonia's agrarian structure first became common knowledge only in connection with the conflict of 1984. The French white settlers (*Caldoches*), own most of the best land. Some 2,000 landowners hold 336,797 ha. of the richest land. See *Financial Times* 16 November 1984.
33. These large farms average 1,640 ha., but according to surveys in 1981–2 the average area under crops was only 168 ha. per holding. See Weiner, Moyo, Munslow and O'Keefe 1985 p. 257. The authors analysed survey results and carried out their own studies and concluded that "roughly two-thirds to one-half of Zimbabwe's prime agricultural land is being neither cropped nor fallowed". Ibid. p. 269.
34. See Munslow 1985 pp. 41–58; and "Yates" 1981 pp. 68–88 from which information has been taken. In fact by 1985 only about 35,000 families were settled compared with 162,000 families envisaged and planned by the government. *Financial Times Survey: Zimbabwe*. 17 September 1987.
35. Kinsey 1983 p. 195 n. 24.

36. Transformation of Customary Land Tenure Systems, etc. 1978 pp. 11–13.
37. In Malawi the Government encouraged the continuation of settler farms and encouraged their expansion. At independence there were 74 estates averaging 200 ha., by 1973 there were 400 estates averaging 300 ha. and occupying three per cent of Malawi's arable land. All politicians, top civil servants and military officials are urged or even compelled to become large landowners (Mkandawire 1980 pp. 5, 14). The estate sector still accounts for 70% of all agricultural exports, but is now in crisis. Commercial banks to which they are indebted are appointing receivers to run them. This much-praised style of development, based on a policy of low prices to turn them into labourers on the estates, is now being reversed. The crisis does not affect foreign concerns, the overwhelming majority of which are British; Lonhro, the British multinational, still reigns supreme in sugar, tea and coffee (as well as textiles, packaging, beer and trade in motor vehicles, agricultural machinery, fuel and oil). See *Financial Times Survey: Malawi* 16 April 1985. When I was in Indonesia in the late 1970s the joke was that the generals had more company directorships under them than privates, being mainly used by the multinational corporations as "sleeping" directors to bypass laws or to ease and reduce costs of the corporations' activities in such matters as acquisition of land, securing import or foreign exchange permits and generally ensuring political support.

Belize does not use a façade. It provides attractive terms and has enticed many smaller individual investors, mainly from the US. Large holdings account for 60% of existing productive land, much of it in foreign hands. *Financial Times Survey: Belize* 16 October 1985.

38. The Mumias Project with Booker McConnell in sugar production in Kenya is an example. In the Ivory Coast, for instance, rubber plantations were developed in the 1950s onwards by French companies. Smallholder plantations have been recently developed by the industrial plantations with state support close by where the latex processing factory also is, to keep some benefits in the country. *Financial Times* 1 March 1985. Belize with Hershey had embarked on a model cocoa nuclear estate. *Financial Times* 16 October 1985.

39. Tate and Lyle with extensive interests in Jamaica, Trinidad, Zambia, Belize etc. began the "disinvestment" process in the late 1960s. The strategy was to expand shipping, trading, distribution and engineering and to become the dominant competitor in these. It was no longer necessary to own physical assets (sugarcane plantations and processing) in those countries for fear of expropriation. They were opting instead for offering services to the local sugar industries. "The company would control the key links between producer and consumer." Between 1970 and 1973 Tate and Lyle sold all or majority holdings in those physical assets, including land. Goldbury and McGinity 1979 pp. 490–495.

40. As was the case in Khuzistan in Iran during the Shah's regime. The Philippine government entered into partnership with the Malaysian-British multinational Guthrie Overseas Holdings for oil palm plantation of 4,000 ha. on land declared "virgin" but actually belonging to the indigenous Monobo tribesmen. *The Observer* 31 January 1982.

41. Disengagement from direct production can be harsh for the labour concerned. For instance a classic banana town like Palmar in Costa Rica can have no reason to exist after United Fruit ends its involvement in banana production. *Financial Times* 3 January 1985.

42. Bénetière 1976 pp. 5–7.
43. *Financial Times* 16 October 1985.
44. Examples abound: The Ethiopian Government and the Dutch HVA in sugar plantations and processing in pre-revolution days; British, Belgian and other plantation companies returning to Indonesia after the Sukarno era seek or have ensured government participation; on the other hand, some governments, e.g. the Bahamas and Belize welcome large-scale farm development and plantations by foreign agribusiness firms.

45. See *Financial Times* 9 December 1980.
46. See Laidlaw 1981 pp. 5–7. The Brandt Commission gave an estimate that "intra-firm trade", i.e. between the parent firm and its affiliated enterprises amounted to over 30 per cent of world trade. See Brandt Commission 1980 p. 178.

47. Hines and Dinham 1981 p. 4. In 1980 three US-based Transnational Corporations

(TNCs) controlled 90% of the banana market in the USA and 80% in Japan; eight TNCs control up to 60% of coffee sales in the world; six transnational tobacco-leaf buyers control up to 90% of all tobacco entering international trade. These and similar examples can be seen in Zorn 1985 pp. 45–50.

48. Girvan 1975 p. 42.

49. United Nations Centre for Transnational Corporations 1983 pp. 212–220.

50. Zorn 1985 pp. 45, 47.

51. Dahlberg 1979 pp. 109–110.

52. President Nyerere of Tanzania is reported to have regretted the nationalisation of the sisal estates and the replacement of their management. BBC Broadcast 25 May, 1985.

53. See e.g.: Vernon 1971 and Johnson 1975.

54. For the reaction of W.R. Grace Corporation, mobilisation of support in its home country, the USA, and the final settlement following its nationalisation by the Velasco government in Peru, see Sigmund 1980 pp. 195–196, 205.

55. Domínguez 1978 p. 435.

56. Modern agribusiness may develop large population concentrations. The Casa Grande in Peru, 75% of which was owned by European and American interests, had in 1970 a population of 32,000 and an economically active population of 4,500. The Paramonga of the W.R. Grace (American) Corporation had 20,000 and 2,000 respectively; here the management lived in a separate district in chalets, white collar employees in brick houses, foremen and skilled workers in adobe houses, unskilled labourers (80% of the work force) in rear blocks of adobe housing or in mat and stick shacks. From Paige 1975 pp. 142–144.

57. Colonial governments have waged war on anti-planter agitation and nationalist movements in Malaya and Kenya, Algeria and New Caledonia, the Congo, Mozambique and Angola. The Colonial Secretary, Oliver Lyttleton went to Malaya in 1951 to reassure the British rubber planters "of our determination to support them by all methods in our power". *The Observer* 3 January 1982 on the release of Cabinet papers under the 30-year-old rule.

58. "The State Department has always held that its duty to extend diplomatic protection to its citizens includes the defence of the property of American-based corporations against arbitrary or confiscatory actions by foreign governments if local remedies are exhausted." Sigmund 1980 p. 328. UN 1973 p. 43, goes so far as to suggest that "multinational corporations may be used by home governments as vehicles for the implementation of their foreign policy."

59. Fagen 1978a p. 119.

14. The United Nations System

Agrarian Reform, FAO and the United Nations System

Background

In the Preamble to its Declaration of Principles the World Conference on Agrarian Reform and Rural Development, held at the Food and Agriculture Organisation (FAO) headquarters, Rome, in July 1979 recognises

> that the United Nations system has a responsibility to formulate a new international development strategy and that the FAO, under the terms of its constitution, has an explicit obligation to elaborate those parts of this new strategy in regard to food, agriculture, nutrition and other areas of its competence, and should play a leading role in assisting developing countries to promote agrarian reform and rural development.

The Resolution of the Conference further refers to FAO's constitution, stressing the direct responsibility this places on FAO to "promote the common welfare by furthering separate and collective action . . ." for *inter alia* "bettering the condition of rural populations".

Formally the role of FAO within the UN System concerning agrarian reform was settled after a debate at the United Nations Economic and Social Council (ECOSOC) in July 1962 on the *Third Report on Progress in Land Reform*. The ECOSOC referred to FAO in Resolution 887 (XXXIV) as the organisation "which has the major role in this field", i.e. in land reform.

The formal position has not changed since 1962 but its practical application has experienced difficulties, especially since the constitutions of many UN agencies and units contain general assignments so that their respective spheres of responsibility tend to overlap.[1]

If the substantive aspects of agrarian reform and technical assistance have become the concern of specialised agencies, mainly FAO and other UN socio-economic and financing units, the UN General Assembly has provided the political support and impetus. In fact it launched the periodic reports on *Progress in Land Reform* as far back as November 1950, expressing its concern to see analysed "the degree to which unsatisfactory forms of agrarian structure . . . impede economic development and thus depress the standards of living especially of agricultural workers and tenants and of small and medium-sized farmers". The General Assembly also called for recommendations for improving the conditions of agricultural populations. This problem has, therefore, been with the UN system formally for almost four decades and the objectives and perceptions have evolved very little in substance despite some changes in handling.

Impulses and their Generation

Agrarian reform is not a "cold" subject or value-free. The UN system cannot insulate its own handling of agrarian reform from conflicting pressures and influences. On the contrary it is open to them more widely than national agencies. It is no accident that it was the General Assembly, i.e. the main political organ of the UN, that launched the system on its involvement with agrarian reform in the late 1940s; the "brave new world" was to be built on the ruins left by a destructive war and there was acute global political and ideological rivalry.

The two prominent champions of UN involvement with agrarian reform in 1950, the USA and Poland, represented the two main contrasting tendencies. The US government had been instrumental in introducing agrarian reform in occupied Japan and in Taiwan and South Korea and strongly advocated it in the newly liberated Philippines. The US was keen to break the power of the class of large landowners whom they considered, with justification, as pillars of the militarist caste that had led a destructive war in the case of Japan, and as collaborators with the Japanese occupation forces in the case of Korea; moreover, the traumatic "loss" of nationalist China was largely attributed to a tide of peasant support for the victorious Communists. The US believed, therefore, that building a class of small property owners, a rural lower middle class, would counteract radical tendencies and gave similar encouragement to Italy in the crucial late 1940s. The USA also had an abiding interest in the countries of Latin America where the rhetoric of agrarian reform served as an anodyne. In its efforts to involve the UN General Assembly in agrarian reform the USA was thus applying at the international level what it had practised or advocated in countries it controlled or influenced.[2]

Conversely, Poland represented the new socialist tendencies of Eastern Europe, freshly reinforced by the Chinese Communist victory, who viewed agrarian reform as the spearhead of that total transformation of the economy and society essential for broad-based development and the liberation of oppressed rural majorities. Before the war the large landowners were the people's oppressors and exploiters, and during the war collaborators with the occupation forces. Poland itself underwent profound territorial changes and was engaged in major resettlement programmes and in reform and reconstruction in the rural economy.

The 1950 General Assembly resolution (401 (V)) shows the system's early involvement in socio-economic matters; agrarian reform was considered central to economic development in developing countries, at least if "the agricultural workers and tenants and the small and medium-sized farmers" were not to be bypassed in the process.

The Operation of Impulses
States initiating impulses must secure sufficient support, especially since in the UN system, particularly in social and economic matters, confrontation and majority decisions are rarely viewed with favour. Support at UN forums is gained by resort to like-minded states and to allies or dependents.

Positive commitment is only one, albeit important, aspect; much numerical "support" springs from a "silent majority", or the belief that it would be inadvisable to oppose agrarian reform in such an innocuous forum. Too much UN "action" has proved to be no more than campaigns on paper. Much of the cynicism surrounding activities in this field rests on the cleavage between easy government "rhetoric" and "utopian" resolution-passing at the UN and inaction, even repression, at home.

As an inter-governmental machinery, the UN System derives its mandate, and financial and political support, from what *governments* decide at UN sessions and from what they do (or permit) in their own countries.

Actors Within the UN System
The main actors within the system are the delegations and secretariats. A government's role is played essentially by its representative(s) at important sessions of various bodies, through correspondence with units of the system, and through visits of UN staff to member countries.

Government Delegations: There is as much variety in the delegation of government role and the manner in which it is discharged as there are countries and occasions.

Discussion of agrarian reform usually features in general or political forums and in technical meetings. Very rarely is a delegation given a detailed or strict brief. How a country operates depends on its status in the particular UN body and the personal standing of its delegate(s). Thus a powerful and influential country is listened to and can have considerable impact with its initiatives or attitudes. An influential member of the so-called group of 77, or of the non-aligned movement, carries considerable weight and its role can be important. The role is, however, potential, and has to be played effectively.

Agrarian reform rarely gets a neutral treatment. Therefore, it requires a whole string of circumstances to get effective championship at any forum. The government brief to its delegation must be committed to, or permissive of, strong support for agrarian reform; the delegation must be interested and must overcome the class or status prejudices of the officials involved; and it must be active and able to operate effectively.

UN Secretariats: The secretariats of UN agencies have at least two main tasks; to suggest policies, action and programmes for approval by governing bodies, and to execute policies, action and programmes duly approved. Their role is clearly influential; they generate most of the ideas, policies and programmes and put their stamp on all action.

The role, therefore, of the UN system depends heavily on the attitudes of the secretariat staff. Agrarian reform is not a routine or low key activity and there can be pronounced bias.

The majority of senior staff, especially those with influence on policy-making, have for many years come from developed countries.[3] They are mostly from middle-class, urban, comfortable backgrounds and have no direct experience of rural poverty and little of rural life. Recently some staff from developing countries have entered policy-making positions, but that staff also come from well-to-do backgrounds, have been mostly educated at institutions of developed countries and have thus assimilated much of the culture and outlook of their *alma mater*. They look for approval and recognition among their "peers", i.e. intellectuals and officials from the universities and institutions of developed countries. Many have ambitions to make their home in developed countries and for reasons of prestige and high reward, to find a career in the constitutions of a developed country. In the final analysis, if one ignores the colour of their skin, there is little to choose among the senior staff in their élitist attitudes.[4]

The net result is that an influential part of the UN Secretariats is élitist, status quo oriented, and imbued with middle-class ideals, such as the right to security (even sanctity) of one's property, stability, orderly progress, due process of law and established procedure; many also have upper class ambitions and mannerisms; they are, therefore, instinctively against agrarian reform, which champions the cause of the underprivileged and aims at redistributing assets and changing power relations. Many have little knowledge of social or political sciences, and are genuinely out of their depth in trying to understand agrarian reform. Others have a diplomatic outlook with habits of obedience, tact and reticence remote from the conflicts inherent in agrarian reform. Nearly all have served as public servants or academics, or even held political office, in their own countries and are likely to return to similar jobs, preferably in developed countries.

In the circumstances, therefore, agrarian reform has no easy passage through the numerous screening and approving processes necessary to become part of the Programme and Budget of large organisations, nor is implementation easy after approval.

Some Special Mechanisms and Occasions

Technical Assistance: An important mechanism that directly affects a country is technical assistance, which, in recent decades, has been practically under United Nations Development Programme (UNDP) finance, although collateral or supporting activities, such as investigations or analysis, may come from regular budgets of UN units. The World Bank is now heavily involved in agricultural and rural development but operates with autonomy within the UN system. Agrarian reform is not easy to fit into "normal" technical assistance, except indirectly and as a long-range activity promoted through studies and training. Usually technical assistance comes into its own on special occasions, predominantly when a country is launching agrarian reform (or its undoing) after a change of regime, or when delaying tactics are resorted to by governments under pressure.

Technical assistance is provided at the request of the country's government. Because of its sensitive nature, agrarian reform does not lend itself easily to bilateral assistance. The UN system, being inter-governmental, tends to provide technical assistance on terms of the given government's choosing or subject to its final decision. In theory, UN assistance has a pluralistic background, is under the government's own control, and need not reflect national bias. However, objectivity and professionalism are not always adequate, either because of bias on the part of the responsible secretariats or from rivalry within the system.

Finally, technical assistance can be a timid affair because the UN system has no muscle of its own or because it treads unduly warily. Too often it eschews its catalytic influence in social and reform issues through overcaution and formalism. Apart from Headquarters conservatism, the composition of UN field staff and their relations with their counterparts in the countries are important. The 1972 annual report of the Administrator of UNDP showed that 15 advanced industrialised countries, which provided 88% of the total voluntary contributions for the system, also supplied 66% of the expertise, 87% of the equipment,[5] and 62% of the training facilities to 118 developing countries.

From time to time critical voices are raised regarding the quality and direction of assistance, including that of such senior UNDP staff as M. Marc Henry in *Le Monde* in January 1981. In the most critical views these agencies are seen as self-serving and self-perpetuating, large bureaucracies and technocracies that monopolise key development instruments, generate an organisational type not fully responsive to real needs, and, through training of aid-receiving country personnel, impart these qualities to the latter, thus increasing their alienation from the poor and powerless of their own countries.[6]

But developing country professional and bureaucratic élites are not always innocent victims. We have already referred to their aspirations to join well paying agencies so that, in pursuit of this aim, they do not exert themselves in negotiations on behalf of their country, while their academic output is geared to what the aid agencies perceive as fashionable.[7] In fact, the offering of posts, or the expectation of posts, in the UN system is often criticised as a strong conditioning factor in dealings between UN élites and national élites, with possible distortions of action or decision in both.

World Conferences and Special Committees: There have been two world conferences and one special committee on agrarian reform within the UN system in the last 20 years. They were attempts to give a shot in the arm to agrarian reform at times when interest within the system sagged considerably. On all three occasions the initiative came from inside and from two persons, one originating the first world conference, the other the second and the special committee. The second originator justified the launching of his two initiatives on the reasoning that, since the UN system normally ignored agrarian reform, "abnormal" attention through special events could allow it to survive and surface.

From what is known, intra-secretariat reaction to promoting agrarian reform through a major event of this kind, at least in its first stages, tends to be hostile. How it survives depends on the balance of internal bargaining and on motives that are difficult to assess. Some considerations are tactical and appropriate to a particular period.[8] If the initiative clears the foothills, the subject has to appeal to the political instincts and calculations of the highest echelons. If it manages to reach one of the governing organs, even as a tentative proposal, it usually attracts attention. Then the processes, and delegates' reactions, described above, permit it to start on its long road to fruition, at least as far as holding the conference is concerned. When, however, a conference becomes an accepted decision and preparations get under way, there is an impressive jumping on to the bandwagon within the secretariat.

It has often been remarked how conferences, even on such a subject as agrarian reform, tend to become large festivals with a good deal of pomp and even feasting; how they are characterised by boasting of a country's achievements and by very few polemics; and how a spirit of "consensus" prevails. Many find this quite unnatural. The simple explanation is that solemn declarations and plans of action agreed upon do not bind anybody.[9]

What then of the hopes and calculations of the originators? Experience has confirmed that the original idea of a real probing of the disturbing facts of rural life and their graphic presentation at a world forum, with urgent questions posed to the influential decision-makers for answers and action, never gets realised.

Does this mean that the whole thing is a waste of effort or, worse, a counter-productive exercise? The following considerations are relevant:

The fact that the issues are raised, in however smooth a form, helps to keep them alive. Light may be shed on the problems and in some countries may, thereby, generate a process of questioning, pressure-building, and even action.[10] Solemn declarations may conceivably be used by pro-reform forces as cheques to be cashed; for instance, oppressed groups may be encouraged to press their own ruling élites to honour their solemn international undertakings. This, of course, presupposes that the oppressed groups already have a voice and that they have knowledge of world conference pledges.

The UN system commits itself to some action in agrarian reform and especially to keeping issues alive. Experience has shown that not much comes out of this but, at a national level, interested parties may use it to press for commitments to be honoured.

The holding of a major conference is a rare event and an ineffectual conference can not only be a wasted opportunity but also serve as a blocking device for effective future action; since any attempt to get a new meeting or other action is frustrated with the argument that a major conference has been "successfully" held.

An ineffectual conference enhances cynicism among both enemies of agrarian reform and its genuine supporters.

The Special Committee set up by FAO with the cooperation of ILO and the UN was conceived by the originator as a means by which eminent people, who had held high office, could visit heads of state, and highly placed élites, in many countries in order to tap and assess experience and ideas at high policy levels; the assessed experience and analysed ideas were to be made an instrument for bringing to bear on action by countries and by the UN system, thus ensuring rapid and effective progress in agrarian reform.

The idea eventually received the approval of the governing organs. Implementation of the proposal was subjected to the internal influences of the secretariat; it resulted in a "balanced" committee membership (meaning the balancing of regional representation and members' outlook) and in an "ambitious" programme of travel. The probe was neither deep nor sustained; visits became essentially "polite" affairs, flattering each host's opinion of the government's performance; and such information as was gathered resulted in a brief and innocuous report of high ideals and general propositions.

The report was duly approved within the UN system and the Committee praised; it was solemnly agreed to keep its functions alive. Nothing was applied and the Committee was never reconvened.

A Much Neglected Vital Role

The UN system possesses unparalleled potential for beneficial influence in a role which it has never taken seriously. This role is the illumination of issues and the propagation of possible ways ahead in agrarian reform, which I have styled the *leadership role*. In 1971 the FAO officially adopted this point of view but never put it into practice. The system can exercise such a role independently, and act as an intellectual and moral force for the progress and welfare of humanity.

Hitherto innocuous, shallow surveys have been accompanied by muted and timid analyses of their implications. Options, if offered, are rarely more than tautologies or statements of the obvious.[11]

The influential voice of the UN system is thus indeed subdued, its contribution to knowledge and understanding well below its potential, and its guidance feeble. Those seeking to learn or to find solutions to their problems are offered no help. Agrarian reform is denied real help from its most hopeful source.

Propagation of principles and operation of conventions sound a weak way and a naïve approach to the UN system's role, especially in a climate of cynicism. Certainly they are not miracle-working instruments, and cannot be expected to produce immediate results. They do, however, raise the sights of those involved, they establish a code and a yardstick by which to make judgements, and through international emulation and one-upmanship, generally create an environment less congenial to obstructive policies.

Thus a combination of publicising facts and solutions with the establishment of standards of effective behaviour can give the UN system a unique place in the struggle for agrarian and other structural reforms and make it a beneficial influence far beyond its present mixed accomplishments. That, however, presupposes a different system.

Special Note on the World Bank

We have already referred to the World Bank in various parts of this work. It is a most, if not the most, powerful international institution in world development and its power is far from diminishing in spite of the ups and downs in the policies towards it of its most crucial and all-powerful member, the USA, who in addition has the privilege of having its own nominee elected as President. In theory the World Bank is a member of the United Nations System[12] but it is so powerful and imbued with such a sense of superiority that it can be considered totally apart from and ahead of the other members, who are, so to speak, its poor relations.

The strength of the World Bank, based on the economic power and foreign policy thrust of the USA, and to a much lesser extent that of the other rich industrialised (Western) countries[13] acting in concert, lies in the fact that it is endowed with funds for investment "beyond the dreams of avarice", compared with other units of the UN System who are very poor relations indeed. According to the Annual Report of the World Bank 1987, in fiscal 1987 the International Bank of Reconstruction and Development (IBRD) part of the World Bank disbursed $11.38 billion; and the International Development Association (IDA) part $3.48 billion.

The United Nations Development Programme (UNDP) is voted funds every two years and spends them through the UN Specialised Agencies and other units. The funds are not only considerably lower, the money is also of necessity distributed far too thinly by far too many agencies of the UN over practically all countries with hundreds of thousands of projects and causes. There is a rough distribution of labour: the UNDP and the Agencies carry out studies and feasibility investigations to be used by the World Bank, if the Bank is interested and approves; sometimes this is done in association with one or more of the Specialised Agencies with whom in many cases the Bank maintains a Joint Cooperative Programme. Such a Programme is largely financed by the World Bank and carries out the feasibility studies. The power remains firmly in the Bank's hands; and the Bank carries out its own feasibility studies and evaluations by its own staff or through a great number of consulting firms and academic institutions under contract to it.

The Bank's main characteristic is that it is a banking institution, in essence financed and controlled by the USA and its allies among the rich industrialised countries. Voting power is also roughly commensurate to a country's financial stake in the Bank. As a banking institution, it also borrows money in the money markets and lends it mainly at commercial rates of interest, except for its International Development Association which is funded with grants from governments and lends at highly concessionary rates. The Bank's strength lies in its engagement in direct action: seeking projects to finance, supervising and/or controlling all stages of study, approval, lending, spending and project implementation and evaluation. It has a permanent or semi-permanent corps of experts and hires, as required, a great number of others. It deploys a vast amount of development research and presents it effectively as authoritative, advanced, deep and penetrating high quality research. It has influenced, almost conditioned, development thinking to an unimaginable degree. It is information power at its most telling.[14] Its critics have neither the means nor the influence to match this near monopoly of output and professional domination.

In all this its effectiveness stems from its role as a powerful instrument in advancing and safeguarding dominant interests in the world: it serves as a fire brigade in conflict, a soothing influence in socially troubled situations, a propagandist or thought-conditioner and, more importantly, as a strong bond-builder with numerous dependent economies, interests and groups therein, who look for benefits and patronage and also political legitimacy; with colossal funds to invest it is received with open arms. The net effect is to enhance dependency. Few countries, if any, have resisted or overcome this aid dependency, although some have been denied the medicine, disqualified for their actions, deemed inimical to dominant interests in the world.

This role is played from a position of prestige as an intelligent and sophisticated development agency capable of "putting its money where its mouth is" or believed to be. Its attitude of superiority and its impressive publications have earned it unrivalled admiration; furthermore the hiring of numerous specialists and academics from many countries and institutions for research, planning or implementation and its own massive but sophisticated publicity have earned it a great number of praise singers and well-wishers among academics and opinion formers with great and widespread influence. Its pay is excellent and its prestige as an employer and user of specialists' work attract many professionals and politicians who become the envy or hope of numerous other professionals and non-professionals who have not yet had the call, but hope it will come.

Developing countries are in its thrall. Major development projects and association with such a prestigious international institution are the dream of every politician; government services and aspiring senior officials vie for links with, and recognition by, its visiting mandarins; Central Banks are flattered that the Bank looks to, and operates in, their countries through them. And jobs may be had – even a short mission for the World Bank brings in high pay and high living and scarce foreign exchange. Many aspire to training offered by the Bank at its Headquarters. In fact, such training prepares minds and habits of senior staff in developing countries to facilitate its work and influence. It may also be a qualification for entry into the employ of the Bank.

In development the Bank's role has been that expected from an international banking institution which has already disbursed many billions of dollars and spent many millions on research and studies, has supported thousands of projects, big and relatively small: infrastructure development (some of it for government prestige reasons rather than for practical usefulness), utilisation of natural resources, and strengthening of services such as banking and tourism, as well as administrative and economic planning capacity. Programmes and projects were chosen to be safe, commercially and politically (as befits the Bank and its major backers).

Agriculture as such was not much affected, but benefited indirectly from infrastructural projects and the development of natural resources, e.g. irrigation. In the 1960s there was a shift as rural credit and inputs for modernisation of production were increasingly paid attention in support of the budding "Green Revolution", sponsored and financially aided (at least at the research centres in Mexico and the Philippines) by American foundations. As stressed earlier, the "Green Revolution" accelerated (and it was hoped it would open the gates to) imports into many developing countries of agricultural inputs from the developed countries. The Bank also initiated or accelerated commercial (capitalist) farming in many countries.[15]

With the settling in of Mr. Robert MacNamara as President of the Bank (1968–1981) there was a marked emphasis in the Bank's publications and pronouncements on the problems of world poverty and income distribution, and some excellent research was promoted. Although at the 1966 World Conference on Land Reform the World Bank was conspicuous by its low or non-existent interest, by the beginning of the 1970s even land was spoken of in bold (for the Bank) terms. Besides (or parallel with) Mr. MacNamara's observation already quoted, the *Agriculture Sector Working Paper* of June 1972 states that "inegalitarian patterns of landownership are a major source of income inequality. Furthermore, the owners of land usually possess political and economic power which can be exercised in ways that harm the interests of the bulk of the rural people".[16]

These were bold words indeed, however carefully chosen. The Bank has never said anything bolder since. In fact, the Bank gradually toned down and abandoned such rhetoric. Action, even at its boldest, was much more restricted. The Sector Policy Paper of 1975 recorded the change in position, and further identified development objectives "to be increased productivity and employment, and social justice. Land reform can be consistent with these objectives and, in some situations, may well be a necessary condition for their realization".[17] New and growing concern

about distribution of income in the rural areas and the relationship between land distribution and income distribution . . . has been reflected both in the (Bank's) technical assistance offered to governments (especially in sector survey and economic reports) and in the types and components of projects in the lending program."

In discussing the Bank's own technical assistance in sector surveys, the Paper, however, emphasises that "many reports do not give appropriate emphasis to issues related to land reform and development".[18] Furthermore, in discussing lending operations, it admits that "few projects have supported land reform as such".[19] The only one mentioned as having been provided "general support" was the Tunisian, which aimed at setting up "unites de production" (or cooperative farms) on recently nationalised French colon-owned farms. I visited these twice in the early years of their formation. They were hastily mounted and as hastily abandoned for internal political (or personality) reasons. Half the Bank loan was eventually cancelled.

The Malawi Lilongwe and other Projects mentioned were really a serious invasion of customary rights and their conversion into alienable land which, as noted earlier, benefited many civil servants and other urban interests at the expense of customary landholders who became the labour reserve army for South Africa. The Bank supported many land settlement projects from Kenya and Ethiopia to Malaysia and Colombia, which were used as substitutes for land reform, all of them as a response to, or diversion because of, pressure for structural reform. Finally, it helped nucleus (or core) plantation farm development and outgrower schemes for export (usually industrial) crops. Such projects were expanded, as in Indonesia, without regard to the land rights of indigenous people and with devastating effects for tropical forests, as in Indonesia again and the Ivory Coast.

Considering its major policy options the Bank concludes[20] in the Paper that "the potential for using the Bank's influence to press or even force the issue of structural reform on member countries is severely circumscribed. Such political decisions are not amenable to ready negotiation with governments". Thus the Bank's brave words of acknowledgement and diagnosis of the key role of land have not been matched by its deeds. The plea that the political issues raised by land reform are acute is, of course, true. But that is because it touches economic, social or political interests of privileged ruling or dominant classes. Unless, however, these interests are touched, "redistribution with growth", the much-flaunted core policy of the Bank in the 1970s, becomes an empty slogan and such growth as occurs is solely for the benefit of a narrow band of interests, mainly a section of the middle classes, especially the upper crust, whom the former support in such policies. The Bank is aware of this and practically said so in the above quotation.[21]

Lipton, who has periodically served on the Staff of the Bank, observed that "even agencies such as the World Bank, justly proud of their success in redirecting much rural lending towards the *poor* bemoan their inability to benefit the *poorest* decile or two".[22] This is no wonder. The assetless, especially the landless, are excluded from benefits accruing from the style of development pursued and pressed for by bilateral and multilateral agencies, prominent among them the World Bank.

Not only this; as seen earlier and stressed repeatedly in this work, aid, trade and general foreign influence and favours have benefited the privileged minority. If anything, that minority tends thereby to become stronger and in a better position to obstruct development which can give those two bottom deciles and other groups, handicapped through lack of assets, a chance to develop and benefit. The condition of the handicapped deteriorates with certainty relatively and often also absolutely, and the vicious circle continues. In other words such aid and loans for development tend to lessen the chances of the poor to develop.

Before concluding this brief account, intended as a note to a vast and complex field of study and assessment, it must once again be recalled that the Bank is a banking institution controlled by the USA and the other rich (Western) industrialised countries. Therefore its pronounced bias against "structural reforms", which are believed to be a "leftists' demand", or worse a revolutionary and "destabilising" threat, is understandable. The Bank, and its local base in any cooperating developing country, the Central Bank and/or the Finance ministry, back projects that yield profits and revenue (and preferably foreign exchange); thus commercially viable farms and larger producing units, preferably geared to export, are their "natural" choice. The basic need of the poor is for food first of all, especially staple food, which, if they can produce, they will eat (and as usual, it may not be enough) leaving no surplus for the urban classes, let alone for export. This has been demonstrated in the case of beneficiaries of land redistribution projects. Thus neither political benefits nor surpluses for profit, revenue and export (economic benefits) are seen or expected to accrue from "structural reforms". No wonder they have been shunned. They are a political liability. Poverty can still be bemoaned. There is no harm in that. In fact, it serves as a substitute for action.

Another striking aspect of the Bank's activities is its obvious shunning of countries which do not enjoy the friendship or tolerance of the Bank's backers. In contrast, lavish help is given to the specially favoured: Kenya, Malawi, Indonesia, Malaysia, Tunisia have been mentioned. Morocco, Turkey, Iran (under the Shah), the Philippines, Thailand, South Korea, Colombia, Venezuela, Zaire and post-Nasser Egypt have invariably been favoured. Brazil under military rule and present-day Chile are also well-favoured. Ethiopia lost its status as a favourite after the 1974 revolution; for a time Chile – under Allende – was estranged and Peru under Velasco lost status. Cuba and Vietnam are untouchable. Nicaragua has become an embarrassment to the Bank because the US and other rich countries disagree.[23]

There is a further specific reason why "structural reform" is offensive in addition to general political discrimination. Even if in theory the Bank acknowledges that land reform may be a necessary condition for achieving its stated objectives and will make its lending more effective, such a structural reform often affects properties such as plantations and other large farms and even processing enterprises and marketing activities owned or run by nationals of the United States and other rich countries, i.e. the Bank's main backers. As already seen, the reaction of such countries can be sharp and the World Bank is used to discipline and in the end punish offenders. As the UN study on Multinational Corporations[24] observed, this can take the form of "bringing pressure to bear on a particular government by influencing foreign official or private lending and insurance agencies, customers and other firms".

The Bank's rhetoric has shifted markedly in the 1980s. The heyday of bold pronouncements has gone. In line with the ideological predilections and the re-conceived interests (economic and strategic) of its rich backers, instead of redistribution with growth, the doctrine now and the goal of lending and other "persuasive" means are: freeing the people from the stranglehold of taxation and economic inefficiency by the state, the institution of a market economy, and giving the market its head everywhere. This will stimulate initiative and enterprise and will save such long-suffering continents as Africa and Latin America from poverty and instability and make them prosperous like Hong Kong, South Korea and Singapore,[25] ignoring the fact that they, as well as Japan itself, have had decades of a state-led and controlled road to development. These countries were, of course, favoured by multinational corporations, foreign aid and investment.

In reality the Bank's activities and practice have not changed much – only its rhetoric. And the Bank has had to go through a few years of disfavour and penance and a change of leadership. Perhaps it is fair to say that the World Bank has not said anything very revolutionary. In fact, a keen observer will note that even its pronouncements quoted above bear strong similarity to what the World Conference on Agrarian Reform and Rural Development said in its Plan of Action and what the Trilateral Food Task Force said in 1978,[26] in effect that wherever redistributive programmes are of critical importance in projects for the utilisation of resources to achieve much-needed agricultural development and food production and the authorities desire it, they can then be considered acceptable, even commendable. This triple agreement may or may not be a pure coincidence.

Notes

1. With regard to the special case and significant position of the World Bank, see the Note at the end of this Chapter.

2. It should be observed that at that time one-third of the 60-odd members of the UN came from Latin America where the USA had strong influence; Europe with the Marshall Plan was indebted to the USA; other countries were also strongly influenced by the USA. The US initiative, therefore, was crucial for a General Assembly decision.

3. The Brandt Commission in its 1980 Report pp. 248–249 observed that in 1978 only eleven of the sixty-five principal officers of the World Bank and IDA were nationals of developing countries and the same proportion of the twenty-four principals of the IMF.

4. Dore 1975 pp. 190–207, makes the interesting point, which, if valid, may be relevant here also, namely that deferential attitudes have been ingrained in the élites of non-western developing countries towards white western élites as the natural leaders in a civilisation which is, after all, their own.

5. Multilateral aid agencies purchase British goods and services equivalent to 120% of Britain's contributions. The *Financial Times* 1 August 1984.

6. Hochschild 1978 pp. 5–6.
7. A view expressed *inter alia* by Goonatilake 1975 p. 7.
8. At a particular juncture the rumour was that a very senior officer occupying a very key post was looking for a new major position at the end of his assignment.
9. I wrote an assessment of the World Conference on Agrarian Reform and Rural Development within a few days of its conclusion for informal consideration by interested colleagues. Because within FAO it took a minority view of the whole matter it received no attention. An extract is appended here at the end of this book.
10. Joshi, as already noted, mentions that the pressures exercised by various UN agencies, including the 1966 World Conference, have impressed on governments the necessity of land reform; and thus a land reform programme has become one of the symbols of international respectability. 1974 p. 182.
11. Evaluating the OECD economic projections, the *Financial Times* of 22 December 1983 commented philosophically: ". . . its 'technical assumption' is in fact a bureaucratic necessity. It is simply not possible for an international organisation of this kind, paid for by governments and working closely with their officials, to do otherwise. If the OECD could be blamed for a run on the dollar – or any other currency – its funds would soon dry up".
12. "In fact, the agreement of liaison which the Bank signed with the UN in 1947 has been described as 'more a declaration of independence from . . . the UN' (Mason and Asher 1973)." Payer 1982 p. 16.
13. At the time of its founding the US held 37% of voting power in the Bank; in mid-1981 the top five "Western" countries (US, UK, Germany, France and Japan) had 43.43% of voting power. Payer 1982 pp. 22, 28.
14. "The financial hegemony is combined with an attempt at intellectual hegemony . . ." Payer 1982 p. 16.
15. Much of the capital for agribusiness was provided by the International Finance Corporation, an affiliate of the World Bank. Bank support for agribusiness is described by Payer 1982 pp. 210–213, including Table 8.1. Many of the enterprises benefiting are subsidiaries or affiliates of multinational corporations.
16. Quoted in World Bank 1975 p. 38.
17. Ibid.
18. Ibid. p. 39.
19. Ibid. p. 40.
20. Ibid. p. 46.
21. The Bank found no difficulty in supporting loans to the larger-scale farmers. Staff members even defended such action. Ul Haq in the IMF/World Bank journal, *Finance and Development* Vol. 15, No. 2, 1978, would argue that it would be easier to help those with tangible assets. See Dunham 1982 p. 165. Furthermore, Lowe in the same journal in March 1977 defended the financing for agribusiness projects on the grounds that it could greatly increase agricultural productivity and allow economies of scale. See Payer 1982 p. 214 where Payer adds that "some of the land . . . that they have financed is in fact *not* developed but held for capital appreciation . . . "
22. Lipton 1983 p. 5.
23. Dunham 1982 p. 167 observes that 63% of World Bank loans to the agricultural sector between 1974 and 78 were for the top ten which included "some of the most conservative and socially unresponsive political regimes".
24. United Nations 1973 p. 43. Lipson 1985 p. 168 observes: "The World Bank has acted at times like the United States' junior partner in protecting foreign investments".
25. In fact the main thrust of the *World Development Report 1987* was to "prove" that outward oriented countries, above all the three mentioned above, register superior performance. As Michael Prowse in the *Financial Times* of 1 July 1987 observes, the sample is uncomfortably small for drawing radical conclusions and in any case if many more countries are equally successful in their industrial exports, the developed countries would not accept the ensuing rise in imports. Michael Prest in the *Independent* of 8 July 1987 comments simply that "such shoddy work does the bank no good".
26. Quoted by Rudavsky 1980 p. 501.

Epilogue: Visions of Some Promise

"For in a nation there be orders three:—
The highest, useless rich, aye craving more;
The lowest, poor, aye on starvation's brink,
A dangerous folk, of envy overfull,
Which shoot out baleful stings at prosperous folk,
Beguiled by tongues of evil men, their "champions":
But of the three the midmost saveth states,
Who keep the order which the state ordains."
Theseus in Euripides *Suppliants*, (V. 238–245)
(Translation by Arthur S. Way)

"You are the State, *you* are the people.
Ruler unquestioned, . . .
You fear no vote; by your mere nod
You . . . decide all issues."
Chorus addressing King Pelasgus in Aeschylus
The Suppliants (V. 72–76)
(Translation by Philip Vellacott)

Epilogue: Visions of Some Promise

The importance of land as an asset is universally attested – an importance enhanced by its special attributes. Its scarcity in relation to demand within an overall fixed quantity[1] increases its value and accentuates the quest for possession, leading to differential access and holding, and monopolistic tendencies that generate whole chains of social, economic and political interrelationships. Its visibility and durability put it in a special category as conspicuous wealth and fruitful resources. As a "natural" resource it raises philosophical or moral issues concerning exclusive possession. Its ultimate desirability depends on its productive capacity, mainly in agriculture, but also as the location of other very profitable uses.

Possession of land, and the quest for it, have shaped historical destinies and provided some of the strongest impulses and driving forces in the dynamics of societies, even of those which have long been only marginally agricultural. In largely agrarian societies it is inevitably the dominant force. Strategic possession confers irresistible power so that sovereignty and control of territory are always linked.

Recognition of a person's or group's "rights" to a particular area needs a supreme authority to acknowledge and protect such rights. Thus land is at the heart of power and political determination and defines both. The social relations arising from access to land are never purely bilateral or entirely private; nor can they remain so, whatever the outlook of the authorities.

The neglect of the issue of land in socio-economic analysis and political evaluations is surprising. Even more surprising is the emphasis on technical treatment of agrarian reform. When international attention focused on rural development and basic needs with a view to dealing with mass poverty, the central and pervasive role of access to land was neglected or buried among long lists of requirements for simultaneous action.

In the midst of concern about food for the millions of hungry people, which climaxed with popular support for famine-stricken people in Africa, emphasis was on modernisation and increased productivity. Writing about the new orthodoxy among aid donors and the need to do "something" about reversing adverse trends in food production per head, Kaletsky quotes an official: "In a sense, we're talking about a kind of recolonisation – about sending smart white boys to tell them how to run their countries".[2] This is,

197

in essence, the message of the Berg report,[3] Lipton is more specific.[4] He recommends a research push—and a smallholder, food linked field test-oriented research strategy, otherwise prices and investment in agriculture in Africa will not succeed. The main flaw here is that they treat farmers (and whole countries), even small farmers, as a uniform mass.

We have shown how the problem of access to food encompasses the problems of access to land: "farmers" or producers are a variable category whose capacity to produce is conditioned by institutional factors governing access to land; access to food has an institutional aspect as well as that of the physical presence of food. As Amartya Sen observed[5] about famine, "It is very largely those with·capital assets who escape; it is those with nothing but their labour to sell on whom the famine is concentrated".

Landlessness and semi-proletarianisation of vast proportions of rural populations make them targets for future famines whatever miracles of productivity are achieved. The rural poor average one-third of the population in ten countries of Latin America (ranging from eight per cent in Argentina to 64 in Honduras) and the proportion will stay almost as high in a larger population as far as A.D. 2000.[6]

In the Ivory Coast, a country which has succeeded in achieving sustained economic growth, 25% of the population in 1975 was below the poverty-line.[7] In Kenya, another country of economic growth, 45% of the population in the mid-1970s were already living in poverty (90% of them in the rural sector).[8] In Asia in 1972 it was estimated that 71% were seriously poor and 42% destitute; for Africa the figures were 69 and 39 respectively; while for Latin America they were 43 and 27. These figures refer to market economies.[9] While famines attract attention and help is mobilised to save the victims, widespread malnutrition and morbidity are more or less accepted. For instance, "there is no such relief for the third of the Indian population who go to bed hungry every night and who lead a life ravaged by regular deprivation. . . . The system takes [endemic hunger] in its stride".[10]

Times of distress push poor farmers and others into greater indebtedness and deprivation. In times of famine they lose their land and other productive assets, with "a net transfer of ownership of land from the cultivating to the non-cultivating classes. . . . A famine, by accelerating the inequality in the distribution of productive assets among rural households, contributes to the long-term process of generation of poverty and inequality".[11]

Availability of food is, of course, fundamental. Emphasis on the relation between food and population at the expense of other important dimensions has, however, distorted discussion. The average annual rate of growth in agricultural production in developing countries for the period 1966–81 was higher than the rate of population growth, "yet diets in many developing countries barely improved." Between 1960 and 1980 population grew by about half, incomes per head roughly doubled.[12] Yotopoulos documents the radical changes in the structure of demand for food in response to dramatic increases in incomes, especially those of the middle classes in both developed and developing countries. In the latter improvement in diets is selective rather than pervasive. Approaching the problem through patterns in cereal use, Yotopoulos suggests that cereals for feed have become a good indicator for the improvement of diets. The developed countries used 81% of the total feed in 1980. Feed use is also rising in developing countries,[13] causing concern in many quarters. In addition to FAO with its figures,[14] it was said that in a Californian feed-lot, cattle for fattening consume enough maize every day to feed 1.7 m. East Africans or one-third of the population of Zambia.[15] Referring to this aspect and to gasohol or bioethanol production from agricultural sources, the Economist Intelligence Unit (EIU) in its *World Commodity Outlook. Food, Feedstuffs and Beverages 1979* observed that "pigs are fed and men go hungry" with "petrol tanks full, bellies empty" and pointed the finger at "the middle class Paulista driving to work on the product of land that could be growing subsistence crops". The EIU then asked: "Does the maximisation of profits within the existing system militate against the long-term survival of the system itself?"[16]

In a belated contribution the World Bank acknowledged these well-attested truths. In February 1986 its President wrote: "Problems in food security do not necessarily result from inadequate food supplies . . . but from a lack of purchasing power . . . and even when [growth] is achieved the present distribution of assets and opportunities means that large numbers of poor people are likely to increase their purchasing power only slowly".[17] That is a striking understatement.

The need to tackle the problem of access to assets, particularly land, is imperative, if people are to be guaranteed that they will not go hungry amidst plenty. Denial of access to land is often presented as inevitable because land area is finite, while population is not. Admittedly, land is scarce and demand for it high; but this is not the essential argument. Within these quantitative limitations access to land is institutionally determined. That, in essence, is the source of agrarian conflict and the target of every effort to change the pattern of access. This work has indicated how complex and pervasive is this problem area.

Land gives opportunity for productive employment and increased productivity enhances the remunerative employment of those with access to it. If unemployment denies the opportunity for remunerative use of human effort, much arduous effort in the world is very poorly remunerated.[18]

If disasters cause the poor to lose their land, "prosperity" and growth are not unmixed blessings. Growth favours those with assets but overlooks large sections of the population. The belief that this Kuznets curve is temporary has yet to be verified. The Matthew effect guarantees that to those who have shall be given while those with little will lose even that. Our analysis of access to land and of the production relations based on it reveals the ultimate roots of agrarian conflict.

The conflict is not confined to these dramatic situations of mass famine and chronic malnutrition – it is universal. Pressures and strains give rise to a variety of contests and provide dynamic forces for socio-political change and even upheaval. Remedies applied in a context of strife turn out to be palliatives or pauses in the contest, with no benefit to those who need them badly or for whom they were destined.

Upheavals and oscillations take place within broad secular changes, the most important of which is the spread of capitalism throughout the world. Its striking characteristic is the concentration of economic power, which implies also social and political power. As inequality and class differentiation become more pronounced, enhanced productive capacity makes affluence conspicuous and poverty relatively more oppressive.

Efforts to tackle acute problems take a variety of forms, of which three are discussed here: spending on the weaker sections of the population; boosting agricultural production; and aid and investment.

Efforts to attenuate the Matthew effect by spending on the weaker sections actually lead to increasing that effect. This applies even to rich countries. The Reagan Administration in its Budget Message pointed out that spending on farm programmes in the United States had increased six-fold over the last five years; most of the Federal money, however, goes to a relatively small proportion of farmers, who own the largest and most efficient farms. For instance, deficiency payments by the Government are tied to output. In 1985, two-thirds of American farmers did not receive price supports. Of the one-third which did, one-fifth reported sales of over US $100,000 and received 70% of the payments. During 1986, some 12% of those receiving subsidies for cotton got more than half the total payments, with some receiving millions of dollars.[19] In 1985 farm bankruptcies continued at record levels.[20]

The European Economic Community (EEC) has itself been facing bankruptcy through the rising cost of its Common Agricultural Policy (CAP), the aim of which was to protect the vulnerable, underprivileged agricultural sector of these rich industrialised countries. Instead it has enriched such classes as the "grain barons" of the UK.

> Buying agricultural land was all the rage among the City's financial institutions in the 1970s. Even as recently as five years ago, some British pension funds, insurance companies and property unit trusts were falling over themselves to purchase farms.[21]

British entry into the EEC gave a substantial boost to this land boom, while agrarian reform in Italy led to the formation of capitalistic enterprises, with the best lands remaining in the hands of landowners who also benefited from the credit and investments offered by the state and eventually from the opportunities and support offered by the EEC.[22]

Agrarian reform in developing countries has often encouraged a similar surge of capitalist farming in two main ways: by conferring title on those already cultivating the land, many of them by no means inconsiderable (relatively speaking) producers, and by acting as a catalyst; the mere threat of a reform and innocuous legislation has galvanised landowners to seek ways to avoid it, resorting to such actions as dismissing tenants (especially dependent ones) and assuming "self-cultivation", often through agents and casual labour or by "modernising" operations (usually superficially) to qualify for exemption from the reform which almost invariably excludes from expropriation "well-developed" farms (especially those with permanent crops).

Such new capitalist reform farms, the "revamped" landlord farms and those not involved, benefit from practically every developing country government's efforts to modernise and promote production and productivity. Aggressive middle level farmers, with reciprocal support and co-operation from the larger agricultural producers, corner subsidies, modern inputs, credit, marketing, organisation and political support lavished by indulgent public services. This universal state of affairs leads to our second main approach.

Nearly all countries have made and continue to make efforts to encourage higher production (and productivity). This seemingly sensible national goal has the support of the economically and politically strong. There is income, wealth and power from these efforts, as dramatically shown by the "Green Revolution". In a wider context the "public economy has . . . become an elaborate network of patronage and subsidies".[23] The greatest gains come from large-scale production, mainly for export and usually with the co-operation or partnership of foreign interests and not infrequently with help from international agencies, especially the World Bank. The emphasis is on industrial crops for rich country markets.

As examples, we have already mentioned the Ivory Coast and Malawi, where in tobacco expansion at first

> most of the newly developed estates were owned by President Banda and a small group very close to him. . . . Management was provided by employing individuals from South Africa and Rhodesia. By about 1974, President Banda decided to broaden the ownership of estates, encouraging members of the political, bureaucratic and military élite to develop estates and arranging for them access to land and to loans from the domestic commercial banking system.[24]

Eventually the latter burned their fingers and the banks took over. Meanwhile much of the population was proletarianised (and this in an African context with traditional rights to land). "Given the extremely low incomes of estate workers, urban unskilled employees and the great majority of small holders, poverty is widespread."[25]

Nigeria, as already seen, introduced public ownership of land but put the powers of allocation into the hands of state governors and the bureaucracy. Given the proneness to patronage and corruption, much of the land is "allocated" to the powerful, including former senior military people and at least one head of state. Efforts to boost agriculture have benefited those interests. The World Bank assisted smallholder projects. The Government has encouraged everyone to invest in agriculture, using *inter alia* import licences as an inducement to large entrepreneurs, including foreign firms, to engage in agriculture. Practically every one of the 100 or so largest firms made plans to produce or process agricultural products. The longest-lasting example of this is a lesson in itself. From 1978 TEXACO tried to produce cassava, at first under an "outgrower" project, which did not attract local farmers, and then directly, for its processing plant of cassava meal, a staple food in Nigeria, but failed.[26] So far efforts to produce food in this way have not succeeded; meanwhile traditional Nigerian holders have been displaced, open unemployment has increased, and some powerful people have profited. If food were available in abundance many people would not be able to buy it. These are some of the vicious circles engendered by such "development" efforts.

They are, however, far from new; Africa is only a latecomer and often propelled by new forces, many beyond its power.[27] Latin America is full of examples and Africa does well to learn from the lessons yielded there. They date from the 1950s and the pattern is like this: Most productive lands often went to agro-export crops, thus requiring restriction of access to land, credit and markets by the peasants so that they would have to work in the agro-export sector at low wages when needed. Those vast majorities are entitled to food only to the degree that they have money to buy or access to land to produce food for themselves or enough to sell at a price permitting them to purchase it.[28]

Independent Africa has experienced other difficulties from the agro-export sector inherited from colonial days, mainly in enterprises taken over by the state from settlers. Cut off from the marketing chain to rich countries' markets and unequipped to run complex enterprises for which they had neither experience nor qualified personnel, they struggled on until the problems overwhelmed them and they had to let multinational companies return (as with Lonhro in Tanzania) or help with operations (as in Mozambique.)

The plight of the American farms mentioned above and EEC troubles with the CAP did not, however, spring from low prices or productivity. Prices were kept high through subsidies; productivity was unprecedented; yet, starvation is widespread in the world. The "surpluses" reflect the incapacity of the starving and malnourished billions to buy the food. Another "scandal" is the low remuneration of commodity producers (outside those rich countries which can afford subsidies and other support on a lavish scale) due to very low prices on the world market, i.e. those paid by the rich countries.

In the 1980s this was further dramatised by the "debt problem", i.e. the too heavy indebtedness of a number of countries to rich countries' banks. The Latin American foreign debt alone is reckoned to be US $382 billion and the net outflow of funds in connection with this was in 1986 (in spite of lower interest rates) still US $22.6 billion or 25% of Latin American exports.[29] Millions of poor people are paying a high price for servicing debt repayment through austerity measures introduced to extract enough surplus to make at least a good show of intentions to pay perhaps some of the interest to secure new loans to avoid (perhaps only postpone) bankruptcy or default. The International Monetary Fund (IMF) is used as the hatchet institution to inflict austerity and tight management on the economy of debtor countries as proof of improved behaviour and promise of repayment.[30]

This heavy indebtedness was not by any means incurred to achieve broad-based development, elimination of poverty or social integration. A good deal of the lending, much of it funds amassed by rich oil-exporting countries being recycled, was by multinational banks, mostly American but also some European and Japanese to a variety of borrowers mainly for short and medium term purposes. As already seen, multinational banks are the financial backers of the multinational companies. Some banks and multinational companies, such as the German and Japanese, are closely connected, if not actually owned by the same interests. Multinational companies are attracted to places where restrictions on repatriating profits and capital are absent or very limited.

In a strict sense, however, the "debt problem" springs from (to continue the Latin American example)

> Governments in the industrial countries [wanting] to integrate Latin America more fully into the world economy and to ensure that it remained essentially western in its political orientation. It is hardly a secret that the US State Department welcomed American loans to countries such as Brazil and Argentina. . . . the overwhelming majority of loans were either to governments or, with government guarantees, to quasi-governmental enterprises or institutions. . . . This . . . has given political élites . . . new pretexts for meddling with the private sector. . . . domestic banks in Latin America [tended] to pass into state hands. . . . There seems no doubt that much of the money was lent to rich individuals who promptly left Argentina and bought apartments in Florida. . . . the banks in Buenos Aires could not get their money back and so went bust. . . . their debts became government liabilities. It fell on the Argentine taxpayer . . . to service them. . . . the harder the IMF tries to extract money on behalf of the international banks, the greater the resentment aroused by its austerity programmes.[31]

Favourites for loans were oppressive military or other dictatorships like Brazil, Argentina and Chile, the Philippines, South Korea, Turkey and Zaire, or one-party regimes like Mexico. As already seen, the Brazil military regime was strongly supported by powerful agricultural and industrial interests who relied heavily "on increased international borrowing, a profound wage squeeze, augmented transnational participation in the economy, repression and conventional expansionary and fiscal policies" to consolidate their economic power and earn the regime "legitimacy".[32] The plight of Brazil's poor reached new depths,[33] but they are now called upon to make new sacrifices to meet pressing foreign debts, even after the military have failed and gone. But the saga of indebtedness, foreign investment, and international agencies' role has new twists.

Since the debt problem reached crisis proportions in the early 1980s developing countries have increasingly opened their doors to foreign capital to offset a drop in bank lending and stagnating development aid. . . . Today the foreign multinational may still be disliked, but it is no longer feared and its capital and expertise is desperately needed. . . . the World Bank is launching the multinational investment guarantee agency (Miga), to insure companies against the expropriation of their assets and other political risks. . . . Large western contractors, desperate for work . . . become part of equity joint ventures . . . to build [and] operate the facility . . . Merchant bankers in London are enthusiastic . . . but . . . less sure how far it overcomes the problem of a developing country's poor creditworthiness.[34]

The country must produce, export and save, i.e. increase its surpluses to achieve that.

It is significant that, while socialist agriculture is criticised for relying on cooperative farming and control of marketing to extract a surplus in support of industrialisation, the extraction of surpluses from the economy of indebted countries to pay for high rates of interest with exports whose prices are so depressed and in markets which cannot absorb them or actually exclude them, especially at the expense of many underprivileged groups, is almost taken as a natural phenomenon beyond dispute. The situation is fraught with so much danger and suffering that the Pontifical Commission on Justice and Peace in a document prepared for the Pope states: "Debt servicing cannot be met at the price of the asphyxiation of a country's economy and no government can morally demand of its people privations incompatible with human dignity".[35] After so many years of North/South "dialogue" that is where matters still stand.

International organisations, prominent among them the World Bank, and regional and international conferences have for almost two decades laid much stress on rural development, which is often styled as integrated. Their concept is such a broad spectrum of action in basic sectors of the economy and in social development, hedged in usually by many pre-requisites and presupposing the availability of impossible levels of resources and experience that it can only be called utopian. All is spelt out in studied "apolitical" terms and contexts. All Specialised Agencies of the UN promote and the World Bank invests in such rural development.

Many governments have tried, none better than India, where successive governments have remained faithful to anti-poverty policies and been backed by unprecedented academic and professional intellectual and administrative talent and skills. India has had to battle with extraordinary numbers of people living in poverty. As late as 1980 they amounted to nearly half the population (i.e. some 300 m.). It is hoped to halve the percentage by the end of the 1980s. Two determined Programmes were put in hand. The Integrated Rural Development Programme attempted to encourage self-employment among the very poor by offering them subsidised credit and assets, mainly dairy cows. Maladministration and corruption plagued this

Programme.[36] The other, the National Rural Employment Programme, attempted to provide the unemployed and landless with food and meagre cash wages in exchange for their labour on public works. Like land reform before, this is dogged by political and economic problems, or, as Professor Suresh Tendulkar puts it: "At some point these efforts, if they are successful, are bound to collide with the established interests who benefit from low wages, the political backwardness and the economic dependence of the very poor".[37] Others observe: "Underdevelopment is . . . a dynamic process which tends to perpetuate itself in the diversity of relationships among classes."[38]

To complete the picture we need to look at other systems outside the capitalist system, but operating and trading in a world dominated by it, where there is a variety of socialist or centrally planned economies. As already discussed, they have reformed land tenure by converting in most cases all or much of the land into public property for cooperative or state use within a system of central management of the economy guided by successive five-year plans. They have reduced income inequalities and raised the relative level of living of the formerly underprivileged strata under a long-standing policy "to provide the people's basic needs, almost free. Staple foodstuffs, accommodation, transport, education, health, gas and electricity have all been very cheap or free for several decades".[39]

These reforms and that pattern of management have not solved problems of production and productivity. Most socialist countries have now adopted new economic mechanisms and approaches to management, including new instruments, in varying degrees. The main emphasis is on stimulating responsibility and initiative at various levels of economic management by decentralising decision-making and passing it on to lower levels within indicative overall plans. Pricing and operation of a market are also increasingly used in inter-enterprise dealings. These reforms seem to offer promise of higher production and labour productivity.

China has gone farthest and fastest. The new economic mechanism in China was agriculture-led possibly because agriculture is of such importance (on account of the households affected) and lends itself to devolving decision-making to smaller, and more "natural", tasks and units. Agriculture, and industries based on it, responded to the call of "getting rich first" with the visible result of a rise in production (China becoming a significant exporter, particularly of maize, soyabeans and cotton) and in the number of high income rural households, especially in suburban areas.[40] They were helped also by higher prices and better access to inputs. Those households specialising in lines of production and services in special demand, reckoned to be over 13% of the rural households in 1984, became "clearly the élite". A revival of hired labour, mainly in the less visible non-field tasks, was also reported.[41]

The situation in China has evolved very rapidly. In the USSR reform is more recent, more cautious but more comprehensive in that it impinges also on the political mechanism, especially after the meeting of the Central

Committee of the Communist Party in January 1987. In fact *perestroika* (i.e. restructuring) combined with *glasnost* (openness) seem to be pervading the Soviet system with profound repercussions for its politics and economics and the whole way of life. In China it was said by non-Chinese critics that the social revolution coexisted with a political fossil.[42] Professor Zhao Fusan of the Chinese Academy of Social Sciences was quoted as stating: "We hope to make the political mechanism much more rational, with democracy and the rule of law as the moving spirit".[43] The path cannot possibly be a smooth one.

China's socialist practice and pride had been frugality, equality and collective effort. On the one hand, early gains in production benefits have, after introduction of the responsibility system, created strains in society since "at the grass roots there are murmurings of discontent over price rises and over how those who have been allowed to 'get rich first' are getting richer and further ahead of the pack";[44] on the other hand, long-run problems will arise from the diminution in, and even disappearance of, investment in infrastructural works especially irrigation projects, which are beyond the interest and capacity of individual households.[45] Political convulsion and ideological conflict, fuelled by social and economic strains, marked the beginning of 1987.

It remains to be seen what will happen in the USSR when reforms have been applied for some time, when individual labour will be able to work on its own account, individuals join in cooperatives to provide services or engage in small-scale manufacture, and when labour will be paid according to productivity and the profitability of their enterprise, which will become the decision of its management. Further influences will come from outside when trade intensifies and economic relations with advanced capitalist economies and their international institutions are vastly expanded.

This sketchy review of broad situations and of issues arising, drawn from a variety of systems, has confirmed two fundamental and inter-linked findings: the development path of all economies, under whatever system, is plagued by the tendency of the rich (a minority) to get richer and the poor at best to be left behind, if not actually become worse off; the springboard for this advance is possession of assets, and this work has indicated in detailed analysis the key role of perhaps the most vital such asset – land. The other, and closely linked, finding is that the possession of assets confers power, basically economic but of key importance also for access to political power.

These findings are not new. What is new is the effort to explore the ways and means by which processes and action function in the case of the vital asset of land and the repercussions they engender. Most importantly, these issues are placed at the centre of the debate. To the extent that there is truth in the analysis and in the interrelationships which we have highlighted, and assuming that they point to a general and key truth about global experience in development and efforts to achieve one world, the question arises whether all that has been achieved is not a world divided, more divided than before.

In my national and international experience I witnessed colonial development, successive post-independence development theories and practice, formula after formula of new strategic approaches backed with ever-increasing funds; and I have concentrated on the crunch issue of structural reform, especially agrarian reform, which raises many socio-political hackles. Well-meaning, sometimes messianic, announcements of new approaches and miraculous breakthroughs (or promise thereof) after so much effort and expense came, stayed and eventually went. Many, if successful, would have brought about a fairer and more prosperous world. There was nothing wrong with approaches, or prescriptions, such as: a unified approach to development (United Nations), redistribution with growth (World Bank), basic needs approach (ILO), integrated rural development (various), and now "development with a human face" (UN). Only they were projected into a world assumed to be ready to take and apply the formula. But the real world was suffering from acquired immunity. What appealed to the decision-makers was what would benefit them and their supporters, what would help them to enhance their constituency, in effect, their power. This investment in the power-holders and power-brokers ensured that any new assets and opportunities would make them stronger and more demanding.

While any new development formula reigned, any scepticism about the feasibility or the effectiveness of the new miracle was met with hostility, as I know from experience. I styled the strategy of integrated rural development, so much advocated, especially within FAO in the 1970s, as the art of the impossible, pointing out that without attention to the structure of asset-holding and to the incidence of opportunity assured for development, efforts would prove self-defeating and achieve more polarisation, not less. I was practically ostracised.

I had the chance to return to FAO and put formally[46] to the 22nd FAO Conference, in Rome in November 1983, the need to eliminate a serious flaw in development, and rural development especially, in that it builds on a narrow range of people, i.e. those with an original real advantage, especially productive assets, and proposed officially that

> FAO should take the lead to study the process of inbuilt marginalisation of the disadvantaged people which fatally flaws the rural development, and all kinds of development, on which we place so many hopes and of which we speak so much. . . . Resources can be found to concentrate on a break-through which will lift this fatal flaw from FAO's efforts which affects all the UN system's efforts, including especially the World Bank.

The source of resources was identified by the Director-General in his Programme of Work and Budget, namely the "resources spent on arms."

The need for study does not arise from an addiction to more and more studies. One is dealing here with one of the most profound and central issues of social-political dynamics. It is so embedded in the behaviour of the social system as to become very nearly an immutable law. This issue has often been (only) hinted at in assessments and strategic formulae and then dropped and ignored as if it can only be exorcised by invocation rather than approached rationally and faced squarely.

Fundamentally, this avoidance of the issue stems from the desire of those who benefit and who hold power to let sleeping dogs lie. There is no knowing how the socialist countries will react when and if within their societies stratification becomes pronounced and tensions acute, i.e. when the reforms now in train get established and yield results. Already critics raise the issue of the political mechanism and its adequacy to manage the repercussions of the economic reforms.

There is less comment on the political mechanisms of other systems. Development literature, technocratic par excellence and, under the leadership of the World Bank, very economistic, has praised as models, the examples of Japan, Singapore, South Korea, Taiwan, Ivory Coast and Brazil (under the military) and even Pinochet's Chile. These regimes are far from based on free popular support. Development literature likes to assume an apolitical stand; it will not escape notice, however, that these models include: an economically highly successful country (Japan), the economic, and especially political, management of which, as astute political scientists have observed, has been for over forty years in the hands of the dominant faction or alliance of factions within the ruling party; two have been for decades under effective personal rule (Singapore and the Ivory Coast); one (Taiwan) for decades ruled by an alien minority with the indigenous people having no voice; another (South Korea) an authoritarian, often military, administration for decades; while the other two cases speak for themselves. The implication seems to be that economic success requires this type of political control.[47]

The apolitical and economistic stand has in recent years been replaced by a sophisticated but transparent attempt to draw a distinction between the *totalitarian* regimes of the left which are both damnable and to be replaced by force and the *authoritarian* regimes of the extreme right which are to be deplored but should be helped to evolve as they are capable of so doing, according to this new dispensation. South Africa has not evolved through "constructive engagement" and how far Guatemala has gone was seen earlier. South Korea, Taiwan, Singapore and the Ivory Coast do not seem to evolve, until and unless internal pressures begin to appear otherwise unmanageable.

In this ostensibly apolitical development climate cultivated with extreme skill and sophistication by international agencies and with other make-believe theories propounded by interests which are overwhelmingly powerful, and disseminated through a universal network of opinion-forming media, most of which are in those interests' monopolistic control, in an era of an explosion of "information" technology, the chances are minimal of achieving a breakthrough in thinking, let alone in the development of operational tools, towards the eminent and vital goals set from time to time internationally (satisfaction of basic needs of the deprived and disadvantaged, achieving redistribution with growth, even effecting a trickle down effect in development, let alone social integration). The international socio-political

scene and practice discourage even minimalist aspirations. Utopian proposals put forward in the circumstances would sound tragic-comic.

One has only to observe the stronger party enforcing his will in an
arrogance of power to be put wise. Here are some examples: in the most
powerful military world alliance the strongest party embarks on a Strategic
Defence Initiative (SDI) to develop an umbrella to shelter itself alone, the
rest are left out in the cold of a nuclear winter; what is more "Japan and
Western Europe are the economic targets of SDI", that SDI technology will
spearhead the American economy into the twenty-first century.[48] The rich
and powerful economic powers fight their own currency and trade conflicts,
trampling under their elephantine capers the weak and poor countries in
another fit of "they can sink into the ocean; it will hardly be noticed";
unemployment of unprecedented proportions and duration afflict even rich
countries where potential resources are idle, but financial *paper* operations,
manipulated by a few and mainly from within, ensure fast profits and huge
incomes for this tiny minority; as already discussed extensively, contrasts in
economic and social fortunes sharpen in the developing countries and
oppressive systems prevail more and more: manifestations of the malaise
are dramatically highlighted by food riots, famines, and scares of deadly
diseases; multinational companies extract profits or abandon activity in
developing countries; multinational banks demand their pound of flesh as
part of the bond entered into by the indebted developing countries' oppressive regimes, which were aided and abetted by rich country interests; the
International Monetary Fund is asked to serve as the disciplinarian head-
master or policeman to make indebted countries conform if they wish to
keep going with injections of funds to stave off bankruptcy; finally, the
international agencies have now sobered up and propound no bold strategies;
the World Bank has been disciplined and preaches what in any case it has
always practised – encouraging and helping enterprise by asset holders in or
towards a market economy.

The question of allocating resources for *new* research and the application
of *promising operational* approaches towards development, which would lift
the scourge of underdevelopment and misery from the lives of the billions
suffering from them, scarcely bears mention. Earlier, I referred to diversion
of resources from the arms race. I sat through the discussions of the United
Nations Economic and Social Council in the summer of 1962 on the economics of disarmament. The discussions were based on a determined and
in-depth study by most eminent experts from a representative cross-section
of countries and socio-economic systems, a study which was both thorough
and authoritative. Even then the militarisation of economic life in so many
countries,[49] in the sense of so much productive activity and cost devoted to
ministering to "defence" needs, was both impressive and disconcerting. The
world has learnt nothing and, if anything, is in a much worse situation a
quarter of a century later. There are no resources for life; there are plenty
for death. Any poor country can ask for arms and will get them; they are the
life blood of many rich countries' economies.

The world situation remains as it has been for many decades; for a far greater number of people it is perhaps worse. Propelled by the dynamic forces operating in highly unequal power structures, gaining momentum from the reinforcing of the already powerful minorities which thereby increases those minorities' capacity to get their own way, it has had its hopes dashed of feeding all the population, the capacity for which exists already, of ensuring satisfaction of the basic needs of everybody, which technically is an attainable goal; or establishing higher levels of wellbeing, amity and peace.

The exploration carried out in this book established the inherent nature of conflict in rural society; it looks as if conflict is inherent in the whole socio-political galaxy of systems in the world; what is important is that it "promises" to continue, if not actually to sharpen further. This book has proposed no utopias. It has commented on realities and processes. The world has to live with conflict.

Conflict is not necessarily negative, nor need it be destructive, except of the participants' illusions and complacency. It can in fact be, and has been in many cases, creative. Furthermore the conflict itself generates momentum for efforts to resolve it. The essential prior requirement for successful resolution is to sense conflict and to recognise its existence, its nature, its functions and implications. This book has tried to shed light on a crucial vast area of conflict and of approaches adopted to deal with it. If it has helped enhance recognition and illuminate the issues involved, it may have made a modest contribution towards the long march in the direction of the promised land.

Notes

1. Or in amusing and poetical terms:
   "I'll let you into a secret, folks,
   I'm buying land. They've stopped
   making it."
   Will Rogers (1879–1930). Quoted by Hutton 1979 p. 186.
2. Kaletsky, Anatole, writing about the famine in Africa, in the *Financial Times* 3 April 1985.
3. World Bank 1981.
4. Lipton 1983 p. 10.
5. Quoted in Robinson 1983 p. 270.
6. See Molina 1982 Table 1, p. 89.
7. Stewart 1985 pp. 84–85.
8. Hunt 1984 p. 42.
9. ILO 1976 Table 2, p. 22.
10. Sen 1983 p. 757.
11. Ghose 1982 pp. 382, 384.
12. Information from Yotopoulos 1984 p. 22.
13. Ibid. pp. 22–25.
14. See e.g. *Ceres* Vol. 13, No. 13, September–October 1980, p. 6.
15. Dumont and Mottin 1980 p. 32, fn. 1.
16. *The Guardian* 3 March 1979.
17. World Bank 1986 p. v.

18. This has been with us for millenia, as the Old Testament reminds us:
The poor rise early . . .
but though they work till nightfall
their children go hungry.
Job 24: 2–12, 14. Quoted in Gutierrez 1983.
19. *Financial Times* 7 January 1987.
20. *Financial Times* 4 September 1985.
21. Andrew Gowers in *Financial Times* 8 February 1986.
22. Di Giorgi and Moscati 1980 p. 52.
23. Bardhan 1984 p. 35. He was writing about India, but it has a far wider application.
24. Kydd and Hewitt 1986 p. 536. See also Chapter 12, note 37.
25. Ghai and Radwan 1983 p. 93.
26. Patti Waldmeir in *Financial Times Survey: Nigeria* 3 March 1986.
27. The penetration of agribusiness into Africa, the plight of commodity producers, and the fate of countries which attempted to practise African socialist ideas as described and analysed earlier and the forces identified should be a salutary lesson. For a full-scale treatment of agribusiness, see Dinham and Hines 1983.
28. See Barraclough 1982 pp. 4–6. This specifically refers to pre-revolutionary Nicaragua, but similar experiences occur in most of Central America, especially El Salvador and Guatemala (p. 12).
29. Data presented to the United Nations Economic Commission for Latin America (ECLA) extraordinary conference in Mexico City in January 1987. Reported in *Financial Times* 23 January 1987.
30. Thirwall 1987 p. 13 observes that the IMF exerts a deflationary bias in the world economy through its asymmetrical treatment of deficit and surplus countries. In reality the bias is against developing countries with no powerful friends. Beenstock 1986 p. 70 commented at a World Bank Symposium, "The US is the Fund's most delinquent member; with its huge budget deficit, overvalued currency, massive public spending on non-productive sectors such as defence, overproductive agricultural sector that was unresponsive to market forces, and increasingly protectionist attitudes". The US is, of course, the dominant force in the IMF; it can preach but need not practise. Furthermore, its massive debt can be reduced "by engineering a devaluation of the dollar", as John Plender writes in the *Financial Times* 14 September 1987.
31. This graphic and eloquent account is taken from Tim Congdon in *The Times* 25 April 1985. There is voluminous literature on world indebtedness. The IMF acknowledged massive capital flight. In the period 1983–85 it was: Africa $28.5 bn; Asia $18.3 bn; Europe $24 bn; non-oil Middle East $6.2 bn; Western Hemisphere $106.6 bn. *Financial Times* 7 September 1987.
32. Hecht 1985 p. 667.
33. For an illuminating discussion of that plight, including methodology, see contributions to the *American Economic Review*, Vol. 70, No. 2, May 1980, pp. 288–292.
34. Christian Tyler writing in the *Financial Times* 13 January 1987.
35. *Financial Times* 28 January 1987. "Between 1980 and 1985 [Third World] debt service jumped from $78 bn to $114 bn, whilst non-oil primary commodity export earnings dropped from $104 bn to $87 bn." Clairmonte and Cavanagh 1987, p. 47.
36. Anatole Kaletsky in *Financial Times Survey: India* 12 May 1986.
37. Both Bhattacharyya 1985 p. 47 and Bagchee 1987 p. 147 in their analysis and evaluation urge a deeper understanding of issues and policies required in what in reality is "an exercise based on progressive discovery of what was not known before" as Bhattacharyya affirms.
38. Di Giorgi and Moscati 1980 p. 57.
39. Writing about the USSR, Patrick Cockburn in *Financial Times* 16 May 1985.
40. Trescott 1985 p. 210.
41. Nolan and Paine 1986 p. 92.
42. Ibid, p. 95.
43. Colina MacDougall in the *Financial Times Survey: China* 18 December 1986.

212 of Non Of

44. Robert Thomson, Ibid.

45. David Dodwell, quoting American experts in the *Financial Times Survey: China* 5 December 1985.

46. As head of my country's delegation, being then Minister of Agriculture and Natural Resources. I was also elected as one of the Vice-Chairmen of the Conference and presided over many sessions, including the one on the Budget.

47. *The Economist*, Vol. 303, No. 7503, 20 June 1987 says so in fact. "Authoritarianism can have economic virtues in the early stages of industrialisation . . . but it becomes a political and economic hindrance when carried on too long . . .".

48. Williams 1987 p. 582.

49. The military expenditure in 1962 was probably $110 billion. The latest figure, given by Tullberg 1986 p. 211, is estimated to have been in 1985 (in current dollars) $850–70 billion [or equal roughly to the developing countries' indebtedness].

APPENDIX: The World Conference on Agrarian Reform and Rural Development (WCARRD): An Assessment

Premises

The World Conference on Agrarian Reform and Rural Development (WCARRD), which took place from 12 to 20 July 1979 at FAO, Rome, should be judged by very exacting standards. A major world event concerning some of the most crucial global issues of our time and a rare occasion calls for critical and deeply probing assessment. Some 150 governments were represented, the majority by ministers, four heads of state visited it, three of whom addressed the Conference, and numerous inter-governmental and non-governmental organisations took part one way or another. Furthermore it had behind it five years of preparation on which FAO and most of the major agencies of the United Nations family were actively engaged. The majority of countries submitted reports on their problems and experience and numerous *ad hoc* studies were prepared for the Conference preparations.

The Conference was based on the consciousness "that past development efforts and programmes have largely failed to reach and adequately benefit the rural areas" and on the belief that the eradication of poverty, hunger and malnutrition is the primary objective of world development. The Conference declared some fundamental principles and guidelines two of which should be underlined: (a) that national progress based on growth with equity and participation requires a redistribution of economic and political power; and (b) that policies and programmes affecting agrarian and rural systems should be formulated and implemented with the full understanding and participation of all rural people.

The Conference could be usefully assessed: (a) by the degree to which it has succeeded in deepening and spreading understanding of the colossal and complex issues involved; (b) by the boost it has given to a strengthening of the will and capacity of governments to take effective action; and above all

213

(c) by the extent to which it has improved the prospects of all rural people to benefit from and participate fully in future development, and thus achieving the primary objective of the eradication of poverty, hunger and malnutrition within the socially and politically necessary time.

Deepening and Spreading of Understanding

Understanding must be at all levels: local and by all groups; national and by all actors and sectors; international and by all participants. Each level requires different content and mode of communication. The local level requires at least understanding of the conditions and processes that control the individual's or the group's circumstances and performance and the avenues and action available for improvement, especially for his or the group's share of effort. The national level comprises the policy-makers and the executives of policies and many interest groups: policy formation, planning, implementation, financing, foreign relations, mobilisation of potential beneficiaries and other resources for action and the share of benefits are the issues, practices and techniques which should be understood. The international level is sometimes tenuous but nonetheless always a real factor, which should be understood in its complexities and articulation: the owners of resources within the country; the direct operators living and practising in the country; the outside operators with strong bearing on the issue; the political and security issues and relations; those and other agents and considerations must be understood, their roles and the implications assessed and the feasible options for action worked out.

The Conference in its preparations has asked and stimulated governments to look at their own countries' problems in all their dimensions and repercussions. The outcome was very variable. Some understanding in some countries must have been enhanced, thereby, and the quantum of knowledge increased. The results were not reassuring, however, if judged by the amount and especially the quality of the reported outcome in official review papers.

The Review and Analysis document prepared for the Conference (WCARRD/INF.3) has put together a certain amount of existing and reported information which could give a fairly general view of the problems, which were presented in the text within the frame of the prevailing conventional wisdom. The material in that document is derivative and where information was easily available the document is fairly informative. In areas where information and thinking are far from advanced the document offers little guidance or really effective analysis. Outstanding cases in point include: people's participation and people's self-reliant action; the nature, dimensions and direct implications of foreign issues in concrete and relevant terms; and the issue of redistribution of economic and political power.

The Conference itself provided no opportunities for ample discussion of issues, findings and differing points of view or for exchange of experiences on substantive matters. The participants and the world at large will rely for such exchange of experience on reading at home each other's contributions in the rather scant literature made available to them. How many will avail themselves of the opportunity to do so is difficult to assess, but clearly they will be very limited in number and social spread.

The class who will find it difficult to obtain access to the deepening and spreading of understanding as contributed by the Conference will be the mass of the rural people themselves, unless they are fortunate enough to get it from participants and from students of the documentation. The work of propagation is yet to start. This leads to consideration of the prospects for government and other people's action after the Conference.

Strengthening of the Will and Capacity to Take Effective Action

Governments through their organs and representatives were offered ample opportunity to take part in the preparations and the sessions of the Conference. They could have expanded their share and opportunities if they cared to take further initiatives. In fact the Conference was primarily theirs from beginning to end. Its success or otherwise is due largely to them as a collective organ and as individual members.

If the will and capacity existed they could, and some governments did, carry out a major reappraisal of their countries' conditions and policies and of their results and of further action required, in response to and on the occasion of the Conference. They could share their experience with others and ask to learn from each other. That the sessions of the Conference itself provided no ample opportunity to share and debate experiences is by commission or omission the outcome of governments' decision or indecision and the responsibility essentially was theirs.

Has the Conference strengthened the will of governments to take new, effective and resolute action? It is difficult to assess any such outcome at this stage and only time will tell. One can ask, though, the legitimate question: how and to what extent has the Conference strengthened the will of governments to redistribute economic and political power; or, put in another way, can the Conference Declaration in this respect realistically be seen as more than an exhortation with little chance to be adhered to? There are other actors who can use the document to good effect. Whether they will do so depends on many factors. To them the Conference Declaration is only one of their weapons.

Concerning the strengthening of the capacity of governments to take action the matter requires a more detailed analysis and it all depends on some key elements of the follow-up action. If a sustained and global programme backed by the requisite political commitment and active cooperation within the international community is effectively implemented with the support of adequate resources, then the capacity of governments to take action will be considerably enhanced. The programme, however, should be prepared and successfully implemented with the full support of the international community, essentially that of the rich countries. Thus this strengthening of capacity will rely on new international development strategies being designed and implemented, new policies by the powerful countries and difficult and tough policies being adopted by developing countries. The Conference merely underlined a set of principles and offered a few general guidelines for action. It has especially called for action by governments and the international community and adopted a stipulated but rather general Programme of Action. The effect of the Conference will be known only when the Programme is implemented, that is how much is put into practice.

The Conference has placed a heavy responsibility on FAO to act as leader among the UN family and as a catalyst and a keeper of the conscience of governments in implementing the adopted Programme of Action. Thus the success of the Conference depends on the will and capacity of FAO to originate, lead and guide and get things done. Thus the results of the Conference and FAO's honour hang together. Will FAO rise to the occasion? Time will tell.

Prospects for Rural People to Participate and Benefit

The Conference in all its documentation and discussions, although eloquent about people's participation as a general principle and a guideline, has avoided being specific or even concrete. As already mentioned development through self-reliance of the rural people is rarely mentioned. Development is assumed to be exogenous and the rural people have to be "reached" and be "targets". Mention is made of their free association and various organisations. The role and action of the rural people and their initiatives are rarely looked into, let alone seen as the main motor (or a main motor) of their own development.

Redistribution of economic and political power will be handed down, as so will many other desirable things, envisaged by the Conference, such as land, employment, and assistance of all kinds, including the rural people's own mobilisation and organisation. Thus it is assumed that rural people are a receptacle, more than as agents with initiatives of their own.

The Conference talked about eradication of poverty, hunger and malnutrition in an unspecified time period but only of "reduction" of rural poverty in targets for the 1980s and 1990s, but never specifying by how much.

The Conference never grappled with two basic issues which constitute the heart of the whole matter: the real causes of poverty and underdevelopment and the processes by which poverty fails to diminish even when growth, even impressive growth, does take place. Without full grasp of those two basic issues and without facing up to the implications for action the Conference has missed the opportunity to raise the prospects of success to levels commensurate with its big claims and the people's expectations. The diagnosis has been rather superficial and the prescribed action runs the risk of addressing the symptoms.

What will the rural people make of the Conference? The question is legitimate and it is a key issue. It is impossible to answer. To begin with it is difficult to tell how much notice they have taken, if any. They have not been heavily involved and they certainly had no direct voice in the Conference deliberations. Some were represented in a manner of speaking by national leaders of their unions or organisations who were included in the national delegations. Their voice in the debates, such as they were, was not very noticeable, even if they could find it useful to say anything.

The Conference could have highlighted one very great truth which is crucial to agrarian reform and rural development, namely that the rural people and their thinking and aspirations are totally ignored in all the talk and rhetoric about their own development; basically very little is known about them and this is a very fundamental and urgent void which has to be properly filled if any hope of effective progress is to be achieved.

Will their leaders when they get back, will their governments which subscribed to the Conference Declaration and Programme of Action, will the international community, will all those people and institutions care enough and will they find the means to spread the findings and explain commitments entered into at the Conference and mobilise the support of the rural people for the follow-up? And yet participation and understanding on the part of the rural people has been solemnly declared as a main principle and guideline at the Conference.

Finally and more importantly will those responsible lay down plainly before the rural people their own commitment to redistribute economic and political power, the acceptance of equitable distribution of land and water, the pledge to eradicate poverty and the basic need for people's organisation and free association to pursue their own development in full partnership with the authorities? Or will they leave it to the rural people to take those issues up themselves and in their own way? That is not the participation as gleaned from the Conference message; it is in fact a replacement of the forces on which the Conference relied. Thus the issues are at present unresolved. The final verdict has to wait before a paean or an epitaph can be written on the Conference.

FAO, Rome
24 July 1979

References

Adams, Dale W. "Colombia's Land Tenure System: Antecedents and Problems", *Land Economics*, Vol. 42, No. 1, February 1966.

Adams, Dale W. "The Economics of Land Reform", *Food Research Institute Studies in Agricultural Economics, Trade and Development*, Vol. XII, No. 2, 1973.

Adams Jr., Richard H. "Development and Structural Change in Rural Egypt, 1952 to 1982", *World Development*, Vol. 13, No. 6, June 1985.

Adedeji, A. (ed.) *Indigenization of African Economies*. Hutchinson, London, 1981.

Adler-Karlsson, Gunnar "Eliminating Absolute Poverty: An Approach to the Problem" in Howard Wriggins, W. and Adler-Karlsson, G. (eds.) *Reducing Global Inequities*. 1980s Project, Council of Foreign Relations, McGraw-Hill, New York, 1978.

Ake, Claude "Kenya" in Adedeji 1981 (q.v.)

Alavi, Hamza "Peasant Classes and Primordial Loyalties", *The Journal of Peasant Studies*, Vol. 1, No. 1, October 1973.

Amin, Samir *Unequal Development*. Monthly Review Press, New York, 1976.

Angell, Alan "The Difficulties of Policy Making and Interpretation in Peru", *Bulletin of Latin American Research*, Vol. 3, No. 1, January 1984.

Appa, Gautam "The Naxalites", *New Left Review*, No. 61, May–June 1970.

Archibald Ritter, R.M. *The Economic Development of Revolutionary Cuba: Strategy and Performance*. Praeger, New York, 1974.

Asian Development Bank *Rural Asia. Challenge and Opportunity*. Federal Publications, Singapore, 1978.

Austin, James, Fox, Jonathan and Krueger, Walter "The Role of the Revolutionary State in the Nicaraguan Food System", *World Development*, Vol. 13, No. 1, January 1985.

Awiti, Adhu "Economic Differentiation in Ismani Iringa Region: A Critical Assessment of Peasants' Response to the Ujamaa Vijijini". Paper presented to an Economic Research Bureau Seminar, University of Dar es Salaam, and circulated at the German Foundation/FAO Expert Consultation on New Forms of Organisation and Structure of Agricultural Production, Villa Borsig, Berlin, 22–31 May 1974.

Baer, Werner "Growth with Inequality" (Review article in) *Latin American Research Review*, Vol. XXI, No. 2, 1986.

Bagchee, Sandeep "Poverty Alleviation Programmes in Seventh Plan [in India]. An Appraisal", *Economic and Political Weekly*, Vol. XXII, No. 4, 24 January 1987.

Bandyopadhyay, D. "Land Reforms in West Bengal", International Foundation for Development Alternatives (IFDA) *Dossier 24*, July/August 1981.

Baran, Paul A. *The Political Economy of Growth*. Monthly Review Press, New York, 1957.

Baran, Paul A. and Sweezy, Paul M. *Monopoly Capital. An Essay on the American Economic and Social Order*. Penguin Books, Harmondsworth, Middlesex, 1975.

Baraona, Rafael and Associates "Tenencia de la Tierra y Desarrollo Socio-económico del Sector Agrícola: Ecuador" Comité Interamericano de Desarrollo Agrícola (CIDA), Unión Panamericana, Washington, D.C., 1965.

Bardhan, Pranab *The Political Economy of Development in India*. Basil Blackwell, Oxford, 1984.

Barraclough, Solon L. y Domike, Arthur L. "La Estructura Agraria en Siete Países de America Latina", *El Trimestre Economico*, Vol. XXXIII, Nm. 130, Abril–Junio 1966.

Barraclough, Solon L. "Agricultural Policy and Land Reform", *Journal of Political Economy*, Vol. 78, No. 4, Part II, July/August 1970.

Barraclough, Solon *A Preliminary Analysis of the Nicaraguan Food System*. United Nations Research Institute for Social Development, Geneva, 1982.

Beckford, G.L. *Persistent Poverty: Underdevelopment in Plantation Economies of the Third World*. Oxford University Press, New York, 1973.

Beenstock, Michael "The Role of the World Bank in a Maturing Capital Market", in World Bank *Recovery in the Developing World*. The London Symposium on the World Bank Role, Washington, 1986.

Bénetière, J.J. "Cooperative Strategies vis-a-vis Multinational Agri-Food Companies", *World Agriculture*, Vol. XXV, No. 4, 1976.

Bennoune, Mahfoud "The Problematics of the Algerian 'Agrarian Revolution' ". Seminar Paper, International Seminar on Agrarian Reform, Land Tenure Center, University of Wisconsin, Madison, 14–22 July 1977.

Bergson, Abram and Levine, Herbert S. (eds.) *The Soviet Economy: Toward the Year 2000*. George Allen and Unwin, London, 1984.

Berman, B.J. and Lonsdale, J.M. "Crises of Accumulation, Coercion and the Colonial State: The Development of Labour Control System in Kenya, 1919–1929", *Canadian Journal of African Studies*, Vol. 14, No. 1, 1980.

Bezzabeh, Mulugetta "Revolution and Land Reform. A study of the Impacts of Land Reform and Agrarian Revolution in Wollo Region, Northern Ethiopia". FAO, Rome, 1980 (unpublished version.)

Bhaduri, A. "Agricultural Backwardness under Semi-Feudalism", *Economic Journal*, Vol. 83, No. 239, March 1973.

Bhaduri, Amit "Class Relations and the Pattern of Accumulation in an Agrarian Economy", *Cambridge Journal of Economics*, Vol. 5, No. 1, March 1981.

Bhattacharyya, Manas "Rural Development in India: A Survey of Concepts, Strategies and Experience", *Economic Bulletin for Asia and the Pacific*, Vol. XXXVI, No. 1, June 1985.

Blaikie, P., Cameron, J. and Seddon, D. *Nepal in Crisis*. Clarendon Press, Oxford, 1980.

Blair, Harry W. "Participation, Public Policy, Political Economy and Development in Rural Bangladesh, 1958–85", *World Development*, Vol. 13, No. 12, December 1985.

Brading, D.A. (ed.) *Caudillo and Peasant in the Mexican Revolution*. Cambridge University Press, Cambridge, 1980.

Brandt Commission *North-South: A Programme for Survival*. Report of the Independent Commission on International Development Issues. The MIT Press, Cambridge, Mass., 1980.

Breimyer, Harold F. "Future Organization and Control of U.S. Agricultural Production and Marketing", *Journal of Farm Economics*, Vol. 46, 1964.

Brietzke, P. "Land Reform in Revolutionary Ethiopia", *Journal of Modern African Studies*, Vol. 14, No. 4, 1976.

Brown, Archie and Kaser, Michael (eds.) *Soviet Policy for the 1980s*. Macmillan, London, 1983.

Byres, T.J. (ed.) "Sharecropping and Sharecroppers", Special Issue of *The Journal of Peasant Studies*, Vol. 10, Nos. 2 and 3, January/April 1983.

Caballero, José Maria "Casual Labour in Peruvian Agrarian Cooperatives" in Stewart, Frances (ed.) *Work, Income and Inequality. Payments Systems in the Third World*. Macmillan, London, 1983.

Cain, Mead "Landlessness in India and Bangladesh: A Critical Review of National Data Sources", *Economic Development and Cultural Change*, Vol. 32, No. 1, October 1983.

Campbell, Bonnie K. "The Fiscal Crisis of the State. The Case of the Ivory Coast" in Bernstein, Henry and Campbell, Bonnie K. (eds.) *Contradictions of Accumulation in*

220   *References*

Africa. Studies in Economy and the State. Sage Publications, Beverley Hills, California, 1985.

Carter, Elizabeth (ed.) *Findings and Implications for AID.* No-SR-LR-70–13, State Department, Washington, 1970.

Castillo, Gelia T. *All in a Grain of Rice.* Southeast Asian Regional Center for Graduate Study and Research in Agriculture, College, Laguna, Philippines, 1975.

Castillo, Gelia T. "The Farmer Revisited: Toward a Return to the Food Problem". *Proceedings of the World Food Conference of 1976.* Iowa State University Press, Ames, Iowa, U.S.A., 1977.

Cehesky, Marta "Redistributive Policy and Agrarian Reform" in Rosenbaum, H. Jon and Tyler, William G. (eds.) *Contemporary Brazil: Issues in Economic and Political Development.* Praeger, New York, 1972.

Chenery, Hollis *Structural Change and Development Policy.* Oxford University Press (for the World Bank), New York, 1979.

Chonchol, Jacques "La Reforma Agraria en Chile (1964–1973)", *Trimestre Economico,* Vol. XLIII (3), Núm. 171, 1976.

Christodoulou, D. "Basic Structural Issues in the Adjustment of African Customary Tenures to the Needs of Agricultural Development". Paper presented to the World Land Reform Conference, FAO, Rome, 1966 (RU: WLR/66/6).

Christodoulou, D. "Towards a Typology of Land Tenure and Land Reform: Some Relevant Issues". Paper presented to the Meeting of the Commission for Agricultural Typology of the International Geographical Union, Verona, Italy, Sept.–Oct., 1970. In *Agricultural Typology and Land Utilisation.* Centre of Agricultural Geography, Verona, 1972.

Christodoulou, D. "Portugal's Agrarian Reform: A Process of Change with Unique Features", *Land Reform, Land Settlement and Co-operatives,* No. 2, 1976.

Christodoulou, D. "Integrated Rural Development and Agrarian Reform in Context: Strategic Options and Operational Requirements. (The Art of the Impossible?)". Paper given at the Seminar on Rural Development of the International Geographical Union, Paris, September, 1975; also Background Paper at the International Seminar on Agrarian Reform, University of Wisconsin, Madison, July, 1977 (1975/77).

Christodoulou, D. "Agrarian Reform in Retrospect: Contributions to its Dynamics and Related Fundamental Issues", *Land Reform, Land Settlement and Co-operatives,* No. 2, 1977.

Christodoulou, D. "Part-time Farming in the Developing World: A Case of Hobson's Choice or the Privilege of Half a Loaf", *GeoJournal,* Vol. 6, No. 4, 1982.

Clairmonte, Frederik and Cavanagh, John "Third World Debt Crisis Threatens Collapse of World Trade and Financial Systems", *IFDA Dossier* 59, May/June 1987.

Clegg, Ian *Workers' Self-Management in Algeria.* Monthly Review Press, New York and London, 1971.

Cline, William R. "Policy Instruments for Rural Income Redistribution" in Frank Jr., Charles R. and Webb, Richard C. (eds.) *Income Distribution and Growth in the Less-Developed Countries.* The Brookings Institution, Washington D.C., 1977, pp. 281–335.

Clower, R.W., Dalton, G., Harwitz, M. and Walters. A.A. *Growth without Development. An Economic Survey of Liberia.* Northwestern University Press, Evanston, 1966.

Cook, Edward "Agricultural Reform in Poland: Background and Prospects", *Soviet Studies,* Vol. XXXVI, No. 3, July 1984.

Cooper, Adrienne "Sharecroppers and Landlords in Bengal, 1930–50: The Dependency Web and its Implications" in Byres 1983 (q.v.)

Country Review Paper. "Agrarian Reform and Rural Development in Sri Lanka", Agrarian Research and Training Institute, Colombo, May 1978. Submitted to the World Conference on Agrarian Reform and Rural Development (1978a).

Country Review Paper. "Agrarian Reform and Development in Kenya 1965–1977", Development Planning Division, Ministry of Agriculture, June 1978. Paper submitted to the World Conference on Agrarian Reform and Rural Development(1978b).

Country Review Paper. "Liberia". Submitted to the World Conference on Agrarian Reform and Rural Development, FAO, Rome, 1979.

Dahlberg, Kenneth A. *Beyond the Green Revolution. The Ecology and Politics of Global Agricultural Development.* Plenum Press, New York, 1979.

Dasgupta, Biplab *The Naxalite Movement.* Allied Publishers, New Delhi, 1974.

Dasgupta, Biplab "New Technology and the Agricultural Labourers in India" in Hirashima, S. (ed.) *Hired Labor in Rural Asia.* Institute of Development Studies, Tokyo, 1977.

Deere, Carmen Diana "The Division of Labor by Sex in Agriculture: A Peruvian Case Study", *Economic Development and Cultural Change,* Vol. 30, No. 4, July 1982.

Deere, Carmen Diana "Rural Women and State Policy: The Latin American Agrarian Reform Experience", *World Development,* Vol. 13, No. 9, September 1985.

de Janvry, Alain *The Agrarian Question and Reformation in Latin America.* The Johns Hopkins University Press, Baltimore, 1981.

Den Tuinder, B. *Ivory Coast. The Challenge of Success.* World Bank Mission Report, the Johns Hopkins University Press, Baltimore, 1978.

DeWind, J., Seidl, T. and Shenk, J. "Contract Labor in U.S. Agriculture: The West Indian Cane Cutters in Florida" in Cohen R., Gutkind, P.C.W. and Brazier, P. (eds.) *Peasants and Proletarians. The Struggle of Third World Workers.* Hutchinson University Library, London, 1979.

Diamond, Douglas B., Bettis, Lee W., and Ramson, Robert E. "Agricultural Production" in Bergson and Levine 1984 (q.v.)

Di Giorgi, Umberto and Moscati, Roberto "The Role of the State in the Uneven Spatial Development of Italy: The Case of the Mezzogiorno", *The Review of Radical Economics,* Vol. 12, No. 3, Fall 1980.

Dinham, Barbara and Hines, Colin *Agribusiness in Africa. A Study of the Impact of Big Business on Africa's Food and Agricultural Production.* Earth Resources Research Ltd., London, 1983.

Dixon, Ruth B. "Mobilizing Women for Rural Employment in South Asia: Issues of Class, Caste and Patronage", *Economic Development and Cultural Change,* Vol. 30, No. 2, January 1982.

Domínguez, Jorge I. *Cuba: Order and Revolution.* Harvard University Press, Cambridge, Mass., 1978.

Dore, Ronald "The Prestige Factor in International Affairs", *International Affairs,* Vol. 51, No. 2, April 1975.

Dore, Ronald "Technological Self-Reliance: Sturdy Ideal or Self-Serving Rhetoric" in Fransman, Martin and King, Kenneth (eds.) *Technological Capability in the Third World.* Macmillan, London, 1984.

Dos Santos, T. "The Crisis of Development Theory and the Problem of Dependence in Latin America" in Bernstein, H. (ed.) *Underdevelopment and Development.* Penguin, Hardmondsworth, 1973.

Dovring, Folke "Land Reform: A Key to Change in Agriculture" and Discussion of the Paper in Islam, Nurul (ed.) *Agricultural Policy in Developing Countries.* Proceedings of a Conference held by the International Economic Association at Bad Godesberg, West Germany. Macmillan, London, 1974.

Dumont, René and Mottin, Marie-France *L' Afrique Etranglée.* Éditions du Seuil, Paris, 1980.

Dunham, David "On the History of Political Economy of Small-Farmer Policies", *CEPAL Review,* No. 18, December 1982.

Esman, Milton J. and Associates *Landlessness and Nearlandlessness in Developing Countries.* Prepared under AID/Office of Rural Development Project No. 931–17–998–001–73. Rural Development Committee, Center for International Studies, Cornell University, Ithaca, New York, 1978.

Fabre, Renaud *Paysans sans Terres.* Dunod, Paris, 1978.

Fagen, Richard R. "Equity in the South and the Context of North-South Relations" in Fishlow, Albert, Díaz-Alejando, Carlos F., Fagen, Richard R. and Hansen, Roger D. (eds.) *Rich and Poor Nations in the World Economy.* 1980s Project, Council of Foreign Relations, McGraw-Hill Book Company, New York, 1978 (1978a).

Fagen, Richard R. "A Funny Thing Happened on the Way to the Market: Thoughts on Extending Dependency Ideas", *International Organization*, Vol. 32, No. 1, Winter 1978 (1978b).

FAO, "Le role des organisations populaires dans l'insertion des populations pauvres dans le developpement rural: Cameroun". Rome, Mars 1978. Working paper prepared for the World Conference on Agrarian Reform and Rural Development.

FAO, *The 1970 World Census of Agriculture*, Rome, 1981.

Feder, Ernest "La Nueva Penetración en la Agricultura de los Países Subdesarrollados por los Países Industriales y sus Empresas Multinacionales", *El Trimestre Economico*, Vol. XLIII (1), Núm. 169, Enero-Marzo de 1976.

Feldman, Rayah "Custom and Capitalism – Changes in the Basis of Land Tenure in Ismani-Tanzania". Paper presented at the Seminar on Problems of Land Tenure in African Development, Leiden, 13–17 December, 1971, Afrika-Studiecentrum, Leiden (Cyclostyled).

Fieldhouse, D.K. *Black Africa 1945–80. Economic Decolonization and Arrested Development*. Allen and Unwin, London, 1986.

Fitzgerald, E.V.K. *The Political Economy of Peru 1956–78*. Cambridge University Press, Cambridge, 1979.

Franda, Marcus *Radical Politics in West Bengal*. M.I.T. Press, Cambridge, Mass., 1971.

Furedi, Frank "The Social Composition of the Mau Mau Movement in the White Highlands", *The Journal of Peasant Studies*, Vol. 1, No. 4, July 1974.

Gaiha, Raghav "Poverty, Technology and Infrastructure in Rural India", *Cambridge Journal of Economics*, Vol. 9, No. 3, September 1985.

Galeski, B. "The Models of Collective Farming" in Dorner, P. (ed.) *Cooperative and Commune. Group Farming in the Economic Development of Agriculture*. University of Wisconsin, Madison, 1977.

Gardner, Richard N., Okita, Saburo, and Udink, B.J. "A Turning Point in North-South Economic Relations". *Triangle Paper No. 3*. The Trilateral Commission, New York, June 1974.

Garza, Hisauro A. "Political Economy and Change: The Zapatista Agrarian Revolutionary Movement", *Rural Sociology*, Vol. 44, No. 2, Summer 1979.

Ghai, Dharan and Radwan, Samir "Growth and Inequality: Rural Development in Malawi 1964–1978" in Ghai, Dharan and Radwan, Samir (eds.) *Agrarian Policies and Rural Poverty in Africa*. ILO, Geneva, 1983.

Ghose, Ajit Kumar "Food Supply and Starvation: A Study of Famines with Reference to the Indian Sub-continent", *Oxford Economic Papers* (New Series), Vol. 34, No. 2, July 1982.

Ghose, Ajit Kumar "Transforming Feudal Agriculture: Agrarian Change in Ethiopia since 1974", *The Journal of Development Studies*, Vol. 22, No. 1, October 1985.

Ghose, Ajit K. and Griffin, K. "Rural Poverty and Development Alternatives in South and South-East Asia: Some Policy Issues", International Foundation for Development Alternatives *Dossier No. 9*, July 1979.

Gibbons, David S., de Koninck, Rodolphe, and Hasan, Ibrahim *Agricultural Modernization, Poverty and Inequality. The Distributional Impact of the Green Revolution in Regions of Malaysia and Indonesia*. Saxon House, Teakfield, Westmead, Farnborough, 1980.

Girvan, Norman "Economic Nationalists v. Multinational Corporations: Revolutionary or Evolutionary Change?" in Widstrand, Carl (ed.) *Multinational Firms in Africa*. African Institute for Economic Development and Planning, Dakar, and Scandinavian Institute for African Countries, Uppsala, 1975.

Goldberg, Ray A. and McGinity, Richard C. *Agribusiness Management for Developing Countries – Southeast Asian Corn System and American and Japanese Trends Affecting it*. Ballinger Publishing Company, Cambridge, Mass., 1979.

Gomes, Gerson and Pérez, Antonio "The Process of Mechanization in Latin American Agriculture", *CEPAL Review*, August 1979.

Goonatilake, Susantha "Development Thinking as Cultural Neo-Colonialism – the Case of Sri Lanka (or Why Visiting Economists are Successful)", *I.D.S. Bulletin*, April 1975, Vol. 7, No. 1.

Gooneratne, W. and Wesumperuna, D. (eds.) *Plantation Agriculture in Sri Lanka. Issues in Employment and Development*. ARTEP, International Labour Organisation, Bangkok, 1984.

Gray, Jack "Rural China: A Strong Strain of Continuity", *Ceres*. Vol. 17, No. 5, September–October 1984.

Griffin, Keith *The Green Revolution: An Economic Analysis*: United Nations Research Institute for Social Development, Geneva, 1972.

Griffin, Keith "Communal Land Tenure Systems and their Role in Rural Development", in Lall, Sanjaya and Stewart, Frances (eds.) *Theory and Reality in Development*. Essays in Honour of Paul Streeten. Macmillan, London, 1986.

Griffin, Keith and Griffin, Kimberley "Institutional Change and Income in the Chinese Countryside", *Oxford Bulletin of Economics and Statistics*, Vol. 45, No. 3, August 1983.

Griffin, Keith and Hay, Roger "Problems of Agricultural Development in Socialist Ethiopia: An Overview and a Suggested Strategy", *The Journal of Peasant Studies*, Vol. 13, No. 1, October 1985.

Gutierrez, Gustavo *A Theology of Liberation*. SCM Press, London, 1983.

Halliday, Fred *Iran: Dictatorship and Development*. Penguin Books, Harmondsworth, 1979.

Halliday, Fred and Molyneux, Maxine *The Ethiopian Revolution*. Verso, London, 1981.

Handy, Jim "Resurgent Democracy and Guatemalan Military", *Journal of Latin American Studies*, Vol. 18, Part 2, November 1986.

Harrison, Paul *Inside the Third World. The Anatomy of Poverty*. Penguin Books, Harmondsworth, 1979.

Hartford, Kathleen "Hungarian Agriculture: A Model for the Socialist World?", *World Development*, Vol. 13, No. 1, January 1985.

Hecht, Susanna B. "Environment, Development and Politics: Capital Accumulation and the Livestock Sector in Eastern Amazonia", *World Development*, Vol. 13, No. 6, June 1985.

Hellman, Judith Adler *Mexico in Crisis*. Holmes and Meir, New York, 1978.

Herring, Ronald J. "Abolition of Landlordism in South India: A Redistribution of Privilege", *Land Tenure Center Newsletter No. 67*, April–June 1980 (summarised from an article in *Economic and Political Weekly (Bombay)*, June 1980).

Herring, Ronald J. "Embedded Production Relations and the Rationality of Tenant Quiescence in Tenure Reform", *The Journal of Peasant Studies*, Vol. 8, No. 2, January 1981.

Hewitt de Alcántara, Cynthia "Land Reform, Livelihood, and Power in Rural Mexico" in Preston 1980 (q.v.)

Hines, Colin and Dinham, Barbara "Export Production – Cause for Famine?", *Development and Cooperation* No. 1/1981 (Jan./Feb.).

Hirsch, Fred *Social Limits to Growth*. Harvard University Press, Cambridge, Mass., 1976.

Hirschman, Albert O. *Journeys Toward Progress. Studies of Economic Policy-Making in Latin America*. The Twentieth Century Fund, New York, 1963.

Hirschman, Albert O. "The Changing Tolerance for Income Inequality in the Course of Economic Development", *World Development*, Vol. 1, No. 12, December 1973.

Hobsbawm, Eric "Peasants and Politics", *The Journal of Peasant Studies*, Vol. 1, No. 1, October 1973.

Hochschild, Steven F. "Technical Assistance and International Development: A Need for Fundamental Change", *Focus*, 1978/3.

Holton, R.J. *The Transition from Feudalism to Capitalism*. Macmillan, London, 1985.

Hong, Ma *New Strategy for China's Economy*. New World Press, Beijing, China, 1983.

Horvat, Branko "Modelo Institucional de la Economia Socialista Autogestionaria", *El Trimestre Economico*, Vol. XLI (1), Enero-Marzo, 1974.

Huizer, Gerrit J. "Historical Background of Peasant Organisations in the Philippines".

Reproduced by the Secretariat, National Reform Council, Diliman, Quezon City, 1971 (Cyclostyled).

Huizer, Gerrit J. "How Peasants Become Revolutionaries: Some cases from Latin America and Southeast Asia", *Development and Change*, Vol. 6, No. 3, July 1975.

Hunt, Diana *The Impending Crisis in Kenya. The Case for Land Reform.* Gower, Aldershot, 1984.

Huntington, Samuel P. *Political Order in Changing Societies.* Yale University Press, New Haven, 1968.

Hussain, A. "Elites and Political Development in Pakistan", *The Developing Economies*, Vol. XIV, No. 3, September 1976.

Hutton, John *The Mystery of Wealth.* Stanley Thornes, Cheltenham, 1979.

ILO *Employment, Incomes and Equality. A Strategy for Increasing Productive Employment in Kenya.* Report of an Inter-Agency Team, Geneva, 1972.

ILO *Employment, Growth and Basic Needs: A One-World Problem.* International Labour Office, Geneva, 1976.

Islam, Nurul *Development Planning in Bangladesh. A Study in Political Economy.* C. Hurst and Company, London, 1977.

Jimenez, Alexis Codina "Worker Incentives in Cuba", *World Development* Special Issue on Cuba's Socialist Economy Towards the 1990s. Vol. 15, No. 1, January 1987.

Johnson, D. Gale "Agricultural Organisation and Management" in Bergson and Levine 1984 (q.v.)

Johnson, Dale L. (ed.) *Middle Classes in Dependent Countries.* Sage Publications, Beverly Hills, California, 1985.

Johnson, Harry G. *Technology and Economic Interdependence.* Macmillan Press, London, 1975.

Jose, A.V. "Agrarian Reforms in Kerala – the Role of Peasant Organisations", *Journal of Contemporary Asia*, Vol. 14, No. 1, 1984.

Joshi, P.C. "Land Reform and Agrarian Change in India and Pakistan since 1947: II", *The Journal of Peasant Studies*, Vol. 1, No. 3, April 1974.

Jupp, J. *Sri Lanka – Third World Democracy.* Frank Cass, London, 1978.

Kaplan, Paul F. and Shrestha, Nanda R. "The Sukumbasi Movement in Nepal: The Fire from Below", *Journal of Contemporary Asia*, Vol. 12, No. 1, 1982.

Katouzian, M.A. "Land Reform in Iran. A Case Study in the Political Economy of Social Engineering", *The Journal of Peasant Studies*, Vol. 1, No. 2, January 1974.

Kay, Cristóbal "Political Economy, Class Alliances and Agrarian Change in Chile", *The Journal of Peasant Studies*, Vol. 8, No. 4, July 1981.

Kay, Cristóbal "Achievements and Contradictions of the Peruvian Agrarian Reform", *The Journal of Development Studies*, Vol. 18, No. 2, January 1982.

Kellner, Peter and Lord Crowther-Hunt *The Civil Servants. An Inquiry into Britain's Ruling Class.* Macdonald, London, 1980.

Kinley, David, Collins, Joseph, and Moore Lappe, Frances *Seven Myths of Aid.* Institute for Food and Development Policy, San Francisco, CA, 1979.

Kinsey, B.H. "Emerging Policy Issues in Zimbabwe's Land Resettlement Programmes", *Development Policy Review*, Vol. 1, No. 2, November 1983.

Klein, Emilio "Agrarian Structures and Employment in Latin America. An Analytical Framework", *International Labour Review*, Vol. 115, No. 1, Jan–Feb. 1977.

Kydd, Jonathan and Hewitt, Adrian "Limits to Recovery: Malawi after Six Years of Adjustment, 1980 to 1985", *Development and Change*, Vol. 17, No. 3, July 1986.

Laidlaw, Ken "Transnational Banks and the Third World", *Development and Cooperation*, No. 6/1980 (November–December).

Laidlaw, Ken "Transnationals and Food Processing", *Development and Cooperation*, No. 1/1981, Jan–Feb.

Lenin, V.I. *The Development of Capitalism in Russia.* Second Revised Edition, Progress Publishers, Moscow, 1964.

Lenin, V.I. *The State and Revolution.* Progress Publishers, Moscow, 1969.

Leo Grande, William M. and Robbins, Carla Anne "Oligarchs and Officers: The Crisis in El Salvador", *Foreign Affairs*, Vol. 58, Summer 1980.

Lewis, Oscar, and Barnouw, Victor "Caste and the Jajmani System in a North Indian Village" in Potter, Jack M., Diaz M., and Foster, George M. (eds.) *Peasant Society*. Little, Brown and Co., Boston, 1967.

Leys, Colin *Underdevelopment in Kenya. The Political Economy of Neo-Colonialism 1964–1971*. Heinemann, London, 1975.

Lipson, Charles *Standing Guard. Protecting Foreign Capital in the Nineteenth and Twentieth Centuries*. University of California Press, Berkeley and Los Angeles, 1985.

Lipton, Michael "African Agricultural Development: The EEC's New Role", *Development Policy Review*, Vol. 1, No. 1, May 1983.

Long, Norman *An Introduction to the Sociology of Rural Development*. Tavistock Publications, London, 1977.

Loveman, Brian *Struggle in the Countryside. Politics and Rural Labor in Chile, 1919–1973*. Indiana University Press, Bloomington, 1976.

Macpherson, C.B. *Property. Mainstream and Critical Positions*. Basil Blackwell, Oxford, 1978.

Martinez-Allier, Juan *Haciendas, Plantations and Collective Farms: Agrarian Class Societies – Cuba and Peru*. Frank Cass, London, 1977.

Martyrov, Vladen "Production of Food and Development of Agro-Industrial Integration in the U.S.S.R. *"Proceedings of the World Food Conference of 1976*. Iowa State University Press, Ames, Iowa, 1977.

Marx, Karl *Selected Works*, Lawrence and Wishart, London, 1945.

McNamara, Robert S. *Address to the Board of Governors*. Nairobi, Kenya, September 23, 1973, World Bank Group.

Mellor, John W. *The New Economics of Growth. A Strategy for India and the Developing World*. Cornell University Press, Ithaca, 1976.

Mintz, Sydney W. "The Proletariat and the Problem of Proletarian Consciousness", *The Journal of Peasant Studies*, Vol. 1, No. 3, April 1974.

Miró, Carmen A. and Rodríguez, Daniel "Capitalism and Population in Latin American Agriculture. Recent Trends and Problems", *CEPAL Review*, No. 16, April 1982.

Mitra, A. "New Directions?", *Institute of Development Studies Bulletin*, Vol. 8, No. 2, 1976.

Mitter, Swasti *Peasant Movements in West Bengal. Their Impact on Agrarian Class Relations since 1967*. Department of Land Economy, Occasional Paper No. 8, University of Cambridge, 1977.

Mkandawire, Thandika *The World Bank and Integrated Rural Development in Malawi*. Working Paper No. 1, Council for the Development of Economic and Social Research in Africa, COD/IFO/I, Dakar, 1980.

Molina S., Sergio "Poverty Description and Analysis of Policies for Overcoming it", *CEPAL Review*, No. 18, December 1982.

Moore, Mick "On 'The Political Economy of Stabilization' ", *World Development*, Vol. 13, No. 9, September 1985.

Mouzelis, Nicos P. *Organisation and Bureaucracy. An Analysis of Modern Theories*. Routledge and Kegan Paul, London, 1970.

Munslow, Barry "Prospects for the Socialist Transition of Agriculture in Zimbabwe", *World Development*, Vol. 13, No. 1, January 1985.

Myint, H. *The Economics of the Developing Countries*. Hutchinson University Library, London, 1969.

Myrdal, Gunnar *Asian Drama. An Inquiry into the Poverty of Nations:* 3 Volumes. Penguin Books, Harmondsworth, 1968.

Nafziger, Wayne E. "A Critique of Development Economics in the U.S." in Lehmann, D. (ed.) *Development Theory*. Frank Cass, London, 1979.

Naiken, L. "Estimation of Rural Participation in Non-Agricultural Employment", *Monthly Bulletin of Agricultural Economics and Statistics*, Vol. 26, No. 1, January 1977.

Nakagane, Katsuji "Review" of John Wong's Book *Land Reform in the People's Republic of China* in *The Developing Economies*, Vol. XIV, No. 3, September 1976.

Newsinger, John "Revolt and Repression in Kenya: The Mau Mau Rebellion, 1952–1960" *Science and Society*, Vol. XLV, No. 2, Summer 1981.

Nolan, Peter and Paine, Suzanne "Towards an Appraisal of the Impact of Rural Reform in China, 1978–85", *Cambridge Journal of Economics*, Vol. 10, No. 1, March 1986.

Nossiter, T.J. *Communism in Kerala: A Study in Political Adaptation*. Hurst and Co., London, 1982.

Nove, Alec "Agriculture" in Brown and Kaser 1983 (q.v.)

Nyerere, Julius K. *On Rural Development*. Address to the FAO World Conference on Agrarian Reform and Rural Development, Rome, 1979.

Nyerere, Julius K. "An Address", *Development and Change*, Vol. 17, No. 3, July 1986. (Given to the Institute of Social Studies, the Hague, 13 March 1985).

Odingo, Richard S. *The Kenya Highlands: Land Use and Agricultural Development*. East African Publishing House, Nairobi, 1971.

Offer, Avner *Property and Politics 1870–1914. Land Ownership, Law, Ideology and Urban Development in England*. Cambridge University Press, Cambridge, 1981.

Ohiorhenuan, John F.E. "The Political Economy of Military Rule in Nigeria", *Review of Radical Political Economics*, Vol. 16, Nos. 2 and 3, Summer and Fall 1984.

Omvedt, Gail "The Left in India", *Journal of Contemporary Asia*, Vol. 15, No. 2, 1985.

O'Neill, Norman "Briefings", *Review of African Political Economy, Special Issue – Sudan*, No. 26, July 1983.

Ortega, Emiliano "Peasant Agriculture in Latin America. Situations and Trends", *CEPAL Review*, No. 16, April 1982.

Osborne, Milton *Region of Revolt. Focus on Southeast Asia*. Pergamon Press (Australia) 1970.

Osofsky, Stephen *Soviet Agricultural Policy: Towards the Abolition of Collective Farms*. Praeger, New York, 1974.

Paige, Jeffery M. *Agrarian Revolution: Social Movements and Export Agriculture in the Underdeveloped World*. The Free Press (Macmillan), New York, 1975.

Papanek, Hanna "Pakistan's Big Businessmen: Muslim Separatism, Entrepreneurship, and Partial Modernization", *Economic Development and Cultural Change*, Vol. 21, No. 1, October 1972.

Payer, Cheryl *The World Bank. A Critical Analysis*. Monthly Review Press, New York, 1982.

Peiris, G.H. " 'Structural' Change in Plantation Agriculture in Sri Lanka", in Gooneratne, W. and Wesumperuna, D. (eds.) *Plantation Agriculture in Sri Lanka*. ARTEP. International Labour Organisation, Bangkok, 1984.

Perlmutter, Amos *The Military and Politics in Modern Times. On Professionals, Praetorians, and Revolutionary Soldiers*. Yale University Press, New Haven, 1977.

Petras, James, Morris, Morley and Havens, Eugene A. "Peru: Capitalist Democracy in Transition", *New Left Review*, No. 142, November–December 1983.

Piekakiewicz, Jaroslaw "Kulakization of Polish Agriculture" in Francisco, Ronald A., Laird, Betty and Laird, Roy D. (eds.) *The Political Economy of Collectivized Agriculture*. Pergamon Press, New York, 1979.

Plutarch *Lives of the Noble Romans* edited by Edmund Fuller, Dell Publishing Co., New York, 1959.

Powell, John Duncan "Peasant Society and Clientilist Politics", *The American Political Science Review*, Vol. LXIV, No. 2, June 1970.

Preston, David A. (ed.) *Environment, Society, and Rural Change in Latin America*. John Wiley and Sons, New York, 1980.

Putterman, Louis "Extrinsic versus Intrinsic Problems of Agricultural Cooperation: Antiincentivism in Tanzania and China", *The Journal of Development Studies*, Vol. 21, No. 2, January 1985.

Radwan, Samir *Agrarian Reform and Rural Poverty, Egypt 1952–1975*. ILO. Geneva, 1977.

Raj, K.N. and Tharakan, Michael "Agrarian Reform in Kerala and its Impact on the Rural Economy – A Preliminary Assessment", in Ghose, Ajit Kumar (ed.) *Agrarian Reform in Contemporary Developing Countries*. ILO Study. Croom Helm, London, 1983.

References   227

Reid, Michael *Peru: Paths to Poverty*. Latin American Bureau, London, 1985.
República de Panamá. Programa de desarrollo inegral de areas rurales. Documento presentado por el Gobierno de Panamá a la Conferencia Mundial de la FAO sobre Reforma Agraria y Desarrollo Rural. Panamá, Septiembre 1978.
Robinson, Austin, "Review" of Amartya Sen's *Poverty and Famines: An Essay on Entitlement and Deprivation* in *The Journal of Development Studies*, Vol. 19, No. 2, January 1983.
Rosenbaum, H. Jon and Tyler, William G. (eds.) *Contemporary Brazil: Issues in Economic and Political Development*. Praeger, New York. 1972.
Roth, Hans-Dieter *Indian Moneylenders at Work: Case Studies of the Traditional Rural Credit Market in Dhanbad District, Bihar*. Manohar Publications, New Delhi, 1983.
Rudavsky, Dahlia "The Grim Reapers: The Trilateral Commission Takes on World Hunger" in Sklar, Holly (ed.) *Trilateralism: The Trilateral Commission and Elite Planning for World Management*. Black Rose Book, Montreal, 1980.
Rudra, Ashok "Organization of Agriculture for Rural Development: the Indian Case", *Cambridge Journal of Economics*, Vol. 2, No. 4, December 1978.
Safilios-Rothchild, Constantina "The Persistence of Women's Invisibility in Agriculture: Theoretical and Policy Lessons from Lesotho and Sierra Leone", *Economic Development and Cultural Change*, Vol. 33, No. 2, January 1985.
Saich, Tony, *China: Politics and Government*. Macmillan Press, London, 1981.
Sánchez, Gonzalo "La Violencia in Colombia: New Research, New Questions", *The Hispanic American Historical Review*, Vol. 65, No. 4, November 1985. (Translated by Peter Bakewell.)
Sanderatne, N. and Zaman, M.A. "The Impact of Agrarian Structure on the Political Leadership of Undivided Pakistan", *LTC No. 94*, Land Tenure Center, University of Wisconsin, Madison, November 1973.
Sanderson, Susan R.W. *Land Reform in Mexico: 1910–1980*. Academic Press, Orlando, Florida, 1984.
Seidman, Ann "Key Variables to Incorporate in a Model for Development: The African Case", *African Studies Review*, Vol. XVII, No. 1, April 1974.
Seidman, Robert B. *The State, Law and Development*. Croom Helm, London, 1978.
Sen, Amartya "Development: Which Way Now?", *The Economic Journal*, Vol. 93, No. 372, December 1983.
Sharpe, Kenneth, E. "Corporate Strategies in the Dominican Republic: The Politics of Peasant Movements" in Malloy, James M. (ed.). *Authoritarianism and Corporatism in Latin America*. University of Pittsburgh Press, Pittsburgh, 1977.
Sigmund, Paul E. *Multinationals in Latin America. The Politics of Nationalization*. The University of Wisconsin Press, Madison, 1980.
Silverman, Sydel F. "The Community-Nation Mediator in Traditional Central Italy" in Potter, Jack M., Diaz, M. and Foster, George M. (eds.) *Peasant Society*. Little, Brown and Co., Boston, 1967.
Simpson, A.W.B. *An Introduction to the History of Land Law*. Oxford University Press, London, 1961.
Stavenhagen, Rodolfo "Collective Agriculture and Capitalism in Mexico", in Hamilton, Nora and Harding, Timothy F. (eds.) *Modern Mexico. State, Economy and Social Conflict*. Sage Publications, Beverly Hills, California, 1986.
Stein, S. *Populism in Peru. The Emergence of the Masses and the Politics of Social Control*. The University of Wisconsin Press, Madison, 1980.
Stewart, Frances *Planning to Meet Basic Needs*. Macmillan, London, 1985.
Streeten, Paul "Trade Strategies for Development: Some Themes for the Seventies" in Streeten, Paul (ed.) *Trade Strategies for Development*. Papers of the Ninth Cambridge Conference on Development Problems, September 1972. John Wiley and Sons, New York, 1973.
Streeten, Paul P. "The New International Economic Order: Development Strategy Options", *Development and Peace*, Vol. 1, No. 2, Autumn 1980.
Syrodoyev, N. *Soviet Land Legislation*. Progress Publishers, Moscow, 1975.

Swainson, Nicola *The Development of Corporate Capitalism in Kenya 1918–1977.* Heinemann, London, 1980.

Szeftel, Morris "Political Graft and the Spoils System in Zambia – the State as a Resource in Itself", *Review of African Political Economy*, No. 24, May–August 1982.

Tai, Hung-Chao "The Political Processes of Land Reform: A Comparative Study" in Uphoff, N.T. and Ilchman, W.F. (eds.) *The Political Economy of Development.* University of California Press, London, 1972.

Tannenbaum, Frank "The Hacienda" in Martz, John D. (ed.) *The Dynamics of Change in Latin American Politics.* Prentice Hall, Englewood Cliffs, N.J., 1965.

Taylor, Lance, Bacha, Edmar L., Cardoso, Eliana A., and Lysy, Frank J. *Models of Growth and Distribution for Brazil.* A World Bank Research Publication. Oxford University Press, New York, 1980.

Thirwell, A.P. "Keynes, Economic Development and the Developing Countries", in Thirwell, A.P. (ed.) *Keynes and Economic Development.* Seminar at the University of Kent, Canterbury, 1985. Macmillan, London, 1987.

Thomas, Clive "Agrarian Change in a Plantation Economy: the Case of Guyana" in Ghai, Dharam, Khan, Azizur Rahman, Eddy, Lee and Radwan, Samir (eds.) *Agrarian Systems and Rural Development.* ILO, Geneva, 1979.

Thorbecke, E. "The Employment Problem: A Critical Evaluation of Four ILO Comprehensive Country Reports", *International Labour Review*, 107(5) May 1973.

Transformation of Customary Land Tenure Systems as a Result of Socio-Economic and Political Change: The Case of Botswana. Working Paper prepared by the Institut d'études économiques et sociales, Paris, 1978, for the World Conference on Agrarian Reform and Rural Development.

Trescott, Paul B. "Incentives Versus Equality: What Does China's Recent Experience Show?", *World Development*, Vol. 13, No. 2, February 1985.

Trimberger, Ellen Kay *Revolution from Above: Military Bureaucrats and Development in Japan, Turkey, Egypt and Peru.* Transaction Books, New Brunswick, N.J., 1978.

Tullberg, Rita "World Military Expenditure", *World Armaments and Disarmament.* Stockholm International Peace Research Institute (SIPRI) Yearbook 1986, Oxford University Press, New York, 1986.

Ul Haq, Mahbub "Employment in the 1970s: A New Perspective", *International Development Review*, Vol. XIII, No. 4, 1971.

United Nations *Multinational Corporations in World Development.* Department of Economic and Social Affairs, New York, 1973.

United Nations *Poverty, Unemployment and Development Policy.* Department of Economic and Social Affairs, New York, 1975.

United Nations "Land Tenure Conditions in South Africa", *Notes and Documnts* No. 37/76, Department of Political and Security Council Affairs, (77–00686), New York, 1976.

United Nations "Salient Features of Economic Cooperation among Developing Countries". Economic and Social Council, Committee for Development Planning, Fourteenth Session 6–17 March 1978. Paper prepared by the Secretariat, E/AC54/L94 of 5 December 1977 (Cyclostyled).

United Nations Centre for Transnational Corporations *Transnational Corporations in World Development. Third Survey.* United Nations, New York, 1983.

Uphoff, Norman, T., Cohen, John M. and Goldsmith, Arthur A. *Feasibility and Application of Rural Development Participation: A State-of-the-Art Paper.* Monograph Series No. 3, Rural Development Committee, Cornell University, Ithaca, January 1979.

Vaitsos, Constantine V. "Power, knowledge and Development Policy: Relations between Transnational Enterprises and Developing Countries" in Helleiner, G. K. (ed.) *A World Divided: The Less Developed Countries in the International Economy.* Cambridge University Press, Cambridge, 1976.

Vernon, R. *Sovereignty at Bay: The Multinational Spread of U.S. Enterprises.* Basic Books, New York, 1971.

Vos, Rob "El Modelo de Desarrollo y el Sector Agricola en Ecuador, 1965–1982", *El Trimestre Economico*, Vol. LII(4), No. 208, Octubre–Diciembre de 1985.

Wallerstein, Immanuel "Dependence in an Interdependent World: The Limited Possibilities of Transformation within the Capitalist World Economy", *African Studies Review*, Vol. XVII, No. 1, April 1974.

Waterman, Peter "The 'Labour Aristocracy' in Africa: Introduction to a Debate", *Development and Change*, Vol. 6, No. 3, July 1975.

Weiner, Dan, Moyo, Sam, Munslow, Barry and O'Keefe, Phil "Land Use and Agricultural Productivity in Zimbabwe", *The Journal of Modern African Studies*, Vol. 23, No. 2, June 1985.

Werner, Jayne "Socialist Development: The Political Economy of Agrarian Reform in Vietnam", *Bulletin of Concerned Asian Scholars*, Vol. 16, No. 2, April–June 1984.

Wilczynski, J. "Towards Rationality in Land Economics under Central Planning", *Economic Journal*, Vol. LXXIX, No. 315, September 1969.

Williams, P. "The Limits of American Power: from Nixon to Reagan", *International Affairs*, Vol. 63, No. 3, Summer 1987.

Wilson, Fiona "Women and Agricultural Change in Latin America: Some Concepts Guiding Research", *World Development*, Vol. 13, No. 9, September 1985.

Wolf, Eric C. *Peasant Wars of the Twentieth Century*. Harper and Row, New York, 1969.

World Bank, *Land Reform*. Sector Policy Paper. Washington, D.C., May 1975.

World Bank. *Accelerated Development in Sub-Saharan Africa: An Agenda for Action*. Washington, D.C., 1981.

World Bank, *Poverty and Hunger*. Policy Study. Washington, D.C., 1986.

World Bank, *World Development Report 1987*, Oxford University Press, New York, 1987.

World Conference on Agrarian Reform and Rural Development *Report*, FAO, Rome, Italy, 1979.

Wright, Steven "Kenya: What Went Wrong with the Picture of Success", *South*, December 1982.

Wurfel, David "Foreign Aid and Social Reform in Political Development: A Philippine Case Study", *The American Political Science Review*, Vol. LIII, No. 2, June 1959.

Yates, Peter "The Prospects of Socialist Transition in Zimbabwe", *Review of African Political Economy. Special Issue on Zimbabwe*, Vol. 18, February 1981.

Yotopoulos, Pan A. "Competition for Cereals: The Food-Feed Connection", *Ceres*, Vol. 17, No. 5, September–October 1984.

Young, Crawford *Ideology and Development in Africa*. Yale University Press, New Haven, 1982.

Young, Ruth "The Plantation Economy and Industrial Development in Latin America", *Economic Development and Cultural Change*, Vol. 18, No. 3, April 1970.

Zorn, Stephen "TNC-Government Relations in Agriculture", *The CTC Reporter*, No. 20, Autumn 1985.

Index